FIRE OF THE
RAGING
DRAGON

BOOKS BY DON BROWN

The Black Sea Affair
The Malacca Conspiracy

The Pacific Rim Series
Thunder in the Morning Calm
Fire of the Raging Dragon

The Navy Justice Series
Treason
Hostage
Defiance

DON BROWN

FIRE OF THE
RAGING
DRAGON

PACIFIC **RIM** SERIES

ZONDERVAN®

ZONDERVAN.com/
AUTHORTRACKER
follow your favorite authors

ZONDERVAN

Fire of the Raging Dragon
Copyright © 2012 by Don Brown

This title is also available as a Zondervan ebook. Visit www.zondervan.com/ebooks.

This title is also available in a Zondervan audio edition. Visit www.zondervan.fm.

Requests for information should be addressed to:

Zondervan, *Grand Rapids, Michigan 49530*

Library of Congress Cataloging-in-Publication Data

Brown, Don, 1960 –
 Fire of the raging dragon : / Don Brown.
  p. cm. – (Pacific Rim series).
 ISBN 978-0-310-33015-8 (softcover)
  1. Submarines (Ships) – Fiction. 2. Children of presidents – Fiction. 3. International
relations – Fiction. I. Title.
PR3602.R6947F57 2004
 813'.6 – dc23   2012018603

Published in association with the Steve Laube Agency, LLC, 5025 N. Central Ave. #635, Phoenix, Arizona 85012-1502

Maps created by Jane Haradine. Copyright © Don Brown.

Cover design: Curt Diepenhorst
Cover photography: Colin Anderson / Getty Images® / Shutterstock
Interior design: Michelle Espinoza

Printed in the United States of America

12 13 14 15 16 17 18 19 /DCI/ 22 21 20 19 18 17 16 15 14 13 12 11 10 9 8 7 6 5 4 3 2 1

This novel is dedicated to Margaret Brown McCaffity, my aunt, who inspired me to read, learn, and think—all those years ago.

ACKNOWLEDGMENTS

With special thanks to my "West Coast Editor," Jack Miller, of La Mesa, California, a distinguished veteran of the United States Army, and who, along with his lovely wife, Linda, remains a generous benefactor of the San Diego Zoo and the Lambs Theatre of Coronado, among other worthy causes.

Also with grateful appreciation to B. T. Prince of Carmel Baptist Church, a friend, mentor, and faithful soldier in the Army of God.

FIRE OF THE
RAGING
DRAGON

PROLOGUE

A million white lights mark the evening skyline, and at a hundred thousand intersections, traffic lights flash green, then yellow, then red. Under the traffic lights, the high beams of thousands of cars and buses flood the roads and streets of the city.

Along colorful stretches of the historic Dongcheng District, along Wángfǔjǐng and Donghuamen Streets, purple and orange electric signs display the names of bars, restaurants, and open-air food stalls, where a sea of pedestrians fill the streets despite the lateness of the hour.

Even at midnight, Beijing is a city that never sleeps.

As midnight passes to the dark hours of the morning, secluded deep in the heart of the city, a man paces back and forth along marble-floored hallways, ignoring a small army of servants and bodyguards.

As night yields to the glow of dawn, he steps to a window and peers out at the city through binoculars. The rising sun reflects off a forest of glass-and-steel skyscrapers. The great buildings tower over bustling alleyways and broad boulevards jam-packed with a colorful blur of bicycles, tricycles, and rickshaws and a deafening chorus of blaring car horns.

Beijing, the national capital, is a kinetic panorama of the Chinese economy flexing its mighty muscle. Each new sunrise marks the start of another day in which the world's largest producer ships "Made in China" products around the globe, raking in riches and credits as Western countries sink deeper in a quicksand of hopeless debt.

Yet despite her appearance of vibrancy, China is not, and never has been, a nation where freedom rings. For deep in the midst of Beijing, far below the towering skyscrapers and just west of the ancient sector known as the Forbidden City—the walled compound from which the Chinese emperors once ruled—there is a fortified compound, shrouded in secrecy, that remains as a modern-day walled fortress.

The Chinese call it "Zhongnanhai."

At the south side of Zhongnanhai, by the "Gate of New China," are two slogans chiseled in Mandarin.

"LONG LIVE THE GREAT COMMUNITY PARTY OF CHINA," the first inscription proclaims.

"LONG LIVE THE INVINCIBLE MAO ZEDONG," declares the second.

Although the outside walls of Zhongnanhai scream the slogans of Maoist Communism, the inside is closed to the public.

Little is known about the inside world of Zhongnanhai except that it houses the headquarters for the Communist Party, the State Council of the People's Republic, and the Presidential Palace of the Chinese president.

And little is known about the new occupant of the Presidential Palace except that his name is Tang, and the Chinese call him the Raging Dragon.

The man lowers his binoculars and steps back from the window. He checks his watch.

It is time for blood.

CHAPTER 1

Three porpoises break the surface of the sea in perfect formation, peacefully oblivious to the thundering rotor blades slicing through the morning air just seventy-five feet above.

From the cockpit of the lead chopper, Lieutenant Wang Ju, squadron commander, looked out to his left at the black attack helicopter beside him, its nose dipped down. Hanging from the chopper's underbelly is a fistful of anti-armor rockets, each one powerful enough to take out any target they might find below. Painted on the tail section of its fuselage is a single orange star.

Wang Ju gave his wingman a thumbs-up, then looked to his right, where an identical black chopper, also armed with rockets and displaying a single orange star, flew in a flanking pattern.

There were ten helicopters. They were Z-10 attack helicopters of the PLA Navy, the People's Liberation Army-Navy.

Thundering through clear skies against a five-knot headwind, they flew so close to the surface of the water that their downdraft cut a wide band of ripples across the sea.

Wang Ju glanced down. The porpoises had vanished.

He checked his instrument panel.

Twelve miles to target. Visible contact expected within seconds. He ran through his combat checklist.

Thirty-millimeter cannon. Armed. Check.

HJ-9 anti-tank guided missiles. Armed. Check.

HJ-10 anti-tank missiles. Armed. Check.

TY-90 air-to-air missiles. Armed. Check.

A burnt orange glow lit the cockpit. The edge of the rising sun draped an orange carpet across the rippling wavelets below.

There! Dead ahead! Twelve o'clock!

Itu Aba Island.

The choppers whacked through a wisp of clouds that swept from left to right, blinding their view. Seconds later, they burst through into the sunlit sky on the other side.

The island looked larger now, and the outlines of two buildings came into view. In the distance, at the end of the airstrip in the middle of the island, a green C-130 cargo plane sat on the tarmac.

As the sun climbed higher, its rays illuminated the red flag flapping in the breeze. But the flag was not all red. A dark blue rectangle dominated the upper-left corner, and in the middle of the rectangle was a twelve-point white sun.

The Flag of Rebellion! Anger flushed his body.

"All units. Tiger Leader. On my lead, break left. Assume attack formation."

They had drilled for this maneuver dozens of times over the mainland and dozens more times in flight simulators with footage of the island.

Wang Ju flicked the yoke to his left. Like a flock of geese banking in a perfect "V" formation, the choppers broke out to the east of the island, where they would regroup and launch their attack from the blinding glare of the rising sun, making them harder targets for any sentries posted on the beach with machine guns or handheld missiles.

"Tiger Leader to all units. Arm missiles and report."

"Tiger Two. Missiles armed."

"Tiger Three. Missiles armed."

"Tiger Four ..."

Three miles to the east of Itu Aba, at one thousand feet over the water, they resumed attack formation.

"All units. Follow me." Wang Ju pushed down on his yoke. The lead chopper started back toward the island. "Lock on targets. Report."

"Tiger Two ... target locked ... Tiger Three ... target locked ..."

"Stand by to fire. On my mark."

Ju checked his airspeed indicator.

Speed, 125 knots. Target ... 3 miles downrange ... 2.75 miles ... 2.5 miles.

He gripped the missile-release button. "Stand by. On my mark ..." Target ... 2.25 miles ... 2.0 miles.

"Fire missiles!"

The Z-10 jumped, then settled onto an air cushion. Below the chopper, a single rocket dropped through the air, ignited, and streaked away, trailing a white stream of smoke. Nine other choppers released weapons. Ten white streaks, like streamers dropping from a Shanghai convention hall at New Year's, raced through the sky in a deadly convergence on Itu Aba.

Wang Ju increased airspeed to 130 knots and watched the missiles close on their targets. A fiery explosion in the middle of the island sent angry flames spiraling a hundred feet skyward. A second explosion sent more flames skyward, although not quite as high as the first. When the third explosion erupted, thick black smoke billowed up, rising from bright-hot flames leaping into the morning sky.

"Reduce airspeed to twenty knots," Wang Ju ordered. "Arm machine guns. Descend to 500 feet. Proceed with caution."

He yanked back on the yoke, slowing the helicopter a half mile from the beach. "Go to hover position."

Like gigantic buzzing dragonflies, the ten choppers hovered five hundred feet above the island, viewing the product of their destructive handiwork. Four separate infernos spewing thick black smoke raged below—one from each building at the airstrip, the third from the flaming mass that a moment ago had been a C-130 transport plane, and the fourth from the fuel depot.

Wang Ju flipped on the helicopter's external video cameras to record the event for posterity. As he watched the video monitor's display of the island ablaze in a fiery display of flame and smoke, it hit him. He was witnessing one of the greatest historical moments in the history of the People's Republic of China!

Historians would hail this moment as the dawn of the full and final reunification of the two Chinas under Communist rule! And at center stage of the story would be the squadron leader! Lieutenant Wang Ju! Billions of children in Shanghai, Beijing, Hong Kong, and, yes, even Taipei, would forever remember his name! Many would worship him as a hero!

The Hero's Medal would soon dangle from his neck. And if not the Hero's Medal, then the Meritorious Service Medal! Perhaps the medal would be awarded by President Tang himself! Ju had always wanted to meet the charismatic and bold new president of the People's Republic. Perhaps this would be his chance!

"Proceed cautiously. Move in for closer observation," Wang Ju said as he forced his mind back to the mission. "Watch for small arms on the ground. Eliminate all potential threats."

He tapped the yoke. The air armada inched forward, hovering over the breaking waves as they headed toward the airspace over the beach.

A figure ran from a burning building.

Suddenly, several figures popped up from behind the sand dunes just beyond the beach. They were carrying rifles and ran away from the approaching choppers toward the burning C-130.

Fools! he thought. What did they hope to accomplish by running? Even if they reached the other side of the island, they would have to swim two hundred miles to the Vietnamese coastline.

As Wang Ju watched the men scamper away from the beach, the one on the far left stopped running and turned around.

Wang Ju squinted his eyes. What was the man doing? He looked down through binoculars and saw the man aim his rifle at the choppers! Wang Ju pulled the trigger on the 30-millimeter cannon. Machine-gun fire cracked the air as a string of flashing tracer bullets shot to the ground. A sand cloud rose around the running men, blocking visibility. When the sand cloud cleared, six bodies were strewn in a zigzag pattern, their rifles scattered around them like harmless toothpicks.

Nothing moved. He waited. Finally, moving slowly, other figures began heading for the beach, their arms up, palms turned to the heavens in the universal symbol of surrender.

Wang Ju switched on the chopper's loudspeaker system and spoke in Mandarin. "To all Taiwanese personnel on the island. Come onto the beach with your hands in the air. If you keep your hands in the air, you will not be shot. Military personnel of the People's Republic will land shortly to facilitate your departure." He switched back to the squadron frequency. "Tiger Leader to all aircraft. Fly to prearranged guard points. Remain on station until further order."

The choppers broke from their straight line and flew to positions surrounding the island, hanging in the sky above Itu Aba like points on a clock, their cannons and rockets pointed down at anything or anyone that might move.

Wang Ju scanned the horizon. The second wave of helicopters approaching from the northwest were not attack choppers of the People's Liberation Army-Navy, but rather MI-17-V7 troop transport choppers from the People's Liberation Naval Air Force. The first of five MI-17s came in two hundred feet over the top of the hovering Z-10s. The transport choppers slowed their approach for landing as first one, then another feathered down in the center of the runway that ran down the middle of the island. Armed Chinese Marines poured from the first chopper as the second MI-17 touched down at the end of the runway.

Marines of the People's Liberation Army-Navy fanned out over the island, pointing their guns at the vanquished Taiwanese, who fell to their knees in the sand and surf before their captors, their hands behind their heads.

Wang Ju watched as two other Marines rushed to the flagpole bearing the red flag with the blue rectangular corner and the white twelve-point sun and ripped down the banner. One set it afire, then tossed it aside on the sand to burn.

A new flag ascended the pole. At the top, the wind unfurled it, revealing a large yellow star sewn in the upper-left corner of the orangish-red banner. To the right of the yellow star were four smaller stars in the formation of a waxing crescent moon.

As the morning sun lit the banner of the People's Republic in brilliant splendor, Ju considered it a moment for the ages, an eternal image forever frozen in time. Tears flooded his eyes and dripped onto his flight suit.

Victory!

"All units! Tiger Leader. Mission accomplished! Break formation! Return to base."

Presidential Palace
Zhongnanhai Compound
Beijing, People's Republic of China

shortly after sunrise

Years ago, as a hard-charging, mid-level information officer at Communist Party headquarters in Beijing, the new occupant of the office of the president of the People's Republic had been struck by an offhand comment by Barack Obama, then president of the United States.

In a difficult moment after his inauguration, President Obama lamented to the American press that "it would be easier to be president of China."

Perhaps there was more truth in that statement than Barack Obama had at the time realized, President Tang Qhichen now knew. For unlike the president of the United States, who, at least in theory, had to worry about constitutional checks and balances imposed on the executive by the legislative and judicial branches of the US government, the president of the People's Republic of China had no such "constitutional" roadblocks with which to be concerned.

Years before the Obama statement, before Tang started his meteoric ascendency up the party ladder as one of the brightest young minds of his generation, he had been studying at Harvard, as had so many other young Chinese and Russian revolutionaries. His concentration there was on the structure of the American government with the intention, even then, to compare and contrast the presidencies of each nation in order to focus on the strengths and weaknesses of each system.

Even at Harvard, as a foreign doctoral candidate, Tang had already set as his life's goal to bolster the power of the Chinese presidency in the event that he ever fulfilled the hot ambitions running through his veins and his soul.

Being "president" in China wasn't the same as being president of the United States. For the Chinese presidency was and is a necessary dictatorship or, at the very mildest, as American political analyst Bill Kristol once said, "the strongest position in an autocratic and thoroughly entrenched and unaccountable political system."

Privately, Tang embraced the notion of dictatorship and had agreed with Kristol's comparison. He even quoted him in his dissertation comparing the two presidencies.

Dictatorship, Tang believed, not only best served the interests of the masses but was also the most efficient means in the operations of government.

But there remained one major inadequacy in the structure of the Chinese presidency, and it had to do with command and control over the huge three-million-member People's Liberation Army-Navy. Despite the enhanced power given to the Chinese president, in one very important area, the president of the United States wielded more power. And that area had to do with control of the nation's military. For while the American Constitution gave the American president very clear command-and-control authority as commander in chief of all United States military forces, the loose conglomeration of the Communist bureaucracy that ran China had led sometimes to ambiguity in how the country was run and about just who ran its military.

Tang's final doctoral thesis at Harvard, published in both English and Mandarin, touched on this very topic and would have been considered boring in most non-academic circles.

He titled it "The Presidency of the United States versus the Presidency of the People's Republic of China: A Comparison of the Strengths and Weaknesses in Command and Control of the Military Under the Constitutional Structure of Each Nation."

The thesis presented a contrasting study of command-and-control power of the US and Chinese presidents over their respective militaries. In it, Tang hypothesized that China, despite her economic potential, could never become a world superpower unless and until a Chinese president wielded efficient and uncontested control over all Chinese fighting forces.

He also hypothesized that the US presidency had assumed increasing control over the American military because of the use of American presidential power in the many wars and conflicts that America has been involved in after World War II. Branding the US presidency as an "imperial" presidency, he cited a long list of non-declared wars that America had been involved in since 1945.

The list of postwar military action was long and revealing, starting with the Berlin Airlift in 1948, the Korean War in 1950, all the way through America's involvement in Iraq and Afghanistan through 2012 and beyond.

The thesis created an international uproar, at least within the international think-tank community. It was praised by American liberals as a brilliant denunciation of the long list of US military interventions and for its conclusion that the US presidency had become "imperial." His supporters at Harvard had said, "Nations must share equal power on a true global stage."

Tang concluded that "America had been a warmonger," and a number of American columnists at the *Washington Post*, the *New York Times*, and the *San Francisco Chronicle* penned glowing analyses agreeing with him.

Tang had been blasted by conservatives, who criticized Harvard for allowing Communists to study there. Conservatives condemned Tang's conclusion that the only way to strengthen the Chinese presidency and to strengthen the Chinese president's command and control over the Chinese military was to use Chinese military force more often, with a tempo resembling the American pattern since 1945.

The *Washington Times* branded Tang's thesis as "more dangerous than the original Communist Manifesto." The *Manchester Union Leader* was more blunt and less diplomatic than the *Times*, claiming that "this dissertation is *Mein Kampf* and Karl Marx all wrapped into the mind of a dangerous madman."

The *Wall Street Journal*, in an editorial entitled "The Rise of the Raging Dragon," suggested that Tang "proposed setting Communist China on a course of military aggression patterned on the Soviet Cold War model." From this editorial, headline writers had branded Tang as the young Raging Dragon, a name that stuck and a name that Tang, frankly, embraced as a badge of honor.

But to Tang, his ideas were neither liberal nor conservative. Instead, they were practical. More military power for the Chinese president was a practical solution and, in fact, the *only* means of achieving Sino superpower status. His vision was to transform China into a military superpower. His doctoral thesis advocating this solution got him noticed not only in America but also within the highest echelons of power in Beijing. The thesis was the solid-rocket booster that had launched his amazing climb through the party ranks.

In the fifteen years since he left Harvard, the uproar created when the document was first published seemed to have been forgotten in the West—until a year ago.

One year ago, when Tang became president of the People's Republic, the same groups in America, both liberal and conservative, reawoke in a loud swell of cacophonous voices of both lavish praise and venomous howling, with conservatives broadcasting bloodcurdling warnings about him. The names of the columnists and talking heads had changed over the years, but the sound of their voices had remained the same.

Despite their cries, despite choruses of both praise and prophecies of doom, the Raging Dragon's time had come.

He had laid out his blueprint for his presidency fifteen years ago. That blueprint included his master vision for energy. His actual plan started with the assault he had ordered against a place called Itu Aba Island.

Once married, now divorced, Tang was a very trim and fit forty-eight. The People's Republic was Tang's playground. The Communist Party of the immortal Mao Zedong was his lover. A million-plus soldiers and sailors of the People's Liberation Army-Navy were his children.

This very day, he thought, was the beginning of his grand opportunity to make the greatest contribution to the People's Republic since Chairman Mao! For China had never had a leader who would spread her political and military influence beyond the sphere of Southeast Asia—until now!

Carpe diem! He had learned the phrase at Harvard. "Carpe diem!" And now, indeed, was his time to seize the day!

Tang looked in the mirror in the bathroom adjoining the presidential bedroom and tightened the knot on the bright red tie against the buttoned collar of his white starched shirt.

His military briefing was six minutes away. Anxious to hear the words of his generals, he donned his navy blue pinstripe suit jacket and buttoned the four buttons down the front.

The "presidential pinstripe," it had been called by fashion writers, first in Hong Kong, then in Shanghai, because of his personal preference for Western-style pinstripes that fit well over his muscular torso.

Tang stepped from the bathroom, then walked out of the presidential bedroom into the hallway, where two captains of the People's Liberation Army-Navy jumped to attention.

"Are we ready, Captain Lo?"

"Yes, Mister President." The officer shot a quick salute to his commander in chief. "General Shang and Admiral Zou are awaiting you downstairs in the secure conference room."

"Good." The president again checked his watch. "Very well, Captain, let us proceed."

They walked thirty paces down the hallway of white marble to an elevator. Captain Lo pushed a button and stainless-steel double doors opened.

They stepped into the elevator, where a soldier had been waiting for them. A few seconds later, the elevator doors opened onto a broad marble-laden hallway. Tang himself had selected the ornate Chinese art, much of it from the Ming Dynasty, that now hung on both sides of the hallway.

At the entrance to the military conference room, Captain Lo pushed open the double doors. Morning sunlight streamed in from the four bay windows that opened onto the inner courtyard of the compound. Four chandeliers hung from the ceiling.

Two men sat side by side at the long conference table. One wore the green full-dress uniform of a general in the People's Liberation Army. The other wore the blue full-dress uniform of the People's Liberation Navy. They stood up, shooting salutes at their commander in chief. Tang thought that perhaps their smiles signaled good news.

"Sit, gentlemen," the president said.

Tang looked first at Admiral Zou Kai, then at General Shang Xiang, the minister of national defense, who was second only to the president in command of all the armed forces.

"General Shang," Tang said, "do you have a report on Operation Lightning Bolt?"

Shang, in his mid-sixties, sported a broad girth that reflected his propensity for whiskey and wonton noodles. He broke into a wide smile. "Mister President, I am pleased to report that Operation Lightning Bolt has been a smashing success! Thirty minutes ago, attack helicopters, with swift and deadly precision, executed the assault that you ordered, sir.

"The traitors on the island were caught by surprise. Two dozen were shot by our choppers on the beach as they attempted to fire their weapons at us. The rest tried to flee like scared rats! Admiral Zou's helicopter pilots were brilliant in the execution of their duties!"

Goose bumps crawled up the president's arms and neck, the sudden realization of total success overwhelming his body in electric excitement.

"After our pilots shot up the traitors like Swiss cheese, troop transport choppers arrived, and our Marines secured the ground. We are in total control.

"At this time, one of our civilian freighters, the M/V *Shemnong*, a freighter which I believe you may be familiar with, is steaming to Itu Aba with weapons and reinforcements for our forces to defend the island."

"Aah, yes. The *Shemnong*." Tang allowed himself a broad smile.

"And may I make a recommendation, Mister President?"

Tang leaned back in his chair and crossed his arms. "Yes, of course, General Shang."

"Thank you, Mister President. Yes, I was about to say that none of this would have been possible without the brilliant work of the PLA Navy, and not only of our Navy assault helicopters but also the crew and commander of the *Shi Lang*." The defense minister glanced at the admiral, who gave a dutiful nod of appreciation. "I recommend, Mister President, that in addition to commending the lead chopper pilot, we should also commend the captain and crew of the *Shi Lang*."

"Ah, yes, the *Shi Lang*.... Bring me a cup of hot tea, will you, Captain?"

"Yes, Mister President," the aide-de-camp said.

Tang smiled as he thought of the ship, of what it would mean in the days and years ahead. "The *Shi Lang*. The great equalizer to the American Navy."

He picked up the white porcelain cup of steaming oolong tea and took a sip. Mmmm ... just as he liked it. "Gentlemen, if there is one thing we should have learned from Napoleon and from the Japanese imperialists at Pearl Harbor, it is this." Another vivifying sip. "That the element of surprise is our best friend." He looked over at the blue-jacketed admiral. "Admiral Zou."

"Yes, sir, Mister President." The admiral's face perked up.

"There will be plenty of time to honor the crew of the *Shi Lang*. But something tells me that the *Shi Lang* may see action again very soon. Particularly if the traitorous pigs in Taipei try something in response to our victory. I think we should reserve that ceremony until another date in the future."

"Yes, of course, Mister President."

"However" — Tang put the cup down and wagged his index finger — "I think we should honor some of the Navy helicopter pilots at a nationally televised ceremony at Tiananmen Square in the next two days. Who is the squadron commander who led this attack?"

"Let me check, Mister President." The admiral flipped through some papers. "Aah, yes. Lieutenant Wang Ju, sir."

"Excellent!" Tang turned his eyes back to the minister of national defense. "General Shang, contact the minister of information and propaganda. I want a national ceremony, full of pageantry, celebrating China's restoration of this territory to its rightful origin. Our people must appreciate our military, and our military needs to know that our people are behind them."

"Yes, sir."

"I must address the nation from Tiananmen Square. Let's decorate this Lieutenant ... What was his name?"

"Wang, sir. Lieutenant Wang Ju."

"Aah, yes. Let's give Wang Ju the Hero's Medal. Find his assistant. We shall give him the Silver."

"Of course, Mister President." The general scribbled notes on a pad.

"This nation needs to create a few military heroes to visualize the fullest extent of what we can become!"

"I do not think either of us would disagree with that, Mister President," General Shang said.

Tang pushed the cup and saucer out of the way, leaned forward, and eyed first the general and then the admiral. "Consider the opportunity before us. We have just taken the first step in transforming the People's Republic into the great superpower of the twenty-first century! Where our Russian Communist adversaries to the North and the West failed, we shall succeed. The Soviet economy was nothing but a dilapidated patchwork of industrial rust, while we, the Chinese, are the world's greatest manufacturer.

"The Russians could not compete economically with the Americans. But we, the sons of Mao, sell our products to them! We loan them money to support their hopelessly bankrupt economy, fueled by their fat and undisciplined politicians who spend money as if there is no tomorrow."

He stopped and eyed the two senior officers again, first one, then the other.

"Gentlemen, we stand on the verge of the great Chinese century." Then, scowling at the general, he declared, "And this shall be the Chinese century because it shall be the century of the Chinese military! Do you understand, General?"

General Shang looked back at the president. "Yes, sir, of course. I understand."

Tang then turned to his Navy chief. "And you, Admiral Zou. Do you understand this?"

"Yes," the admiral answered immediately. "I embrace this glorious opportunity. And I am with you, sir."

"Very well!" Tang said. "Then let us, the three of us, toast this glorious moment of victory. Captain Lo!"

"Yes, Mister President!"

"Captain Lo, bring our finest baijiu with three shot glasses. In fact, bring a fourth. One for you too. We shall allow ourselves a toast of celebration! To victory!"

"To victory!"

USS Emory S. Land
northern sector of the South China Sea

4:00 a.m.

The young officer stood alone on the forward deck of the ship. Through the infrared binoculars that she held to her eyes, the black, rolling waves of the South China Sea morphed into a ghastly green abyss.

She scanned the entire sector of the sea, first at the distant horizon, sweeping from left to right, and then in closer to the ship, to an area where she expected the submarine to surface.

No sign of a conning tower. Only rolling swells.

"Morning, ma'am."

She recognized the voice. "Morning, Senior Chief Vasquez."

Another enthusiastic voice came from the dark. "Get you some coffee, Miss Surber?"

"I'm fine . . ." This time she lowered the binoculars and squinted at the sailor's nametag, dimly lit by the faint glow of one of the running lights. "Uh . . . Seaman Martin. But thanks for asking."

Seaman Martin's enthusiasm was typical of the incessant attention she received. The command had promised to keep it quiet for security reasons, but any dummy could figure it out, and most had.

Her last name.

Pictures in the media.

The whole "no talk" policy was a joke.

People talk.

After only a few weeks at sea, she had learned that scuttlebutt on board a Navy ship could erupt like a gas drum ignited by a match.

Why was the Navy protecting her? The thought of it hacked her off. Her grades at Annapolis should have earned her a spot in flight school at Pensacola. She had earned it. She deserved it. Others with a lower class standing than hers had gotten their choice of billets, including flight school.

Of course, the thought had occurred to her that the thought had occurred to them that the daughter of the president might be safer on the deck of a submarine tender than in the cockpit of an F-18 fighter jet or an SH-60R Seahawk helicopter.

Her father had promised never to say a word to any of his admirals or captains about her. And she believed him. He was a man of honor. He would never lie.

Still, she had her suspicions. Some busybody admiral, she surmised, was trying to stay in her father's good graces by giving her orders to a "safe" billet—not that any billet in the Navy was absolutely safe.

She had masked her disappointment when she got the orders. They had "sold" her the typical bill of goods. On the *Emory Land*, she would become the "weapons officer," the detailer said.

"It's unheard of for an ensign straight out of the academy to become a weapons officer, but with your record, you're a natural," the detailer claimed. "This will give you a big jump on your classmates."

Right.

It was true. She was good with a gun and could fire the .50-caliber machine gun. Word had gotten around that she was on the academy's women's rifle team. But still, the title was like a lollipop given to a kid by a bank teller at a drive-through window. It wasn't like she was going to be in charge of antiballistic missile systems or Tomahawk cruise missiles or anything like that. The facts were these. USS *Emory S. Land* had a total of ten weapons on board, and every one of these guns was World War II vintage. The weapons had their value ... against pirates and other small vessels. But a sub tender's mission was to operate under the protective cover of other ships as it supplied the Navy's submarine fleet with food and fuel and torpedoes.

In a real firefight, *Emory Land* would be in trouble—unless her opponent was another sub tender or a tugboat. Everyone on board knew the *Emory Land* was operating outside the protective umbrella of the Navy's cruisers and destroyers. In a word, if something were to go wrong, she was in the wrong place at the wrong time.

Stephanie's role as the weapons officer was in reality her secondary role aboard this ship. She was also the replenishment officer, in charge of transferring supplies from the ship to submarines when they surfaced. The replenishment job was far more time-consuming and germane to the ship's mission than the weapons part.

But hey, she was the weapons officer. That would look good on her FITREP.

Or so she was told.

The sea had brought one positive change in her life, ending, for the time being, a perpetual nuisance that had driven her batty. The Secret Service wasn't out here.

The wind whipped up off the portside, and she caught a whiff of cologne.

"Morning, Ensign Surber."

"Morning, sir." She lowered her binoculars and turned to see the well-cut, handsome figure of Commander Bobby Roddick approach out of the predawn darkness.

"New message from SUBPAC. The sub will be surfacing a little late. It's going to be another thirty minutes." Commander Roddick spoke in the low-country, southern accent of his native Charleston, South Carolina.

"Do we know which sub yet, sir?"

"Just got the word. USS *Boise*. *Los Angeles* class. Skipper is Commander Graham Hardison. A good guy."

A sailor popped a hatch behind them, giving her a glimpse of the XO's blue eyes before the hatch clicked shut again. Then all she could see was his rugged silhouette.

"We want her replenished in an hour," he said. "We want her back under before sunrise. You got that inventory of all the food supplies we're offloading?"

"Yes, sir." She tried suppressing in her own voice any hint of the star-struck tone she normally was the recipient of.

"Look, Stephanie ..." He hesitated.

"Yes, sir."

"We must move faster than yesterday when we replenished the *Georgia*."

"Yes, sir."

"I know the *Georgia* is a lot bigger than the *Boise* because she's a *Trident*-class. But still, we took an hour and forty-five minutes. That's too long."

"That's my responsibility, sir."

"Good." He looked off to the horizon. "These budget cuts make all of our jobs a lot harder. We're short-handed. Makes it tough to meet our self-imposed deadlines. And that's not your fault. But if we don't get that sub replenished within sixty minutes, the skipper will be all over my butt. And that means I've got to come down here and chew you out."

"We'll move faster with the *Boise*, sir. I guarantee it."

"Good. Meet me with a copy of the inventory in the wardroom in fifteen minutes."

"Aye, sir."

"Also, there's something else I need to talk to you about. Bring a notepad."

"Yes, sir."

Commander Roddick turned and walked off, an irresistible rock of a man disappearing into the dark. This was the first time she had ever enjoyed getting chewed out by a superior officer.

"Composure, Stephanie," she mumbled as she walked to her stateroom to get the submarine's food supply inventory. She stepped through the hatch and found the report on the stand beside her rack. What to do for the next thirteen minutes?

Go up now?

She decided to lie down and set her watch for ten minutes. Closing her eyes, the images raced in a whirlwind. The academy commencement ceremony. Her father's speech to the graduates. Their commissioning. Covers flying into the rich blue Maryland sky at Memorial Stadium. The montage of memories swirling in her head gave way to a few moments of sleep.

Beep-beep-beep-beep. She opened her eyes from her quick doze. Five minutes had passed. She grabbed the report and a legal pad and stepped into the passageway. Three minutes later, she walked into the officers' wardroom.

The wardroom was empty. She heard only the distant hum of the ship's engines with an occasional clanging of dishes in the adjacent galley. The rich aroma of fresh coffee filled the air. Bright fluorescent lights hung over the long table.

She sat down just as the XO walked in from the passageway. She stood as he entered, but felt disappointment to see Senior Chief Vasquez with him. Nothing against the senior chief. It was just ...

"Sit, Stephanie." The XO motioned to the seat beside the head of the table. "Got that food inventory?"

"Right here, sir." She slid the papers across the table in his direction. He picked up the report and began perusing it. A steward rolled a silver tray into the wardroom from the galley.

"Coffee, sir?" the steward asked.

"Black please, Ben." The XO flipped through the inventory. "Stephanie? Senior Chief?"

The steward poured steaming coffee into three white mugs, starting with the XO and descending by rank.

"Looks good." The XO laid the report on the wardroom table.

"Thank you, sir," Stephanie replied.

"Ensign Surber." His blue eyes shot her a stare. "You're an academy grad, but you're new to the Navy." He sipped his coffee. "I assigned the senior chief to your division to give you the practical benefit of a sailor who's experienced the Navy for over twenty years." He flashed a slight smile. "Senior chief has seen everything you can imagine."

"I understand, sir," Stephanie said. "I value having Senior Chief Vasquez in my division."

"Stephanie, as you know, we're not a combat vessel. We're light on weapons. Still, you're our weapons officer, and that's one of the most important positions on the ship."

"Yes, sir."

"I know we've been through this before, but things may be getting hot, and I want to go over it again. You're comfortable and familiar enough with the ship's armament if something goes wrong?"

"Yes, sir, XO. Four .50-caliber machine guns, four 20-millimeter antiaircraft guns, and two 40-millimeter antiaircraft guns. Half on port. Half on starboard."

"Very good." The XO's smile broadened. "To make matters worse, back in 2009, the Navy came up with a harebrained idea that this ship should carry around a crew of half civilians and half military, which means that if we have to defend ourselves, we've got a bunch of worthless landlubbers running around and only half the military personnel that the ship was designed to carry."

"I understand."

"Well, I'm not sure that you do understand."

"Sir?"

"There's a war out there between Taiwan and China. We don't know if it will be contained or if it will escalate. As you know, the president" — he did not say "your father" — "has ordered elements of the Seventh Fleet into the South China Sea to … shall we say … discourage this war before it gets out of control."

"Yes, sir."

"Ordinarily, we'd be operating behind a screen of cruisers, frigates, and destroyers. But things are happening so fast that Seventh Fleet has not had time to reposition our missile cruisers. So we have to stay here and fulfill our mission, to resupply our attack submarines. But we're short on ammo and short on guns. We're out in this sector of the sea all alone."

"Yes, sir."

"After we refuel that sub, and they go back under, there's not a friendly ship on the surface within a hundred miles. The *Vicksburg* is on the way, but she won't be close enough to help much for a while if something goes wrong. The administration prior to the Williams administration neglected the military, spending taxpayers' money on sinkhole social programs instead."

"Yes, sir, I know all about that."

"I figured you did. But that's not the reason I called you down here."

"I don't follow you, sir." Don't tell me that you're going to transfer me to a safe shore location, she wanted to say, but didn't.

"Ensign, I want to make sure you're up to speed on the operation of the machine guns and the antiaircraft guns on board. Just in case."

"Aye, sir."

"I know that as part of your training you've had some experience firing the .50-caliber."

"Yes, sir."

"After the replenishment, I want you to get with the senior chief and review the procedures for firing these weapons. Make sure you're prepared to fire each one if we get into a hot situation. Senior chief is a gunner's mate, one of the best in the Navy. So you'll be in the hands of one of our best."

"Aye, sir."

"We're going to be running battle-station drills. Fire a few practice rounds on the fifties to make sure they're all working. But be conservative. Maybe ten rounds max. We don't have enough ammo to waste any."

"Understand, sir."

"And Stephanie ..."

"Yes, sir?"

"Call this a gut feeling, but if things get hot, be careful."

"Aye, aye, sir." Stephanie swallowed hard, her heart pounding from the sudden realization that combat may be imminent. She stood and shot a sharp salute. "Permission to return to my station, sir?"

"Permission granted."

CHAPTER 2

USS Vicksburg
Ticonderoga-*class cruiser*
forward vanguard of the Carl Vinson *Strike Group*
South China Sea

three days later
predawn hours

The officer stepped onto the forward deck of the gray warship and looked out over the dark sea. The starry host blanketing the seascape to the right revealed that the night had not yet surrendered to the coming day. But off to the left, from the direction where the sun would rise, the waters reflected that faint iridescent glow that belonged more to the day than the night.

USS *Vicksburg* was alone in this sector of the sea, with no sign of any other vessel all the way to the horizon.

Yet they were out there.

Somewhere.

The Chinese and the Taiwanese.

His sixth sense screamed it as loud as the Mississippi thunderbolts that preceded the driving rainstorms that as a boy had turned his sandlot football games into hot summer mud slushes.

Something bad was about to happen.

But what? An errant missile attack? A wayward torpedo slamming into the *Vicksburg*?

Lieutenant Commander Fred Jeter dismissed those thoughts and reached into the pants pocket of his wash-khaki uniform and extracted a lighter. He started to put a Benson & Hedges in his mouth.

"Morning, sir." The voice came from an approaching silhouette—a member of the forward watch.

"Morning, Petty Officer."

As the watchman passed by, he put the cigarette between his lips, struck the lighter, shielding the tip of the cigarette with his left hand, and sucked in hard. The miniature flame from the lighter leaped to the tip, kissing it long enough to light it. The dim orange glow revealed the gold oak leaf pinned to his right collar—showing his rank as a lieutenant commander in the US Navy—and on his left collar, a branched oak leaf with a miniature silver acorn—the emblem of the Navy Medical Corps.

Sweet relief.

Fred sucked more nicotine into his lungs, defying the warnings of the surgeon general.

A strong-willed Mississippi boy who once rabbit hunted with a .12-gauge on his granddaddy's farm, Dr.—and now Lieutenant Commander—Fred Jeter never liked being told what to do. In fact, if the surgeon general and all the politically correct, shove-it-down-your-throat activists hadn't made such a hullabaloo about smoking, he probably would've never started. But Fred wanted to prove a point to himself, if to no one else. His thirst for independence triumphed over even his desire for good health.

When the Navy came along and offered to pay his way through medical school and pay him a salary to boot, the deal sounded like a no-brainer—even though it contradicted the career path planned out for him by his father, who ran a long-standing family practice in Hattiesburg. The booming Jeter Medical Clinic had awaited the arrival of its favorite son, and with it came a thriving business, membership in the country club, and his pick of any number of blonde, well-endowed debutante-sorority-sister coeds freshly graduated from Ole Miss.

But Fred Jeter had other plans. Sure, he caught some flak from some who called him crazy, including his father. But he fell in love with the Navy.

And here he was, sucking cancer sticks and standing watch on a warship on the other side of the world, about to get in the middle of a war, all because he was as stubborn and bullheaded as a rebel-yelling infantryman at Manassas.

A voice boomed over the ship's 1MC: "All officers report to the bridge."

Fred cursed and checked his watch. He dropped the cancer stick on the deck, kicked it overboard, and watched the breeze sweep it into the drink.

He stepped into a steel passageway illuminated by bright fluorescent lights. A moment later, he stepped onto the bridge.

"Sorry to interrupt your smoking break, Doc." The ship's commanding officer, Captain Leonard Kruger, was standing behind a wooden podium, making a point of looking at his watch. Affectionately known by his wife and crew members behind his back as "Lenny," the punctuality-conscious captain blazed an irritated stare right at Fred. "Long night in sick bay?"

"My apologies, Skipper." Fred took the last seat in the semicircle of chairs around the CO.

"Very well," Kruger said, "let's get started." The captain pointed to the XO, who hit a button that projected a map of the South China Sea on the overhead. "Gentlemen, pay close attention." The skipper sipped hot black coffee. "As you know, the president has ordered the *Vinson* Strike Group into the South China Sea. Our ship, the *Vicksburg*, is at the tip of that strike group. Our mission: step into a hornet's nest and stop a war.

"As I speak to you now, we're just entering the South China Sea." The captain slowed his cadence. "This mission may be the most dangerous that the US Navy has undertaken since World War II."

The officers on the bridge raised eyebrows and exchanged concerned glances.

"The only American surface ships in the area right now are the USS *Vicksburg*, our sister ship USS *Shiloh*, and the USS *Emory S. Land*, which is a lightly armed sub tender. *Emory Land* is one hundred miles out in front of us. It was already in the area before the president issued his order.

"*Shiloh* is twenty miles off our left flank, just behind us. The carrier and the rest of our naval firepower are way back to our rear, just sailing from Japan. Since we're the lead warship entering the fray, our position is vulnerable. Some of you know Lieutenant Commander Gunner McCormick." The skipper nodded at a trim, muscular officer wearing wash-khakis and sporting closely cropped hair sprinkled with a few grays.

Fred had heard of McCormick, who had a reputation as a swashbuckling intelligence officer who had served with SEAL units in Afghanistan and had been awarded two Navy Crosses for heroism—one for some questionable activities he was involved with in Korea.

"Commander McCormick is the senior intelligence officer on the carrier group staff. Admiral McPherson has flown him out here by chopper to brief us." The skipper glanced over at the commander. "The deck is yours, Gunner."

"Thank you, sir." McCormick, a former college quarterback who still had the build of one, stood and moved to where the captain had been behind the podium. "Good morning, gentlemen."

"Morning," a few mumbled.

"The skipper's right. Our naval task force is steaming into a dangerous situation. Let me start with a bit of history about the relevant players." McCormick slipped on a pair of black plastic government-issued reading glasses.

"As many of you know, Taiwan and Communist China hate each other." He adjusted the glasses. "This mutual hatred reignited just after World War II, when Communist rebels waged a civil war against Chiang Kai-shek and the nationalist government on the mainland. By December of 1949, the Commies had pushed the good guys off the mainland, and Chiang Kai-shek moved the nationalist government to Taipei, on the island of Taiwan. Mao Zedong established the Communist government in Beijing.

"Chiang Kai-shek maintained that the government in Taiwan was the legitimate Chinese government, and the US recognized that position up until 1979, when President Jimmy Carter finally recognized the commies in Beijing. However, we kept Taiwan as an ally, even though we didn't grant it diplomatic status or put an official embassy there or even recognize it as a nation. Still, the US has made a commitment to protect it."

The skipper nodded at the supply officer. "Lieutenant?"

The supply officer hit a switch and a map appeared on the overhead.

"This, gentlemen," McCormick continued, "is the South China Sea ...

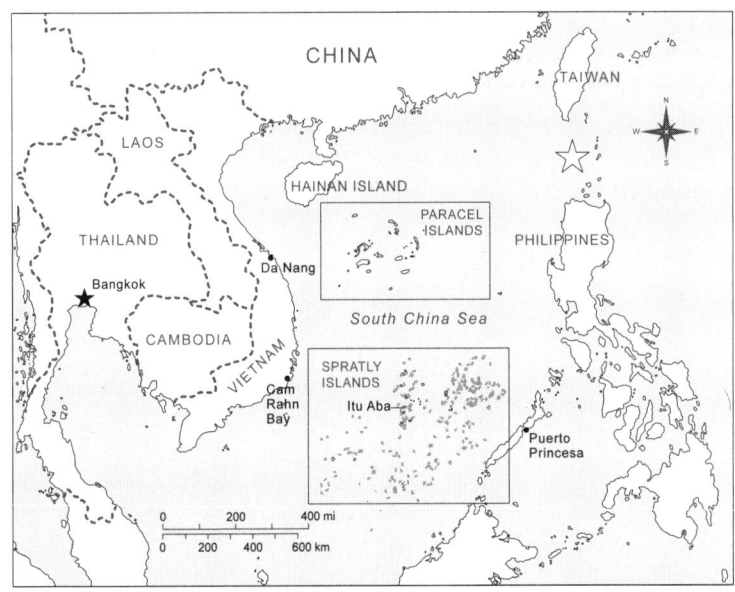

Area of the South China Sea, with the Paracel and Spratly Island groups

"The area within the lower rectangle shows the Spratly Islands. One hundred islands are scattered throughout these waters.

"Vietnam, Malaysia, and the Philippines claim parts of the Spratlys. But Taiwan and China each claim them all. They're uninhabited, except for small military units on forty-five of the islands claimed by these five nations. Minor skirmishes have occurred between the countries, but there's been nothing like what's brewing between China and Taiwan right now."

A hand shot up.

"Yes, Lieutenant?"

"Excuse me, sir," the weapons officer said. "What's the value of these islands to these countries?"

"Good question, Lieutenant," McCormick said. "The answer is natural gas." A brief pause. "China"—he tapped at the top of the map—

"decreed last year that all cars manufactured there over the next four years be fueled by natural gas.

"China's become the world's largest producer of goods, and their consumption of fossil fuels has skyrocketed. So they adopted this natural gas mandate to reduce their dependence on foreign oil. Then Chinese petroleum engineers discovered huge natural gas reserves in the waters around one of the Spratly Islands, an island known as Itu Aba."

He nodded at the supply officer. "Lieutenant, a close-up of the middle of the first map, please."

"Aye, sir."

Another map screen flashed up.

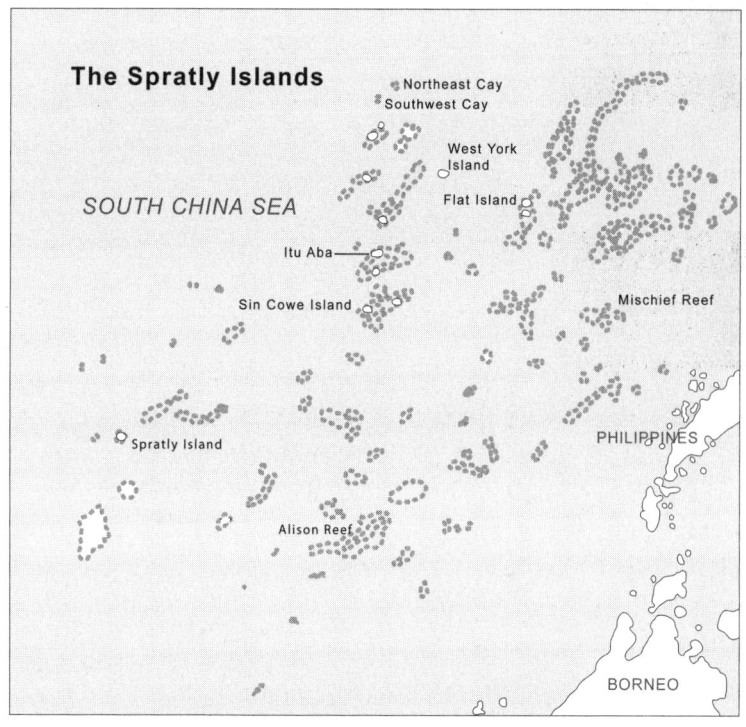

The Spratly Islands and Itu Aba Island

"Here's a close-up of that sector, showing the Spratlys in the middle of the South China Sea. You can see Itu Aba in the upper portion of this map. This is the grand prize in the fight between China and Taiwan, gentlemen. Itu Aba. Huge natural gas reserves are below the shallow waters around it.

"Less than a mile in length, two-tenths of a mile wide, Itu Aba was a Japanese sub base in World War II. China controlled it after the war, and then Taiwan controlled the island after the Communist revolution in China. Yes, Lieutenant?"

"Sir, how far is the island between the Philippines and Vietnam?"

McCormick set down his coffee mug and picked up a bottled water. "Lieutenant, put the map back up on the screen, full scale, will you?"

"Yes, sir." The image of the South China Sea region reappeared.

"Very well. Now Itu Aba is here, represented by a diamond on this chart."

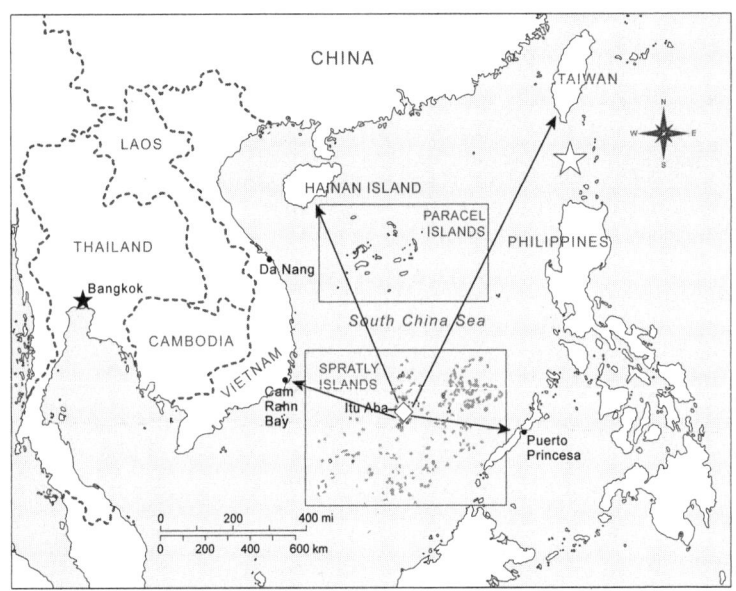

The South China Sea region

"Itu Aba is 900 miles from the southern tip of Taiwan. So looking at this graphic with the center of the clock being the diamond from which these arrows radiate, Cam Rahn Bay, Vietnam, is at 9:30 on the clock, almost 400 miles from ground zero. Hainan Island in China is at 10:30,

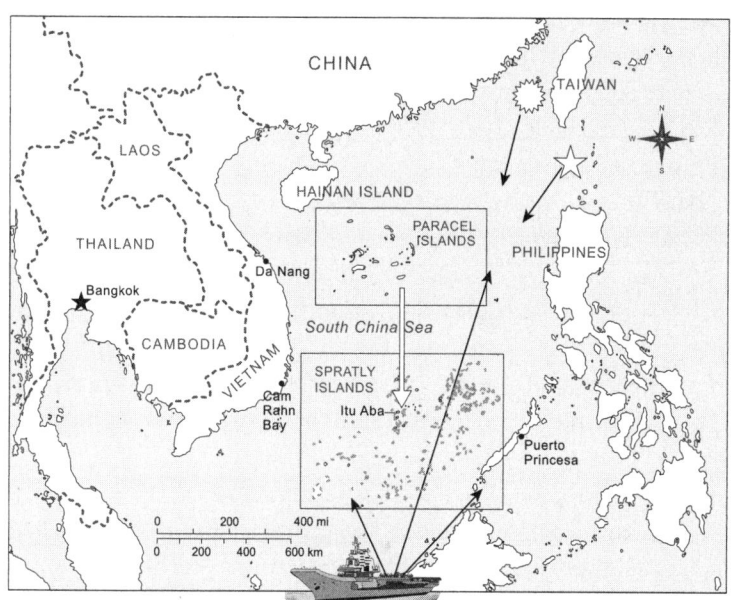

Arrows indicate possible locations of the Chinese aircraft carrier
Shi Lang in relation to Itu Aba Island. The Taiwanese fleet's position is shown
with the white sun. The USS *Vicksburg's* is shown with a white star

"Now let me say a few words about the Taiwanese threat. We believe
that the Taiwanese task force consists of two frigates, a destroyer, a
troop carrier with a Marine expeditionary unit, and one submarine out
front in the lead." The skipper sipped coffee. "At our current rate and
course, we should intercept them before sundown today."

The skipper turned away from the chart. "But either way, we are *not*
to fire on them. Unless, of course, they fire on us first, which I doubt
they'll do. We're more concerned about the Chinese firing on us. Especially with that carrier out there. Now if the Taiwanese task force sails
past us and continues on toward Itu Aba, then at that point, we begin
electronic jamming."

"But Skipper." The engineering officer raised his hand.

"Lieutenant?"

"Sir, couldn't our e-jamming be construed as a hostile act by either
of the parties?"

The captain nodded. "Yes, to answer your question, our jamming might be considered hostile. Will we get fired on? Possibly. And we must be ready to defend against anything."

For a few seconds, there were no questions.

Fred raised his hand.

"Doc?"

"What can the medical staff do to prepare?"

"Thanks, Doc. Prepare for anti-ship missiles. Remember what the French Exocets did against the British frigates *Ardent* and *Antelope* during the Falkland Islands war. Remember the missiles that hit USS *Stark* in the Persian Gulf. The danger from missile attacks is explosion and raging fire. Advise the medical staff to prepare for severe burn treatment."

Fred nodded as he jotted notes on a small pad.

"Meantime, Doc, we are going to General Quarters one hour before we reach the intercept point with the Taiwanese. I'd like you to make rounds with all the men to observe their psychological state and let me know if you're concerned about the possibility of anybody cracking as this thing gets closer."

"Aye, Captain."

Bridge
Chinese freighter M/V **Shemnong**
Gulf of Tonkin
fifty miles west of Hainan Island, People's Republic of China
course 135 degrees

predawn

Plowing to the southeast through the dark waters of the Gulf of Tonkin in the predawn hours, the Chinese freighter M/V *Shemnong* was passing fifty miles west of China's Hainan Island.

The distant glow of the coming morning, fueled by a still-invisible sun somewhere off to the east over the Pacific, cast a dim, opaque gray off to the ship's port, out toward Hainan.

Captain Fu Cheuk-yan, awash at the moment by the nostalgic

memories of his glorious days as a young naval officer, stood on the bridge and fixed his binoculars in the direction of Hainan. For it was in Hainan, in April of 2001, that as a junior lieutenant in the People's Liberation Army-Navy, Fu had witnessed history.

A United States Navy surveillance aircraft, an EP-3, after colliding with a Chinese military jet, made an emergency illegal landing on Hainan Island, in the territory of the People's Republic.

When it landed, soldiers of the People's Liberation Army-Navy surrounded the American plane and took the crew into custody.

The twenty-four Americans had looked worn, tired, and afraid, Fu remembered. Ten days later, after then US President George W. Bush penned an apology to Foreign Minister Tang Jiaxuan, they were released.

Fu later concluded that Hainan Island marked a historic turning point wherein the People's Republic of China eclipsed the United States as the world's foremost power. That moment, the Hainan Island incident, a moment in which "mighty America" apologized to the PRC, marked the beginning of the twenty-first century power shift from America to China.

And he was there as an eyewitness!

Captain Fu smiled at the thought, struck a match, and held it at the end of his cigarette.

Much had changed in Fu's life since that glorious experience at Hainan. He had gotten out of the People's Liberation Army-Navy, had gone to work for several shipping companies, and was now part owner and captain of the *Shemnong*, doing what he loved most and making far more money in a month than he had in an entire year as a young naval officer.

But his presence all those years ago at Hainan Island had opened many doors for him. Prospective employers and business partners had peppered him with questions about the interrogation of the Americans. In fact, his experience at Hainan had led to the ownership group for the *Shemnong* offering him a stake in the company. Indeed, life had been good. And each day brought more promise than the last.

By the time the sun appeared on the eastern horizon on this day, *Shemnong* would have slipped outside the protective waters of the Gulf of Tonkin and into the open waters of the South China Sea, headed to

Itu Aba Island to deliver military supplies for which he would be paid handsomely.

His final port of destination on this voyage was Thailand, where he would deliver secret medical supplies under the new transportation contract he had signed with the Qinzhou Medical Group, a contract he believed would make him filthy rich.

The exclusive contract over the next three years to carry this medical cargo from the *Shemnong*'s home port in Qinzhou, China, to Bangkok was the break he had been hoping for. His special connections in Beijing had been helpful in securing both the Itu Aba contract and the even richer Qinzhou Medical Group contract.

"Mr. Chan." He beckoned to the ship's first officer, who was manning the wheel.

"Yes, Captain."

"Turn the wheel over to Mr. Liu and punch up our navigational chart. I want to see where we are and how long until we clear the coast of Hainan."

"Yes, Captain."

The ship's navigator, a younger sailor named Liu, took the wheel as the first officer punched in some numbers on a keyboard.

A second later, a real-time navigational chart popped up just under the bridge windshield.

"Here is our current position, Captain, marked by the white arrow just west of Hainan Island, a place you are most familiar with, sir." The first officer nodded and smiled in unspoken tribute to what had happened there all those years ago in 2001. "We have just turned on a course of one-three-five degrees, sir. By the middle of the morning, around ten o'clock, we will have cleared Hainan Island and will be steaming in the South China Sea toward the Paracel Islands. Then we will turn to one-eight-zero degrees, heading south on the next leg of the voyage, followed by another course change, to one-three-five degrees to head to the Spratly Islands. There, as you know, we will rendezvous with military helicopters from Itu Aba Island for the airlift of supplies for our forces there. That should take no more than one hour.

"From there, our course will be two-five-zero degrees, heading southwest, to a point in the South China Sea south of Long Xuyen, Vietnam. From there our course is three-one-five degrees to the northwest, steaming into the Gulf of Thailand, past the Cambodian coast, before making a final course adjustment to three-six-zero degrees on our final approach to Bangkok."

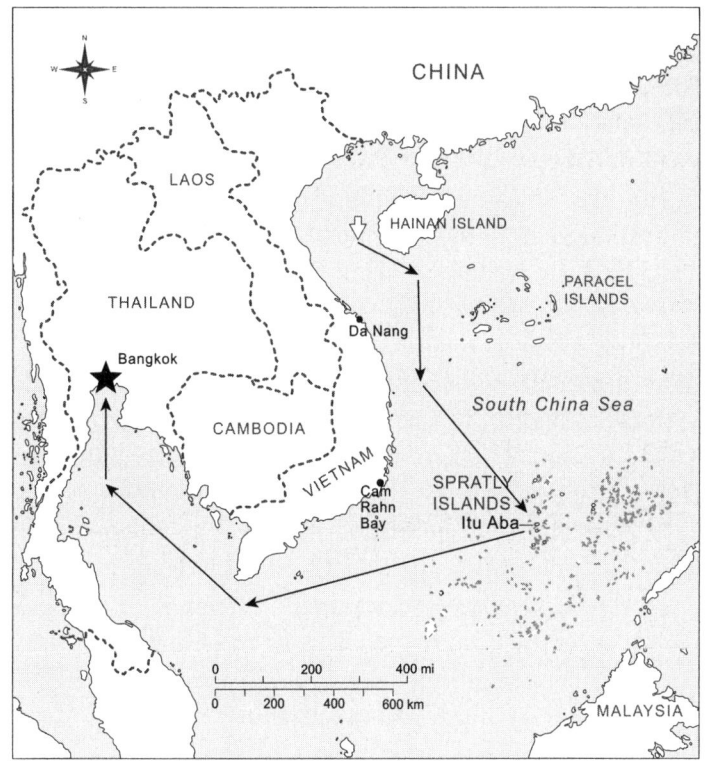

Route of M/V *Shemnong*

Fu sucked on the cigarette and studied the chart. "Looks good, Mr. Chan. But we must remind the crew to go to high alert once we enter the South China Sea. The Taiwanese may not be happy that our first stop is to deliver military supplies to our forces. Make sure you keep someone glued to the radar until we clear the Spratlys."

"You do not think the Taiwanese would interfere with the high-seas passage of a civilian freighter, do you?"

Fu flicked gray ashes into an ashtray and rose from the captain's chair. "Nothing about them surprises me. They have fought the People's

Republic since 1927. Any vessel, civilian or military, flying the flag of the People's Republic is a potential target for them. Remember, the danger of this mission is one of the reasons we are being paid so handsomely under this contract."

They lapsed into silence, the humming of the ship's engines the only sound.

The first officer said, "Captain, may I ask a question?"

"Of course," Fu said.

"Are you not curious about the cargo?"

Fu smiled, then took another drag from the cigarette. "You mean the military cargo destined for the Spratlys?"

"Actually, I was wondering about the secret medical cargo," Chan said. "After all, we are being paid a lot more for that than for delivering machine guns and antiaircraft rockets to Itu Aba."

"Why be curious?" Fu tipped his head back and released a cloud of smoke from his mouth. "The first installment has been deposited in our Hong Kong account. Freedom of navigation exists on the high seas. And besides"—he snuffed out the cigarette—"we have been told that the cargo is medically related and that we are not to ask about it. Even you, my dear Chan, will become rich from this, I am sure."

The first officer nodded. "I am grateful, Captain Fu. But still, given the size of the contract, are you not curious about our cargo?"

Fu smiled. "Whatever it is, it is boarded in crates. If you are all that curious, Mr. Chan, go down into the cargo bay and have a look. Just make sure you bring your jacket. The refrigeration system is on, and it is very cold. That refrigeration system in the cargo bay will make us tons of money." He smiled as he pondered that last thought.

"Yes, sir." Chan nodded.

"Oh. And one other thing."

"Yes, sir?"

"Whatever you find down there, do not share that information with me. I do not have a need to know nor do I wish to know."

"Yes, Captain."

"Navigator, maintain course one-three-five degrees. Steady as she goes."

"Aye, Captain."

Helipad
US Navy SH-60R Seahawk helicopter
USS Vicksburg

T he sun peeked above the eastern horizon, casting a bright orange glow across the sea. Lieutenant Commander Gunner McCormick watched from the cargo jump seat as the pilot reached forward and pushed the start button. The helicopter's engines sputtered. Rotors turned. Engines fired, sending the rotors into full rotation. A sonorous roar drenched the ship's fantail.

US Navy crewmen, wearing sound-protection gear, scrambled away as the chopper roared on the deck, awaiting permission to fly.

"You strapped in, Commander?" The pilot, his olive-drab flight suit zipped up to his neck and white flight helmet strapped to his chin, turned around from his left cockpit seat and looked over his right shoulder at his passenger. His copilot, seated in the right cockpit seat, continued his preflight checklist.

"Good to go, Lieutenant," Gunner said through his chin microphone, responding to the pilot's voice through his headset. "You got enough gas in this bird to get us out to our next stop? You know I don't like to swim."

"We do now, courtesy of the *Vicksburg*," the pilot said. "We'll need to gas up again when we get there."

"Just what I envisioned when I joined the Navy." Gunner chuckled. "Long helicopter rides from ship to ship in the middle of the ocean, flying on fumes, and trying to land on tiny helipads on a moving target, with barely enough gas to avoid ditching."

"Hey, look on the bright side, Commander," the pilot said, chuckling. "A tender's got a bigger fantail than a missile cruiser. So you've got a smaller chance of landing in the drink."

"That's comforting to know," Gunner quipped. "I know how you flyboys are. Taking bets on which passengers reach for the barf bag first."

The copilot chimed in. "We'll have to try the barf bag thing on this leg of the flight. I think we'd both lose our wings if we try it on the way back."

"That's for dang sure," the pilot said. "You can never have any fun when you've got VIPs on board. Even if you outrank the VIP. No auto-rotations. No fake fuel losses. No nothing."

"Seahawk Three. *Vicksburg* control."

Gunner heard the ship's air traffic control through his headset.

"Seahawk Three. Go ahead, *Vicksburg*."

"Seahawk, you are clear for takeoff."

"*Vicksburg*. Roger that."

The roar of the engines grew louder, and the helicopter shook on the *Vicksburg*'s helipad. Gunner felt separation from the fantail, the lofty feeling when an aircraft first leaves the surface. The chopper rose, climbing into the morning sky. A moment later, the sleek gray missile cruiser was cutting through the water off to the left as the chopper climbed high above her.

"Seahawk Three. *Vicksburg* Control. Go to two thousand feet. Set course for two-two-zero degrees. Good luck and Godspeed."

"*Vicksburg*. Seahawk Three. Climbing to two thousand. Setting course for two-two-zero degrees. Thank the skipper for his hospitality. Hope to see you next time."

The Chinese (PRC) freighter M/V Shemnong
South China Sea
between Da Nang, Vietnam, and the Paracel Islands
course 180 degrees

Against the swirling tropical wind, two long gongs rang out over the length of the ship. These gongs were followed by a pause, followed by two more gongs.

Like most freighters and merchant ships on the high seas, M/V *Shemnong* operated on six separate watches of four hours each, with the forenoon watch beginning at 8:00 a.m. and running until noon. The gongs of the ship's bell were used to signify the beginning, middle, and end of each of the ship's watch.

The two gongs, separated by a pause, and followed by two more gongs, signaled that the forenoon watch was half over.

First Officer Kenny Chan, walking along the windswept portside deck when the gongs sounded, checked his watch. Ten o'clock sharp. Right on time.

M/V *Shemnong* had cleared the waters of the Gulf of Tonkin and was now steering a southerly course at full speed in the warm waters of the South China Sea. Chan, halfway through his rounds, had just stepped out of the galley and come topside.

He extracted a pair of sunglasses from his pocket, slipped them on, and gazed out across the aqua-blue sea, in the direction of the Spratlys and beyond toward Borneo.

How could such placid-looking waters harbor such danger as the captain had warned? Yes, it appeared the war between China and Taiwan was about to erupt in the Spratlys, and from that one of two good things could happen. China could establish total control of the Spratlys and all their natural gas reserves. Or, even better, Chan thought, the war could escalate and lead, finally, to the toppling of the traitorous regime in Taipei.

Still, Chan wondered why he had a sense that the danger lurking over the horizon somehow paled when compared to the danger lurking in the belly of his own ship. How odd, he thought, that the captain was not interested in the contents of the cargo.

Why would the shippers of medical supplies not want the captain to know what he was shipping? And why would all the supplies be boarded up so they could not easily be inspected?

"Forget it," Chan mumbled. He stuck a cigarette in his mouth and reached in his pocket for a lighter. If the captain wasn't concerned about it, why bother? There would be plenty of options for spending the bonus money from this voyage. Chan would take a two-week vacation to Tahiti and spend the rest on a down payment for a high-rise flat in Hong Kong.

Time to get back to work, he decided. Chan glanced at his clipboard. He had already checked the galley, the boiler room, and the engine room. Still to be checked, the crew's quarters, the radio room, the cargo bay ...

The cargo bay. He remembered the captain's words: "But if you are all that curious, Mr. Chan, go down into the cargo bay and have a look. Whatever you find down there, do not share that information with me. I do not have a need to know nor do I wish to know."

He had to check the cargo bay anyway. It was part of his routine on watch. Besides, the cargo was boarded up, so what could one see? The captain was right. The refrigeration system was running full blast down there. Going down there would feel like stepping from the tropical heat onto a polar ice cap.

Why bother?

Why not?

He bypassed the radio room and crew's quarters. Stepping through an open hatch, leaving the bright sunlight behind, he entered a windowless space lit by fluorescent lights. He started down the ladder. The cargo bay was one more flight down. He stopped to permit his eyes to readjust from the sunlight, then descended the ladder down one more deck.

The entrance to the cargo bay consisted of three doors. The middle door was a large metal garage-like door, large enough to drive several forklifts through. It was flanked on each side by two regular-sized door hatches.

Chan opened the door hatch on the left. Freezing cold air hit him. He stepped into the chill. The grated steel walkway stretched back for a hundred feet from the front doors. On each side of the grated steel walkway, separated by a distance of eight feet, dozens of unpainted plywood crates were stacked up to the ceiling.

The sides of the crates were screwed together. Painted in red on the outside were the words: MEDICAL SUPPLIES.

DO NOT OPEN.

GLASS. FRAGILE.

Something seemed odd about it all, Chan decided. Glass? Fragile? Inside a wooden crate?

Chan was all alone in the cargo bay. He stood for a while, looking over the cargo, then walked down the center aisle between the rows of crates, looking up and down.

Whatever was inside these mysterious wooden crates, these "medical supplies," as they were labeled, was valuable enough for them to be paid a great deal of money that would change all their lives forever.

The captain was right. No need to know.

On the other hand, he could remove about six screws to open one of those crates. He could just take a look.

Chan stopped. He stared at one of the crates, feeling oddly paralyzed. "Forget it."

He started to leave the cargo bay. On his way out, bolted to the bulkhead just to the right of the hatch, the industrial toolbox caught his eye. He stopped and eyed the toolbox. He turned and looked back at the crates.

Why not?

He popped open the latch on the toolbox.

Wrenches, bolt cutters, pliers, soldering guns and irons, electrical testing devices, hammers, and wire cutters filled the toolbox. Three power screwdrivers lay side by side.

Chan picked up the second one and slid the "screw" button forward. The Phillips head spun like a drill. Instant response. Plenty of charge.

He laid his clipboard on the toolbox, took the screwdriver in his hand, and walked back down the steel walkway to the third row of crates. He stared at one of the crates that was stacked about five feet off the deck.

Eight Phillips-head screws held down the plywood side of the crate. Three along one side, three on the other side, and one on each end.

The power screwdriver whirled counterclockwise. Two seconds later, the first screw spun out and fell to the deck. Finally, only one screw remained.

Chan grasped the top edge of the plywood with his left hand to prevent it from falling to the deck. As he gripped the plywood, his knuckles pressed against a cool glassy-feeling surface behind the plywood.

The power-driver swirled again. The screw slipped out, and Chan removed the plywood and propped it on the deck by his boots.

"Oh, dear God!"

Chan gagged and almost vomited.

He needed air! He dropped the screwdriver in the toolbox and rushed out the door, up the ladder, and back onto the portside deck.

The rush of warm sunshine on his face relieved some of the queasiness in his stomach. But it was not enough.

He leaned overboard and puked into the sea.

CHAPTER 3

Bridge
USS Emory S. Land
South China Sea

10:15 a.m.

Much better job getting the *Boise* replenished this morning," Captain Auclair Wilson said. "I don't know what you did, XO. But we got her replenished and under way with ten minutes to spare."

"Thank you, Skipper." Bobby Roddick breathed a sigh of relief that his commanding officer was pleased. "I just gave Ensign Surber a little pep talk."

"You're amazing, XO. When you retire from the Navy, you should write a book called *My Pep Talks with the President's Daughter.*"

Roddick chuckled. "Catchy title, Captain. But I wouldn't feel right writing that book alone. I'd want to coauthor that with you, sir."

"Now that's funny, XO. When I retire, I'll be too busy elk hunting to worry about even writing a check, let alone a book. But right now, I've got to worry about the Chinese hunting the Taiwanese."

"Or vice versa, sir," Roddick said.

"Ya got that right, Bobby."

"Sir, we have a TOP SECRET FLASH message from Seventh Fleet."

Roddick turned around. Lieutenant Bill Rogers, communications officer for the *Emory S. Land*, had just stepped onto the bridge with an envelope in his hand. He walked over to Captain Wilson and handed him the envelope.

"Thank you, Lieutenant."

Commander Roddick watched Captain Wilson unfold the message and read it.

"Unbelievable," the skipper muttered, shaking his head in a disapproving manner. He handed the message to Roddick. "The money they waste for one naval officer."

Roddick read the message and handed it back to the skipper. "She's not going to like this."

"No, she isn't," the skipper said. He gave the message back to the communications officer. "Log the message in and lock it in the safe. You're dismissed."

"Aye, captain," the communications officer said.

The skipper turned back to the XO. "Do you want to tell her?"

"Up to you, Skipper. You're the boss."

The captain looked out to sea. "Well, Bobby, she seems to have taken a liking to you. Your last pep talk worked. Sounds like XO-type of duty to me. Maybe she'll think this was your idea and report you to her daddy instead of me." The skipper looked back at the XO and chuckled.

"Aye, sir. I'll break the news."

"Appreciate it, Bobby. Let me know how it goes."

"Aye, sir."

USS Emory S. Land
Fantail
South China Sea

10:30 a.m.

The M2 "Browning" .50-caliber machine gun, a workhorse weapon that was developed prior to World War II and put to extensive use by all five US armed forces in every war since then, was mounted on a movable post on the aft deck of the ship.

Stephanie had fired the weapon once before — during her last midshipmen's cruise off San Diego a couple of years before.

The USS *Stockdale*, the host ship for the cruise, had been operating in the Pacific, in international waters twenty-six miles southwest of San

Diego, just off Mexico's Coronado Islands. A friendly, private competition erupted that day between Stephanie and her roommate at the academy, Ensign Julianne McCall of Colorado. Stephanie would fire a few rounds at the practice disks, and Julianne would fire right behind her.

Both midshipmen shot well, bursting the circular airborne targets being flung into the air by a chief petty officer.

Soon a group of junior officers had gathered on deck in a semicircle around the midshipmen, wagering on which of the two would win the shoot-out. Each burst of machine-gun fire had caused another round of whooping and hollering from the JOs, that is, until the XO came along and ordered everyone back to their stations.

Before the XO rained on the party, Stephanie had busted three more targets than Julianne, which meant that Julianne had to buy drinks at the Hotel Del Coronado when the ship returned to San Diego and the Thirty-Second Street naval station.

A handful of the junior officers who had been making bets accompanied the women to the Coronado later that day and bought them both several rounds inside the perimeter of Secret Service agents, who had cordoned off half the bar so the officers and women could have their fun.

That was then.

Today was anything but fun. Stephanie didn't know what she would face, but the adrenaline had kicked in. This was real, and her performance might make the difference between life and death.

"Pull!"

Whish ...

Whish ...

Whish ...

Three Frisbee-sized clay disks whirled out in perfect symmetry, arcing in formation out over the South China Sea.

"Fire at will, Ensign," said the venerable senior chief petty officer, who stood behind her shoulder.

Stephanie swung the gun from left to the right, aiming it at the sky, leading the movement of the three flying disks.

She pulled the trigger. A powerful blast from the .50-cal.

Chug-chug-chug-chug-chug-chug ...

The disks exploded in the morning sunshine. Stephanie exhaled.

"That's some pretty impressive shooting there, Ensign Surber."

She looked around, recognizing the XO's voice.

"Thank you, sir. I didn't see you standing there. I got some practice with the .50-cal a couple of summers ago on a midshipmen's cruise."

"So I hear." The XO smiled. "Got into a little shootout wager with your roommate?"

"You heard about that?"

"Word gets around." He smiled. "XOs talk. The XO of the *Stockdale* is a buddy of mine."

"I don't know what to say, sir."

"The XO of the *Stockdale* said you were a great shot. I see that he's right."

"Thank you, sir." She fumbled for words, unable to restrain her own smile. "Hopefully I can shoot like that if things heat up out here."

The XO winced. "Stephanie, we need to talk."

"Yes, sir?" Something wasn't right.

"Let's take a little walk."

"Yes, sir."

Commander Roddick motioned toward the stern. A few sailors meandered about the empty flight deck. Sailors snapped salutes at the XO as they strolled by.

They walked back as far as anyone could walk on the flight deck, just under the American flag flapping at the stern. The XO stopped at the ship's steel-cord railing. He gazed down at the white water churning behind the ship with its powerful 20,000-shaft horsepower engines and propellers.

"Stephanie." He looked at her. "We got a TOP SECRET FLASH from Seventh Fleet."

Her heart pounded. "Seventh Fleet? Are we going into combat?"

"I can't say. But if we do, there are some high-ranking officers at Seventh Fleet who apparently don't want you to be involved."

"With respect, sir, may I ask what that means?"

"First off, neither the captain nor I knew about this, nor do we approve of it. But it's not our call."

"I don't understand."

"Ensign Surber, they're sending a helicopter for you."

"A helicopter?" She covered her mouth with her hand. Fear flushed her body. "Oh, dear God! Please don't tell me something's happened to my dad!"

"No. No. Nothing like that," the XO said. "Your father is fine."

"Thank God." Her worst nightmare was the fear of someone assassinating her father.

"But I think it's because of your father that the chopper is now en route."

"Because of my father?"

"They don't want you on the front lines of a naval battle."

"Who is 'they,' if I may ask, sir?"

"They," the XO said, "is Seventh Fleet. I don't know. Probably the admiral. The message was from the admiral."

Stephanie wanted to explode. "And just where are they planning to take me?"

"Anywhere other than the front lines of a naval war. Probably the carrier. Then to Japan."

She crossed her arms and looked out at the white water churning behind the ship. "Sir? Permission to speak freely?"

"Absolutely. Speak away."

"Well, sir, I know as a naval officer, I'm bound to obey orders. But this is the most ridiculous set of orders I could imagine. I'm a US Navy officer. My performance at the academy was upper third in my class. I can't imagine how much taxpayer money is being wasted to send a helicopter out here to fly me out of harm's way." She turned to look at him. "Is there something you can do, XO? Can the captain do or say anything to stop it?"

"I wish we could. But someone at Seventh Fleet with a lot higher rank than we have thinks it's too risky to have the president's daughter in combat."

Frozen, she stood in the tropical breeze fuming at the news, yet not wanting to reveal the extent of her anger. "That's the first time you've mentioned anything about me being the president's daughter."

"That's because I see you as a naval officer, Stephanie. And a fine one at that. I don't view you as Douglas Surber's daughter. I see you for who you are. Not for who you're related to."

All at once she felt hot and cold. She wasn't sure why. She was furious that some high-brass admiral had taken it upon himself to protect her, yet she had to control herself.

"How long before the chopper arrives, sir?"

"They're in the air now. They're due within two hours. They land long enough to grab food, refuel, then fly you out of here before things get hot."

"I guess that means there's no point in me taking any more target practice."

He turned and put a reassuring hand on her shoulder.

"Look, from what I saw of your shooting back there, even if you were staying aboard, I don't think you need any more target practice. That was some impressive marksmanship."

"Thank you, sir."

"You better go pack your sea bags."

"But ..." The directive saddened her. "But what about my shipmates? I don't want to let them down. I don't want to let the skipper down. I don't want to let you down."

"You're not letting us down, Stephanie. Hang in there. Stick with the Navy. I've got a feeling we'll all be together again soon."

"Is that a promise, sir?" Oh, what a stupid thing to say, she thought.

He looked at her and smiled. "Yes, I promise, Ensign Surber." A more formal tone. Referring to her again as *Ensign* instead of *Stephanie*. Distancing himself from over-familiarity. "You don't hide your anger well. Let's take this one day at a time. Now go to your quarters and get packed."

"Aye, sir." She shot him a salute, gritted her teeth, turned, and headed to her quarters.

The Chinese freighter M/V Shemnong
South China Sea
between Da Nang, Vietnam, and the Paracel Islands
course 180 degrees

In a small one-man lavatory-head, Kenny Chan bent over the stainless steel commode and heaved for the fourth time in the last fifteen minutes. More yellow spew. More cursing. His stomach kept heaving, and it had worsened when he returned to the cargo bay to screw the plywood sheet back onto the side of the crate.

He had tried looking away from the sight behind the glass. But unable to resist, his eyes locked into a tractor-beam stare. Then he had slammed the plywood back on, drilled the screws back in, and rushed out of the cargo bay. He should've heeded the captain's advice. He should have left this matter alone.

There.

That felt better.

He hit the flush button, then splashed his face with cold water from the small sink. Now maybe that was that. Fortunately, none of his men had seen him vomiting. Rumors would have spread, to the chuckles of the crew, that the first officer was suffering from seasickness, the ultimate symbol of wimpish femininity on a ship.

He splashed more water on his face, blew air from his mouth, and stepped out of the head. The warmth of the sunshine provided a temporary antidote, and he caught his breath.

To tell the captain or not . . .

The ethical tug-of-war wrenched his conscience. In fact, Kenny Chan had for years forgotten that he had a conscience. But somehow, what he saw in the cargo bay had awakened him from a slumber of sorts that spanned four decades.

But why?

Why was he now thinking about his childhood? Did his childhood somehow hold the key to the answer? Feeling like a hapless baby looking for a pacifier to suck, Chan thought of his mother. He closed his eyes. The image of her sweet, smiling face helped counterbalance the horrific sight.

She was a gentle, caring woman despite what he considered her philosophical shortcomings and her activity in one of those underground home churches, always speaking of her love for "Jesus the Nazarene," as she called him. She believed that a man who had been dead for two thousand years was still alive. Or so she claimed. In fact, all the members of the secret, illegal church swore with a straight face that he was alive, that they talked to him.

What nuts, he thought.

Betty Chan had named her only son after his great-great grand-father, an American who was a Christian missionary to China. And Betty was named for his great-grandmother. So he was American in his blood and even bore an American first name, although no one would know by his strong Asian facial features.

His mother took him with her to those illegal underground church meetings. She had tried to indoctrinate him to have a relationship with this imaginary Jesus the Nazarene. About the age of thirteen, he once considered it.

Now, at this moment, he had a feeling he could not explain. He felt within his heart almost like the time that they nearly brainwashed him into "accepting," as they called it, Jesus the Nazarene. It was as if what he had seen in the cargo bay had somehow rushed him back to that moment in time.

His mother had passed away long ago. Fortunately, he thought, his teachers at the government schools in Hanin taught him that religion was merely the opiate of the people. Only the state should be worshiped.

In keeping with his worship of the mighty state, he had applied for and been accepted into membership by the Communist Party and he swore allegiance to the immortal chairman of the Chinese Communist Party, Mao Zedong. That was the happiest day of Chan's life. The local party officials never discovered his mother's "subversive" activities.

But now he did not feel good even about his party membership. Standing on deck, he couldn't shake the hallucination that his soul was being ripped in opposite directions by two dead people: Chairman Mao and the state Communists on the left, his mother and her philosophy of Jesus the Nazarene on the right.

Chan wasn't sure he should tell the captain.

But he did resolve one thing. He wanted no part of the bonus money being offered for this voyage.

"First Officer Chan to the bridge!"

The ship's loudspeaker system broke into his thoughts. The urgency in the captain's voice signaled trouble. Chan hurried along the side deck to the ladder and headed up three levels to the bridge. When he came onto the bridge, the captain, the navigator, the helmsman, and the radar officer were huddled around the radar screen.

The captain turned around. "We have a problem, Mr. Chan."

"What is it, Captain?"

"Radar has spotted an unidentified surface contact. Twenty miles to the northeast. Electronic feedback looks like the signature of a warship. Possibly Taiwanese. Appears to be headed in this direction at full speed."

ROCS Kee Lung (DDG-1801)
South China Sea
course 225 degrees

The destroyer ROCS *Kee Lung*—the letters standing for "Republic of China Ship"—was in an earlier life known as the USS *Scott*, which was decommissioned by the United States Navy in 1998.

For seven years, the *Scott* sat in America's decommissioned fleet, a warship without a home or a mission, destined for the Navy's mothball fleet in Philadelphia, to be lost on the scrap heap of naval history.

But at the end of 2005, the *Scott* and three other *Kidd*-class destroyers were purchased from the United States by the Republic of China—known to most of the world as Taiwan.

And with the change-of-name ceremony, ROCS *Kee Lung* became the lead ship in a class of warships that was the largest and most powerful in the Taiwanese Navy. The *Kee Lung* and her three sister ships, all guided-missile destroyers, carried antisubmarine helicopters and enough firepower to send any Communist Chinese warship to the bottom of the sea.

Only the crème de la crème of Taiwan's Navy was selected for command of and service on the former *Kidd*-class destroyers. On the bridge of the 563-foot *Kee Lung*, Captain Won Lee, surrounded by his staff, studied the blip on the SPS-55 surface search radar screen.

Still some twenty miles to his southwest, the blip, reflecting the presence of an unidentified vessel in the sector, generated a bit of concern.

"What do you make of it, Mr. Chen?" he said, directing his question to his radar officer, who sat right in front of the radar screen.

"Too big for a warship, Captain," the radar officer said. "Resembles a cargo ship. Perhaps bringing ammunition to the Spratlys. We need a visual to know for sure."

"XO?"

"Sir, I recommend we launch one of the choppers for a better look. Recommend we send along a Marine boarding party in case there is a need to board the freighter."

"Very well," Won Lee said. "Navigator, set intercept course with unidentified vessel. All ahead full. Aviation officer, launch the S-70s and get boarding parties on those choppers just in case. I want a closer look and a report back on that ship. Sound the alarm. General Quarters. All hands to Battle Stations."

"Aye, Captain. All ahead full! Sounding General Quarters! All hands to Battle Stations!"

US Navy SH-60R Seahawk helicopter
en route between USS Vicksburg and USS Emory S. Land
over the South China Sea

Flying southwest across the tropical morning skies above the South China Sea, the chopper's engines roared in an almost hypnotic drone that made for a good sleeping aid.

Gunner, strapped into the jump seat in the cargo bay of the chopper, had closed his eyes and become immersed in the constant drone, knowing that sleep for a naval officer often working sixteen-hour days had to be taken whenever and wherever possible.

But he couldn't sleep. Maybe that was because this flight was a stupid waste of taxpayer money. Even the British had left Prince Harry on the front lines to face combat in Afghanistan.

Maybe they were doing this because the First Daughter was a girl. If so, what an insult to women! Gunner didn't know Stephanie Surber from Adam. Or, in this case, from Eve.

All he knew was what he'd seen on TV and in the papers. She was attractive, photogenic, and well thought of by the public. And from what he had heard, she had done fine at the academy and had the potential to be a fine naval officer, to the extent that an ensign—a butter bar—can be evaluated this early in her career.

He tried to remove Stephanie Surber from his thoughts and felt his mind beginning to drift. Acres of sundrenched peanut fields, oak leaves swaying in the backyard in an early autumn breeze under the warm Virginia sun. Fishing for marlin off Cape Henry. Colonial Williamsburg at Christmas … football games at Lane Stadium on the VPI campus … Christmas at Corbin Hall …

The rough bump against turbulence popped open his eyes. The engine was sputtering, like a staccato string of sixteenth notes.

The chopper shook, jarred again, and started dropping.

This wasn't the first time he'd been up with cowboy chopper pilots who got their kicks out of trying to start a barf-fest among non-aviator passengers by practicing autorotations.

Gunner squinted and looked up into the cockpit. "You guys are funny!" he shouted.

But this time, no typical over-the-shoulder smug grins of satisfaction from flyboys showing off autorotation skills. Both the pilot and copilot were flipping switches on the control panel with a serious urgency. Something wasn't right.

"Check the backup fuel line," the pilot's voice came over Gunner's headset.

"I'm flipping the switch!" the copilot's voice was less calm than the pilot's and seemed to crack. "Nothing."

More midair bumping.

The engine caught, then sputtered, then caught and sputtered again.

"Commander," the pilot said, "recommend you put on your life vest, sir. We've got fuel-line problems. I'm sending out a distress signal."

Fear crossed the copilot's face.

Gunner reached over for his life vest as the pilot's voice blared over the headset: "MAYDAY! MAYDAY! To all ships and aircraft in the vicinity. This is US Navy SH-60R Seahawk. Mark position at fifteen degrees north latitude, one hundred fifteen degrees, forty-two minutes, eight seconds east longitude. Altitude ten thousand feet and dropping. Course two-seven-zero degrees. MAYDAY! MAYDAY! We're losing fuel and descending rapidly!"

Bridge
USS Emory S. Land
South China Sea

Bridge! Radio!" The radioman's urgent tone blasted over the bridge's loudspeaker system.

"Radio. Go ahead," Captain Auclair Wilson said.

"Sir, we've got an emergency distress call from SH-60R Seahawk en route from USS *Vicksburg*! They're still airborne but having engine problems."

"Radar! Bridge! Range to that Seahawk?"

"Seventy-five miles inbound, Captain."

"Radio! Open a channel to that chopper!"

"Aye, Captain!"

Captain Wilson looked over at Commander Roddick, who was biting his lip and running his hand through his hair. Another squelch from the loudspeaker.

"MAYDAY! MAYDAY! To all ships and aircraft in the vicinity. This is US Navy SH-60R Seahawk, altitude now nine thousand feet! Still on course two-seven-zero degrees and still dropping!"

"Seahawk. This is USS *Emory S. Land*. Keep talking and keep that baby in the air, Lieutenant. We're headed your way." He looked at the ship's navigator and barked orders over more incoming chatter from the helicopter. "Navigator! Helmsman! Set course zero-nine-zero degrees. All ahead full!"

"Zero-nine-zero degrees. All ahead full! Aye, Captain!"

The voice over the loudspeaker said, "Don't know how much longer I can keep us airborne, Captain!"

"We're coming, Lieutenant!" Wilson said. "Keep the faith."

The helmsman spun the wheel to the right, and the *Emory S. Land* listed hard to starboard. Captain Wilson grabbed the brass railing in the center of the bridge and kept barking orders. "XO. Notify the crew. Prepare for search-and-rescue operations. I don't have a good feeling about this."

"Aye, Captain."

Junior Officers Quarters
USS **Emory S.** Land
South China Sea

The First Daughter of the United States, standing in the small shower adjoining her cabin, eyes closed, enjoying the warm water running through her auburn hair and down her face, lost her balance when the *Emory S. Land* made its turn, suddenly listing to starboard.

Her feet slipped, but she managed to latch on to the grab bar to avoid falling.

Her heart pounding, she wondered what happened. She thought a rogue wave might have rolled the ship, which had leveled off again. Stephanie stepped out of the shower, having washed the smell of gunpowder out of her hair and off her face. She grabbed a towel and wrapped it around herself.

A shrill two-toned whistle blared from low to high over the ship's 1MC, the shipwide intercom system controlled from the bridge.

"Now hear this, this is the XO. We've just received an emergency distress call from the US Navy helicopter inbound to our position from USS *Vicksburg.*"

Static ... then ...

Commander Roddick's voice came back on. "Communications with the chopper indicate that the situation is critical. We're steaming at full power on a projected intercept course with the chopper. Be on high alert. By order of the captain, prepare to conduct search-and-rescue operations. This is the executive officer."

Silence.

She stood there, wrapped in the towel, staring at the small mirror inside her small gray metal locker.

Her face flushed crimson and her body was awash with anger. They had sent a chopper to pick her up because of who she was, because some captain or admiral wanted to curry favor with her father when he hadn't asked for the favor, for the chopper.

And now ... now ... someone might die because of her.

"Dear Jesus, please no," Stephanie said.

What could she do? She felt like smashing the mirror, but "destruction of government property is an offense under the Uniform Code of Military Justice" played in her mind.

Smashing wouldn't help. Not now. Not ever. Neither would anger. She dropped to her knees in front of her rack. "Lord, protect that helicopter. Please, somehow get it here in one piece. Please don't let anyone die because of me." She paused. She had to get dressed. "In Jesus' name, amen."

US Navy SH-60R Seahawk helicopter
en route from USS Vicksburg to USS Emory S. Land
over the South China Sea

Gentlemen, we're dropping fuel fast. Barring a miracle, we won't make it to our rendezvous point with the *Emory S. Land*." The pilot paused. "And even if somehow we could make it that far, I wouldn't want to try and set this bird down on the ship. Not in this condition."

Gunner had once been aboard a light aircraft that ditched in the sea. That ditching, off the coast of North Korea, was part of a planned mission when the pilot had purposely crashed a Beechcraft Bonanza in the cold waters of the Sea of Japan. Gunner almost lost his life.

"How much longer do we have, Lieutenant?"

"Right now, the engine is stabilized. We're still flying, making headway. The problem is, we're still losing fuel. Maybe a leak in the fuel line. Unless we can get it fixed, we'll run out of gas. To answer your question, ten maybe fifteen minutes, Commander."

Thirty seconds passed. "Lieutenant, how can I help?"

"We're going to have to jump before the chopper hits the water. Otherwise we could be decapitated by the whirling blades. I'm going to bring us down to fifty feet over the water to hover position. Pray that our fuel holds. There's an inflatable life raft back there. Copilot Hodges will go back there and the two of you will drop that baby overboard. When it hits the water, it should inflate. Then jump. Lieutenant Hodges will jump right after you. I'll put the chopper in forward and I'll jump.

"With the chopper flying forward, it'll crash far enough away from us. We'll be okay. Here, strap this on. After you hit the water, activate it."

"What is it?"

"It's a homing beacon. But when you hit the water, first swim to the raft. Secure it. Then hit the homing device. It's working if you hear it beeping. That's our only chance for getting spotted."

"Got it." Gunner tightened his life vest.

"Okay, I'm bringing her down."

Gunner's heart was pounding as the pilot brought the chopper down closer to the water. The copilot, his life jacket strapped on, crawled back to the cargo bay area.

"Okay, Commander, hang on tight," the copilot said. "I'm gonna open the cargo bay door."

"Got it," Gunner said.

"Altitude one hundred feet," the pilot said.

The cargo bay door slid open. A powerful gust of whirling wind and noise rushed in from the overhead rotor blades.

"Altitude seventy-five feet," the pilot said. "Okay! Drop the raft!"

"Roger that, Skipper," the copilot said. "Commander, give me a hand here."

"You bet," Gunner said.

The copilot was standing next to an orange cylinder about the size of a small oil barrel. "Raft's in here. We're just going to walk over to the edge and toss it. When it hits the water, the cord from the chopper should cause it to inflate. You grab that side, I've got this side. Don't get your foot snared by the cord."

"Okay," Gunner said.

"Let's pick it up."

"Okay."

"It's cumbersome but not heavy," the copilot said as he lifted one side and Gunner lifted the other.

"Let's just ease it over here to the side. Don't get too close to the edge."

"Got it."

They inched toward the open cargo bay. Gunner hated heights. He hated leaping off the thirty-five-foot tower at Officer Candidate School in Newport, Rhode Island. He tried not to look down as they inched closer to the edge, but could not avoid it. They were at least three times as high as the diving tower at Newport. And in the tank at Newport, there were no sharks in the waters.

"Close enough," the copilot said.

"Step it up, Lieutenant!" the pilot said. "We're dropping fuel fast."

"Roger that. Commander, on three, we'll toss this baby out."

"Got it."

"Ready?"

"Ready."

"On my mark. One thousand one . . .

"One thousand two . . .

"One thousand three!"

They hurled the barrel out over the sea, the cord uncoiling as it fell.

The copilot stepped to his left, right into a loop of the cord on the floor that swirled around his ankle and snapped tight, yanking him toward the open bay, smashing his head against the floor as he was dragged from the aircraft.

"Dear Jesus, no!" Gunner yelled. "Lieutenant! Copilot overboard."

"Okay! Hang on!" the pilot said.

The cord uncoiled as fast as a line from a fishing reel with a big fish on the hook, then stopped with a snap.

"When the raft inflates, detach the line and jump overboard," the pilot yelled.

Gunner looked down. The copilot was floating face down in the water, one leg being yanked up toward the chopper by the line that was wrapped around his boot. The orange life raft, complete with an orange tent, was inflating, like a butterfly emerging from a cocoon.

"Commander! Detach the cord and jump!"

Gunner looked down at the floor of the chopper. The end of the cord was attached to a steel loop on the floor just inside the cargo bay, held there by a spring latch. He reached down, unlatched it, and the end of the line slipped out the open bay.

With one hand on the homing device that was strapped around his waist, he took a running step and leaped over the edge, feet first. His stomach seemed to slip into his throat. His feet angled up. As he dropped, he knew this would not be a vertical landing.

His right knee and thigh struck first. Somehow, his entire body, life vest and all, submerged in the warm water. The sound of the rotors faded to a garbled bubbling.

When he popped back up to the surface and bright morning sunlight, he heard the sloshing sound of the waves and felt the wind on his face.

He squinted and looked around.

Where was the raft? Paddling with his arms and hands to pivot himself around in the water, he turned to his right.

The orange pup tent bobbed in the water, in and out of sight in the big waves, perhaps two hundred yards in front of him.

He started swimming toward the raft. He couldn't see the copilot or the pilot.

Off to his right was the helicopter, just skimming the surface.

KA-BOOM!

The percussion from the explosion hit him like a wall. The helicopter vanished in a huge fireball that hit the water.

Chinese freighter M/V Shemnong
South China Sea
between Da Nang, Vietnam, and the Paracel Islands
course 180 degrees

Captain!" the radar officer shouted. "Radar shows two aircraft approaching from the northeast! Range ten miles. Airspeed two hundred knots. From the direction of the unidentified ship."

Captain Fu Cheuk-yan looked over at his first officer. At that moment, for the first time, First Officer Kenny Chan saw a look of concern in his boss's eyes.

"No doubt attack helicopters," Fu said. "Which tells me that we are dealing with one of the *Kidd*-class destroyers that the traitors bought from the US Navy."

Chan glanced at the radar screen. "I think you are right, Captain."

"Perhaps we should turn and steer a course into Da Nang."

"Are you asking my advice on this, sir?"

"Yes. What do you think?"

"I think it would be pointless, sir. Their choppers are faster than we are and so is their warship, if that is a *Kidd*-class ship."

The captain seemed to think about that. "Perhaps you are right." He wiped his forehead. "Well, grab your binoculars and let's step out on the flybridge and have a look."

"Yes, Captain." Chan could not shake the image he had seen in the bowels of the ship, nor could he shake the queasiness from his stomach. Yet he had to focus on the danger to the ship. He reached into a utility drawer and grabbed a pair of binoculars, then followed the captain out onto the open flybridge.

"There! Out on the horizon." The captain pointed off to the northeast. Two helicopters, flying in tandem, were lit by the morning sun. A slight smokescreen trailed each one. Just a moment later, they heard a sonorous roar.

"Helicopters," Captain Fu said.

"Headed this way," Chan said. He wrestled with a surrealistic sense of relief, almost, as if the enemy—the Taiwanese or even the Americans—would do something about what he had seen. As he watched through the powerful lenses of his binoculars, the choppers grew larger, more distinct—definitely two military choppers. The only question now was their origin, their nationality. Taiwanese or American.

"I do not like this, Mr. Chan," the captain said, his eyes fixed on the approaching helicopters as he looked through his binoculars. "What . . . what should . . . I do?"

The captain's voice had morphed from swaggering confidence to uncertainty—almost a hint of fear. He lowered his binoculars. His face was dazed. He looked at Kenny.

"We must determine who they are, Captain. If they are Taiwanese, we must radio for help to the PRC Navy. Either way, we steam forward on course."

The roar of the choppers was almost deafening off the portside. Then, as the choppers banked to the right, Chan saw it. Painted on the fuselages was the red flag with the blue rectangular corner and the white twelve-point sun.

"Enemy choppers, Captain! Taiwanese!"

South China Sea
somewhere between USS Vicksburg *and USS* Emory S. Land

Gunner kept treading water, working his arms, as he tried to decide where to swim.

He looked from the barely visible floating orange pup tent to the leaping flames and black smoke from the downed chopper. The raft and chopper were drifting in opposite directions, getting farther apart.

"The pilot!" he thought. "Help the pilot!" If he could get to the pilot, maybe he could pull him back to the raft. He started fighting through the warm tropical water, swimming toward the burning chopper. The wind had picked up. The waves were getting bigger. Against the larger swells, Gunner tried a breaststroke. He rode the next swell down into the trough and wound up with a mouthful of seawater.

He resorted to a freestyle stroke and swam up the next swell to its crest. The smoke and fire came into full view. And then he was carried back down again, hidden in a trough. The next swell pushed him up, back up to the peak again. This time ...

No flames! No billows of smoke! Just a remnant of smoke hanging in the air. The chopper was gone. He looked for the pilot and copilot, the raft.

Dear Jesus ... He rode the swell back down into the trough ... Help me find them! Please help me find it!

Was he swimming in the wrong direction? The next wave brought him back up to the crest again. He looked all around again. Nothing.

No chopper!

No life raft!

Nothing anywhere except water!

ROCS Kee Lung
South China Sea

Captain!" the radio officer said. "Our choppers have a visual on the ship."

"Put them on the loudspeaker!"

"Yes, Captain!"

"Dragon One. This is the captain! Report."

At first only static, then the roar of helicopter rotors. "*Kee Lung.* Dragon One. Ship is a PRC freighter. We have a visual. She is the M/V *Shemnong.* I see guns on deck. Chained down. Looks to be transporting antiaircraft guns, Captain."

"Hmm." Captain Won Lee glanced at his executive officer. "They are cruising toward the Spratlys. Probably to deliver weapons to the enemy occupants."

The executive officer nodded. "That is a reasonable assumption, Captain."

"Then we must intercept that ship, and if we determine that these are in fact military supplies, such as weapons and ammunitions for the enemy, we must interdict the delivery of such weapons and supplies. Do you agree, XO?"

The XO nodded. "Yes, Captain. I agree."

"Very well." Won Lee nodded. "I shall order our helicopters to prevent the freighter from making a land run, and then we will bring the *Kee Lung* to General Quarters. We are going to board that freighter."

"Aye, Captain," the XO said.

Captain Won Lee flipped the talk switch to the helicopter.

"Dragon One. This is *Kee Lung.* I want both choppers to fly a screening pattern between that ship and the Vietnamese coast. Under no circumstances do you let that ship break for land. If she tries to break away, warn her to hold course. If she disregards your warning, then spray her with machine-gun fire. Do you copy?"

A staticky burst. "*Kee Lung.* Dragon One. Copy. Fly screen to avoid break for land. Warn and fire if necessary to contain."

"Very well," Won Lee said. "Execute screening maneuver."

"Roger that, Captain. We are flying to her starboard now."

The captain turned to his executive officer. "XO. Bring the ship to General Quarters. Alert boarding parties. Be prepared to board."

"Aye, Captain." The XO flipped the switch for the 1MC. Bells rang all over the ship. "General Quarters! General Quarters! All hands to Battle Stations!"

Sailors began running across the deck.

"Boarding parties. Prepare to board Communist freighter believed to be carrying military supplies to Itu Aba. Estimated time to intercept, twenty minutes! General Quarters! General Quarters!"

Chinese freighter M/V Shemnong
South China Sea
between Da Nang, Vietnam, and the Paracel Islands
course 180 degrees

Captain!" First Officer Kenny Chan said. "The choppers are flying from port to starboard!"

"Let's go," Captain Fu said.

They cut through the bridge and headed for the starboard flybridge. As they passed through the bridge, Fu yelled, with a nervousness in his voice, "Steady as she goes," which brought the response, "Steady as she goes. Aye, sir!"

They stepped out onto the starboard flybridge. The choppers, their Taiwanese markings and flag now visible, were flying about two hundred yards off to the starboard. They had slowed their airspeed to parallel the speed of the *Shemnong*.

"Captain," Chan raised his voice to speak over the roar of the enemy helicopters, "I think that they do not want us to change our direction."

The two men exchanged glances.

"What do you think we should do, Mr. Chan?"

The captain's indecisiveness put Chan in an uncomfortable position. "Captain, I think we should radio the People's Liberation Navy and alert them of our predicament, and then continue to steam toward our rendezvous point off the Spratlys, as if we have nothing to hide."

The captain seemed to think about that. "Mr. Chan, you are correct. Let us step back onto the bridge. We are not being productive standing out here in the sun gawking at these traitorous helicopters."

"Yes, Captain." Chan, still battling queasiness in his stomach, was pleased to hear a little more confidence in the captain's voice.

They stepped back onto the bridge, sealing the hatch behind them. This diminished the noise of the helicopter engines buzzing in the sky outside the ship.

"Mr. Wu," the captain said in an authoritarian tone, "open a channel to the People's Liberation Navy. Tell me when you have raised them."

"Yes, Captain," the radio officer said. "Switching to their hailing frequency now." He flipped several switches and punched several buttons on the radio control panel. "People's Liberation Navy. This is the PRC freighter M/V *Shemnong*. Do you copy?" Static. No response. "Once again, People's Liberation Navy. This is the PRC freighter M/V *Shemnong*. Do you copy?"

A puzzled look crossed the radio officer's face. He re-flipped several of the same switches that he had flipped earlier and tried again. "Once again, People's Liberation Navy. This is the PRC freighter M/V *Shemnong*. Please respond."

More static. No response. The radio officer flipped several more switches.

"Hailing all ships or aircraft in the area. This is the PRC freighter M/V *Shemnong*. Please respond."

The radio officer spun around in his chair and looked at Chan and the captain. "Captain. I cannot raise the Navy, nor can I raise anyone even on our open ship-to-ship channel. I am receiving nothing but electronically generated static."

"What do you mean by 'electronically generated static'?" the captain asked.

"That means, sir, that someone, or something, is jamming our communication capacity. We cannot reach anyone on ship-to-ship or ship-to-shore radio."

The mariners looked at one another.

"The Taiwanese," Captain Fu said.

"Agreed," Chan said. It hit him that the *Shemnong* was about to get caught up in the burgeoning naval war. He thought about his five-year-old son, Kenny Chan II, and his wife, Won-Hu. Both lived in their government-issued flat back in Harbin in the heavily industrial sector of northeastern China. He continued to sail the seas at Won-Hu's insistence because, despite the long periods apart, the shipping job paid far more than most jobs in the People's Republic. This allowed them to build for the future. When he left home three weeks ago to begin this voyage, the boy had cried in his arms and begged him not to go.

He promised his son to come back with toys from Bangkok. But now, the terrifying thought entered Kenny Chan's mind that he might never see his boy again.

"Now what?" The tone of uncertainty had returned to the captain's voice.

"Captain," Chan said, "we have a mission. And that mission is to deliver cargo to the Spratlys. We are not a military vessel. But we have been ordered by the government in Beijing to deliver this cargo, and we are being paid to deliver it. And we are dependent upon the government for our license to operate."

The captain paced four steps to his left, folded his hands behind his back, pivoted, and paced four steps to his right. He stopped and looked at Chan.

"My problem with that, Mr. Chan, is that the weapons on board make us a military target. Some of the military equipment is sitting on deck in broad daylight, and I am sure that they have spotted it."

The captain's point was hard to argue with. Chan decided to play devil's advocate. "But Captain, the fact remains that we are not a warship. We are a civilian freighter. I would hope that Taiwan would be deterred from firing on a freighter by the prospect of UN sanctions. They are already sensitive about their lack of recognition in the UN." Kenny Chan was not even convincing himself with his words.

"Mr. Chan, you are speaking about a group of people who are traitors to the People's Republic. And you speak as if they are civilized, as if they will play by rules of civilized behavior and would allow a freighter with military supplies to pass those supplies along to their enemy."

"Captain!" the officer of the deck yelled. "Warship on the horizon!"

"Where?"

"There, sir! Off the port bow!"

Chan and Captain Fu stepped over to the left side of the bridge. They both saw the outline of a sleek gray warship.

Chan, looking through binoculars, said, "Looks like an American *Kidd*-class destroyer, Captain. Which means if she belongs to Taiwan, she's probably the *Kee Lung* or one of her sister ships. They have four ships in that class, as I recall, that are helicopter capable."

"I agree, Mr. Chan," Captain Fu said. "And it looks like she's steering an intercept course with us. At that angle, I would estimate the intercept to be ... what ... maybe three miles if she stays on that course."

Chan studied the broadside of the ship in his binoculars. "Captain, from this angle I cannot determine if she is on an intercept course or paralleling us. It looks more like she is paralleling us."

Captain Fu watched the ship for a few more seconds. "Even if you are right, Mr. Chan, even if they are on a parallel course, I do not like it. I am going to order a course change. New destination: Da Nang, Vietnam. We will go there, wait, and request a naval escort to complete our mission."

"But Captain," Chan lowered his binoculars. "I would remind you, sir, that Vietnam also claims the Spratlys. Once they discover that our cargo contains military equipment for PRC forces on Itu Aba, I fear that we would not receive the warmest welcome by the Vietnamese."

Fu fixed his gaze on the warship. "We have no choice, Mr. Chan. We are a civilian ship and we have no chance against a man-o'-war. I have a feeling that if we continue on this course, we are on a collision course with them."

"Yes, Captain, but if we turn toward Da Nang, those helicopters off to our starboard might have something to say about it."

"There is freedom of navigation on the high seas, Mr. Chan," Fu snorted. "We can sail wherever we like. And right now, I am more concerned about that warship than those helicopters. Now please return to the bridge and instruct the navigator to plot a course to Da Nang." The captain donned a pair of aviator sunglasses.

"Yes, sir." Chan's stomach double-knotted, his mind on Kenny Junior. "I shall pass your order to the navigator."

ROCS Kee Lung
South China Sea

Captain!" the radio officer said. "Our choppers report the freighter is executing a course change."

"Let me guess," Captain Won Lee said. "They are turning toward the Vietnamese coast." He picked up his binoculars and peered off to starboard. The turn was visible, even at a distance of three miles. "Put Dragon One back on the loudspeaker!"

"Aye, Captain."

Won Lee said, "Dragon One. *Kee Lung*. What is going on out there?"

The muffled sound of helicopter engines preceded the pilot's voice. "Sir, the freighter is executing a turn to two-seven-zero degrees."

"Due west," Won Lee said. "Why am I not surprised." No response from the pilot. "Lieutenant, patch me through to your chopper's loud-speaker system. Then I want you to fly a holding pattern right over the bridge of the freighter at an altitude of two hundred feet. I will order them to turn back to their original course.

"If they do not comply, you are instructed, upon my command, to open machine-gun fire into the ship's bridge." Officers and sailors on the bridge of the *Kee Lung* exchanged nervous glances. "Do you understand my orders, Lieutenant?"

More roaring spilled from the loudspeakers. "Copy your orders, Captain. We are maneuvering into position over the freighter."

Bridge
Chinese freighter M/V Shemnong
South China Sea
between Da Nang, Vietnam, and the Paracel Islands
course 270 degrees

Captain!" Kenny Chan tipped his head back and looked skyward. "One of the choppers is flying right over us!"

Captain Fu rushed to the front windshield of the bridge and looked up.

The chopper hovered over them like a giant dragonfly, blocking the sun and casting an ominous shadow over the bridge.

"What are they doing?" Fu shouted.

"Perhaps they are preparing to drop troops on board," Chan said.

"Perhaps we should get the rifles from the arms locker!" Captain Fu blurted out.

"Now hear this! To the Freighter *Shemnong*! Now hear this!"

Chan and Fu looked at each other. "That's coming from the chopper!" Fu said.

"To the captain of the freighter *Shemnong*! This is the captain of the ROCS *Kee Lung*. I am speaking to you from the bridge of my ship, which is three miles to your stern. Now hear this! You are suspected of transporting illegal arms to aid the war effort in support of the illegal invasion by Communist forces against sovereign ROC territory on Itu Aba Island."

Captain Fu blurted out, "That is not sovereign ROC territory!"

The voice from the helicopter continued. "Your communications ability has been electronically disabled. You are unable to communicate with anyone.

"Now hear this! Moments ago you changed course from one-eight-zero degrees to two-seven-zero degrees. This is unacceptable. You are ordered to steer your course back to one-eight-zero degrees."

"What did he say?" Fu asked.

"Repeat. You are ordered to steer course back to one-eight-zero degrees. Should you fail to comply, you will be fired upon. This is the captain of the ROCS *Kee Lung*."

The helicopter's PA system fell silent. Captain Fu began pacing around the bridge again. "I will not be blackmailed," he said. "I will not be threatened!" He looked at Chan. "Mr. Chan, order the master-at-arms to post armed sentries forward, aft, and amidships. Order sentries to fire on any intruder attempting to board. Bring all remaining firearms to the bridge! We are going to shoot those choppers out of the air!"

"But Captain," Chan said, "we are going to fire at the helicopters with small arms? Even if we got lucky and brought one of them down, I remind you, sir, that the *Kee Lung* is three miles away. And she is armed with Harpoon missiles, Mark-46 torpedoes, and five-inch cannons. I am concerned that firing on those helicopters would be the functional equivalent of suicide."

"Carry out my orders, Mr. Chan!" the captain snapped. "If you cannot carry out my orders, I will replace you with someone who can, and I will cut you out of the bonus that we are to be paid from this mission!"

All eyes on the bridge were on Chan and Fu.

Chan hesitated. "Yes, Captain. I will carry out your orders. My apologies, sir, if my question signaled any intent to the contrary. That wasn't my intention."

"Very well," the captain said.

Chan picked up one of the bridge telephones and punched the number for the ship's master-at-arms. A voice answered.

"Master-at-Arms, this is the first officer. By order of the captain, post armed sentries at the forward, aft, and starboard, and on both gunwales. Until further order of the captain, sentries are to shoot any intruder attempting to board the *Shemnong*. Bring all remaining small arms to the bridge. Immediately! This by order of the captain."

The captain looked at Chan with a scowling nod of approval. He barked another order. "Helmsman. Maintain course two-seven-zero degrees to Da Nang. All ahead full!"

ROCS Kee Lung
South China Sea

K*ee Lung*! Dragon One!" the pilot's voice boomed over the bridge's loudspeaker. "The freighter has increased speed. Still maintaining course two-seven-zero! No sign of course change as you ordered, sir."

Captain Won Lee cursed under his breath and glanced at the sweeping second hand on the clock on the bridge bulkhead. "She's got one minute, Lieutenant. Stay out in front of her and let me know if she starts a course correction."

"Yes, Captain."

Won Lee kept his eyes on the second hand. Several junior officers watched the show through their binoculars.

"Captain!" The helo pilot on the loudspeaker again. "They are coming out onto the flybridge with weapons. Small arms. Rifles. Perceived hostile intent!"

Won Lee could wait no longer. "Open fire, Lieutenant! Now!"

ROC Sikorsky SH-60 Seahawk
altitude 250 feet
above the Chinese freighter M/V Shemnong

T**he chopper turned broadside to the ship below it, and a petty officer slid open the cargo bay door. Morning sunlight brightened the cargo bay. At the edge of the door, the copilot slid behind the door-mounted M60D machine gun, his finger resting on the trigger, his eyes glued on the four men standing below on the ship's starboard flybridge, rifles in hand.

As the man on the right brought his rifle skyward, the copilot pulled the trigger.

Like a powerful jackhammer, the American-built M60D shook as it fired, spraying a burst of lead bullets at the rate of 550 rounds per minute.

The copilot kept firing on the four men, squeezing the trigger against the gun's powerful vibrations. The men's heads and chests exploded in multiple red geysers of blood. Only after their bodies fell lifeless on the sun-drenched steel flybridge did he let up on the trigger.

Lowering the angle of his aim brought his crosshairs down to the bridge itself.

He again squeezed the trigger. Shards of glass burst in a spectacular spray from the windshield of the bridge.

If anyone survived inside the bridge, it was by the grace of God.

CHAPTER 4

South China Sea
somewhere between USS Vicksburg *and USS* Emory Land

The sun had climbed high into the sky, its rays beating down with a pulsating heat. The warm tropical water felt like bathwater. The morning had passed to what was probably high noon. The wind had subsided, and calmer winds brought calmer seas.

Still, there was no sign of anything except water in every direction. The orange pup tent on the life raft had vanished. Perhaps it had sunk, or had been carried away by the wind or an ocean current.

Questions kept flashing through his mind. How long could he survive? A day? Two? Three?

The problem, inevitably, would be thirst and sunburn.

A silver flash broke the surface of the water ten or so feet in front of him!

Were his eyes playing tricks?

He squinted.

Nothing.

There! Again!

"Dear God, no." The triangular fin was coming at him! Fifteen feet. Ten feet. Five feet. Then, gone.

His heart pounded like a machine gun. He reached for a sidearm. It was gone. Why hadn't he strapped on a pistol before he jumped?

A bump against his leg from the back!

"Dear Jesus!"

The fin resurfaced in front of him, cutting through the water, swimming away, then swirling in a wide circular motion, then disappearing again.

Did the fin have a white tip? "Dear God, no! I think I saw a white tip! Stay calm, Gunner."

He tried breathing slowly to slow down his pulse. But he couldn't shake the memories of the crew of the USS *Indianapolis*, the Navy cruiser that delivered parts of the atomic bomb to Tinian Island for the attack on Hiroshima. The cruiser was torpedoed by the Japanese at almost this same latitude in the nearby Philippine Sea. She had sunk in twelve minutes and wasn't discovered missing for four days!

As an intelligence officer, Gunner knew the fate of the *Indianapolis*. Of the 1,200 men aboard, only 300 survived. Most died after four hellish days in shark-infested waters. Some died from salt-poisoning, some from starvation, some from dehydration. Most had their limbs ripped off by the razor-sharp teeth and powerful jaws of oceanic whitetip sharks.

The Discovery Channel had produced a documentary claiming that the *Indianapolis* sinking resulted in the most shark attacks on humans in history!

The triangular gray fin with the white tip resurfaced.

A whitetip shark! No doubt!

A second fin cut through the surface! They swirled in the warm water, perhaps twenty feet in front of him. Now, a third gray-and-white-tipped triangular fin had joined them!

One of the fins turned toward him, but remained stationary, as if treading water. And then the beast started toward him, slowly at first. It picked up speed. As it approached, it suddenly disappeared. A powerful bump hit his legs, spinning him around in the water.

"Dear Jesus!" Were his legs still there? He reached down to feel.

Thank God. He still had his legs. But now he realized his hands were a target! He jerked his hands out of the water.

This was a heck of a way to die.

When he was attached to the SEALs as an intelligence officer, he'd won the Navy Cross for heroism in Afghanistan and again for a commando mission behind enemy lines in North Korea. In those cases he'd faced deadly enemies with guns and knives and explosives and never flinched nor felt an ounce of fear.

But here? Here he was out of his habitat. He was like a sitting duck in the habitat of the enemy, helpless and without a weapon.

What to do?

Lieutenant Commander Gunner McCormick, a US Navy hero, had never been much on prayer. Prayer was his mother's job at the family's estate back in Suffolk, Virginia. And just about every day that Gunner had ever been around her, Virginia McCormick had spent some time on her knees.

Maybe her prayers had just run out.

Maybe he'd better try himself.

"Jesus, somehow, some way, I know I don't deserve it, but if you can help me out of this one, get me out of here alive … I promise … I promise to turn things around … live right!"

Bridge
M/V **Shemnong**
South China Sea
between Da Nang, Vietnam, and the Paracel Islands
course 270 degrees

The burst of bullets that sprayed into the bridge had stopped. From the deck in the far corner of the bridge, First Officer Kenny Chan raised his head and opened his eyes. The ship's helmsman, radioman, and navigator, the three sailors who moments ago had been standing just behind the windshield, all lay on the deck in a nest of shattered glass, bleeding.

Three sailors were sprawled around the perimeter of the bridge in pools of blood. Three others were up front, motionless under the shot-out windshield.

Strained groans came from the mound of human carnage—the faint sounds of life. Some movement. Some stirring.

Chan got up and winced at the gruesome sight of one man lying on his back in the center of the deck, his mouth and eyes frozen open in a bloody mask, a bullet hole in the center of his forehead, with blood still oozing from the back of his head. He was at first unrecognizable.

Then Chan realized that he was looking at the lifeless body of Captain Fu. Command of the ship had now passed to the first officer.

"I am in command," he mumbled aloud, shocked at the very thought of it. "I must react before they fire again."

He stepped to the ship's wheel. Wind from helicopter rotors above blew in through the broken glass.

He turned the wheel to the left, putting *Shemnong* into a course change. Thank God … if there was a God … that the gunfire had not damaged the ship's steering capacity.

He watched both the navigational compass and the electronic GPS directional compass showing the ship's heading as it went from

270 degrees …

265 degrees …

260 degrees …

ROCS Kee Lung
South China Sea

K*ee Lung!* Dragon One!"

"Dragon One. Go ahead," Captain Won Lee said.

"Sir, the freighter is executing a turn! She's turning back toward the south, just as you ordered."

Won Lee exhaled. "Excellent. Hold all fire unless it appears that you are about to be fired on by the freighter. Advise when the ship has completed her turn."

CHAPTER 5

South China Sea
somewhere between USS Vicksburg *and USS* Emory S. Land

The fins kept circling him now, like Indians in an old western movie circling a covered-wagon train in the moments before an attack. The bloody ambush, which would rip him apart limb by limb, was near.

Gunner had never feared death. But he had always hoped that whenever death came, that he would die with honor. Perhaps in battle, fighting for freedom.

But now, facing an imminent and gruesome end, his mind flew in all directions, remembering a string of regrets he would never be able to make right. He'd never settled down to marry, and thus no children. He'd once met an attractive young intelligence officer, Lieutenant Mary Jefferies. But he'd gotten redeployed, and she got away, and that was that.

Settling down was hard with the Navy as his mistress. Now he would never have a wife or children to carry on his legacy.

The fins stopped still in the water. Then, three fins pivoted, swirling and lining up one behind the other. Based on the direction of the fins, he could tell that the sharks were facing him, just sort of floating near the surface.

They had closed to within fifteen feet ... straight in front of him. The shark in the middle raised its snout out of the water as if to get a better look at him, its black eyes peering down at him. The snout seemed to be at least three feet wide. The shark opened its mouth, displaying a full set of white teeth that looked sharper than razor blades!

The gray snout disappeared under the water, and all three fins started swimming straight at him. This was it!

Gunner closed his eyes. Splashing erupted in the water, spraying water in his face. He felt bumping against his legs.

More splashing. More water in his face. Almost as if a fight had erupted in the water around him!

He opened his eyes. Fins! Tailfins! Splashing all around him! There must have been six or seven of them now. Were they fighting over which one would take the first bite?

"Get it over with!"

More splashing by tailfins and flippers slapping the water between him and the gray-and-white-tipped dorsal fins.

Suddenly, the sharks turned and swam away, disappearing under the surface.

Gunner heard chirping behind him. He turned, looking for a stray seagull.

No birds in sight.

More chirping.

Gunner jerked his head to his left.

The bulb-nosed dolphin lay almost sideways in the water, chirping and smiling at him. It splashed him in the face with its flipper, then disappeared under the water.

Now only the sound of the wind and sloshing waves.

More chirping cracked the air behind him. Gunner whirled around. Two more dolphins broke the surface of the water, spouting air from the blowholes on the top of their heads, chirping and chattering as if playing a game of hide-and-seek.

When the third one surfaced, the three dolphins swam laps around him for several minutes, splashing him in the face with their flippers and chirping and laughing and spouting water at him. A moment later, the trio disappeared, leaving him alone again with the wind and the sea.

His life had been spared ... for a bit longer. Then he remembered. How had he forgotten? "Here, strap this on. Then after you hit the water, activate it ..."

The homing device strapped around his waist!

He reached down and felt for the activation button. There. That feels right.

With his thumb, he pushed down hard.

Beep ... Beep ... Beep ... Beep ...

"You'll know it's working if you hear it beeping."

"Thank you, God!" he said.

He was still lost at sea, but he wasn't alone.

And he was alive.

For now.

Bridge
M/V Shemnong
South China Sea
between Da Nang, Vietnam, and the Paracel Islands
course 180 degrees

The M/V *Shemnong* now maintained a course of one-eight-zero degrees, heading due south through the sparkling waters of the South China Sea, just as the Taiwanese had ordered.

Kenny Chan looked at the death and carnage around the bridge.

Why was he the only man left standing?

He needed answers, but more than that, he needed help.

He reached down and switched on the ship's PA system.

"To all hands! Now hear this. This is the first officer. The captain has been incapacitated as a result of the helicopter attack on the ship." He had decided not to reveal the news of the captain's death. Not yet anyway. "I have assumed command of the ship.

"We have a medical emergency on the bridge. All medics, along with the ship's engineering officer and all sentries, report to the bridge. Medics bring stretchers, surgical supplies, first aid materials.

"Lay down your weapons. Do not engage the helicopters. This is the first officer."

ROC Sikorsky SH-60 Seahawk (codename Dragon One)
altitude 200 feet
above the Chinese freighter M/V Shemnong

The lead chopper, codename Dragon One, flying at two hundred feet, drifted in a slow-moving pattern just in front of the freighter's bow. The backup chopper, codename Dragon Two, followed at two hundred feet off the stern. The freighter was cutting through the water at twenty knots, and the choppers were matching her speed, flying bookend guard positions in the front and back.

There had been no change in the freighter's course in the last few minutes, so the pilot pressed the broadcast button, back to the *Kee Lung*.

"*Kee Lung!* Dragon One."

"Go ahead, Lieutenant."

"Captain, the freighter is maintaining a course of one-eight-zero degrees, just as you ordered, sir. We see some medics scrambling on the outer decks. But there is no threat from the ship, and there has been no course change in the last five minutes, sir."

"Very well, Lieutenant. Open up a patch for me through the PA system."

Bridge
M/V Shemnong
South China Sea
between Da Nang, Vietnam, and the Paracel Islands
course 180 degrees

Two of the ship's three medics arrived on the bridge. They slid the captain's body out of the middle of the deck, off to one side.

"Mr. Chan, your arm," a medic said as he approached Chan, who was standing watch at the ship's wheel.

Chan looked down and noticed for the first time blood oozing from his upper arm.

"You have been hit, First Officer. You're bleeding. We should treat that. It could become infected."

"I cannot abandon the helm," Chan said.

Just then, the engineering officer arrived on the bridge. "Oh, dear God!" he exclaimed, his eyes displaying stunned shock.

Chan found irony in men devoted to the Communist Party who, at the sight of such bloodshed, were calling for God when the official Communist position was that the state was the only god.

"Zhu Yan," Chan said to the engineering officer, "relieve me at the helm so the medic can attend to my arm. Maintain course one-eight-zero until further notice."

"Yes, First Officer." Zhu took the helm, and the medic took a pair of scissors to the bloody sleeve on Chan's left arm.

"Aaahhh!" The alcohol against the open wound burned like fire, bringing sensation back to the wound that moments ago had been numb.

The second medic was kneeling on the deck, attending to the radio officer, Mr. Wu, who was stretched out on his back. After tying a tourniquet around Wu's bleeding arm, the medic cradled Wu's head with his hand. "He's going to make it."

"Thank God," Chan replied, again betraying the philosophical underpinnings of the atheistic Communist Party to which he had sworn allegiance. "I thought that I was the only survivor on the bridge."

"Good news, Mr. Chan," the first medic said.

"I could use some good news," Chan said.

"The bullet grazed your arm. It did not lodge in you. But we will need to stitch this wound."

"To the captain of the freighter *Shemnong!*" Chan looked up. The enemy helicopter's PA system boomed again. "This is the captain of the ROCS *Kee Lung.*"

"Silence on the bridge!" Chan ordered.

"You were wise to resume the course I ordered." The enemy captain's voice echoed off the deck of the freighter. "You will continue to maintain this course. In a few minutes, we shall board the *Shemnong* with teams of Marines. They will inspect your ship to determine if you are transporting weapons to aid the illegal war effort.

"I warned you before, and I now warn you again. If you attempt to interfere with our boarding or if you fail to cooperate with our boarding party once they are on board, you will be sunk. This is your only warning. This is the captain of the *Kee Lung.*"

CHAPTER 6

Headquarters
United States Seventh Fleet
US Naval Base
Yokosuka, Japan

On a narrow Japanese street not one hundred yards from the pier to which the aircraft carrier USS *George Washington* was moored, on the second floor of a plain stucco building built by the Japanese Imperial Navy to plan the destruction of the United States Pacific Fleet during World War II, high-ranking officers of the United States Navy had just concluded a meeting to discuss the unfolding naval tensions in the South China Sea.

The time was half past noon, the mid-August weather outside was hot. After fierce thunderstorms all morning long, a resurgent sunlight blazed against the puddles, raising steam from the streets and sidewalks.

A US Navy captain wearing his summer white uniform stood looking out on the ships in Tokyo Bay, his arms crossed. Then he did an about-face, turning his back on the view, and walked back to his desk.

How had he gotten himself into such a predicament?

A few weeks ago, he had been working at his desk at the Joint Chiefs of Staff "tank" at the Pentagon, in the "Operations," or "J-3" Directorate, which made him familiar with the work of all United States Navy operational fleets around the world. But because of flashpoints around the Pacific Rim, most of his work, it seemed, at least in the last six months, had involved joint staff coordination with Seventh Fleet.

Like all fleets within the United States Navy, the Seventh Fleet was under the command of a three-star vice admiral. That commander is not only responsible for sixty-some warships spread over half the world's ocean space in the Western Pacific and Indian Oceans but is also responsible for the defense of US allies, including Japan, South Korea, Australia, India, and Taiwan.

Captain David Draxler still remembered the phone call from Japan from Vice Admiral Jim Wesson, commander of Seventh Fleet, that had changed his life. He still remembered every word and every inflection of the admiral's voice as if the call had happened three minutes ago.

"Dave, my chief of staff, Captain Bobby Montgomery, just got picked for rear admiral. I want you to come out here to Yokosuka and replace him."

Less than twenty-four hours later, he was aboard a US Air Force C-17 on final approach to Yokosuka, excited about his new assignment.

Today, his exuberance had faded. He was in crisis mode. His hopes of making flag officer had gone up in smoke. Draxler paced back and forth, in heated conversation with his assistant and Naval Academy classmate Commander Wesley Walls, who was sitting in a black leather chair in the corner of the office.

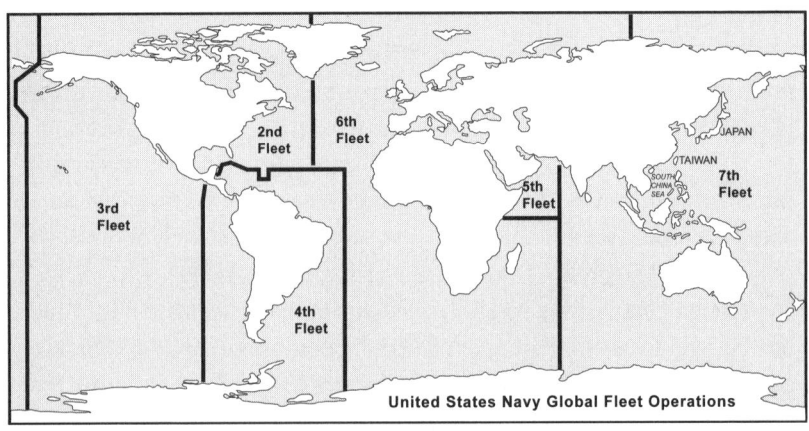

United States Navy Global Fleet Operations

US Navy fleet operational assignments, South China Sea, Taiwan, Japan

"I don't know, Wes." Draxler studied the chart of the fleet operational assignments, at the distance between Japan and the South China Sea. "We got a real problem. Maybe this wasn't such a good idea."

Walls leaned forward in the chair and looked up at the chart. He didn't respond. The two were best buddies from their Naval Academy days, and Walls' silence did nothing except tighten the knots in Draxler's stomach.

"Spit it out, Wes. You've always been a straight shooter. That's why I asked the admiral to approve you as my number two."

"I think you're right, Dave. We screwed up. I think not telling him in advance was a horrible idea." He nodded toward the hallway, in the direction of the admiral's office.

Draxler nodded. "I've been in the Navy a long time, and this is the first time I've ever felt like my head might roll."

"Look, Dave, this whole thing was my idea. Let me go in there and take the heat. I've been passed over for captain. My career is almost over anyway. But you're going to be on the list for admiral, and this idea wasn't even your baby to begin with. No point in both of us losing our careers."

Draxler paced back across the floor. He folded his arms behind his back, shaking his head again. "Can't do that, buddy. You thought of it, but I authorized it. And I'm his chief of staff. I should've brought the idea to him for his approval. But I didn't. I threw my weight around, and now we're in a pickle." More pacing back and forth. "I'm going to get it over with. Right now."

Walls raised an eyebrow. "Captain." A switch from "Dave" to "Captain." A somber tone. "Let me take the fall. Don't run the risk of losing a star because of this."

"Wes, I appreciate your loyalty, but that wouldn't be right. Leaders take responsibility. If I take the fall, I take the fall."

Bridge
USS **Emory S. Land**
South China Sea

1:00 p.m. local time

XO! We've got a homing signal! Thirty-two miles dead ahead, sir!"
"Where?" Commander Bobby Roddick leaned over the radio officer's shoulder.

"Pinpointing right here." The radio officer marked the position on the sweeping amber radar screen.

"Yes!" Roddick pumped his fist. "Dead ahead! Sounds like somebody's alive out there." He hoped that saying it would make it so. "Notify the captain. He's on the fantail."

"Yes, sir," the radio officer said.

"Also, have Ensign Surber report to the bridge."

CHAPTER 7

Headquarters
United States Seventh Fleet
Yokosuka, Japan
Office of the Commanding Admiral

Commander Wes Walls picked up the FLASH message from USS *Emory S. Land* and stepped out of his office into the hallway.

"Hang on, Dave!" Walls stopped Draxler just as he was approaching the admiral's office.

"Wes, I told you I've got to do this," Draxler said. "That's final."

"Wait a minute, Captain. We just got another FLASH message from *Emory S. Land*. They've received a homing signal in the water in the approximate location where the chopper transmitted the last distress signal. She's steaming to that position right now."

Walls handed the message to Draxler. "Thought you might need this for your meeting."

"Thanks, Wes," Draxler said.

The admiral's office was down the hall to the left, guarded by two United States Marines standing on each side of the entryway.

"Good afternoon, sir," the senior Marine guard said as Draxler approached, then walked by the guards into the ornate waiting area. The admiral's American secretary, a sixty-year-old widow named Maddie Hite, sat at one desk. She greeted Draxler with a smile. At the other desk, the admiral's flag aide, Lieutenant Commander Marcus Weatherman, in his summer white uniform with a gold cord draped around his shoulder, rose to his feet.

"Afternoon, Captain."

"Marcus, I need to see the admiral."

"Yes, sir." The flag aide picked up his phone. "Admiral, Cap'n Draxler's here to see you, sir." A short pause. "Yes, sir." Weatherman stepped from around his desk. "He'll see you now, sir. Right this way."

The aide opened the door, revealing a large, yet simple office, considering that this was the office of a vice admiral. Photos of the ships Wesson had served on over the years hung on the walls. On the large wooden desk was a model of the USS *Nimitz*, the supercarrier that Wesson commanded just before ascending to vice admiral.

"Admiral, Captain Draxler," the flag aide announced, prompting the admiral, who was seated behind his desk with his face buried in the *Navy Times*, to look up from the newspaper.

"Dave, have a seat." Wesson laid the paper down on his desk. "Coffee?"

"No, sir."

"Suit yourself." Wesson took a sip from a navy blue mug with three white stars emblazoned on it. "What's up?"

Draxler sat in one of the two chairs just in front of the boss's desk. "Admiral, it appears we've got a chopper down."

"What?" The admiral raised an eyebrow. "What chopper? Where?"

"Seahawk, sir. South China Sea. En route between *Vicksburg* and *Emory S. Land*."

Wesson removed his reading glasses. "Why would we have a Seahawk flying a route between *Vicksburg* and *Emory S. Land*?"

"Sir, I have to apologize to you. I authorized it."

"What?"

"Sir, Ensign Stephanie Surber is on board *Emory Land*. I sent the chopper out to pick her up to get her out of the potential line of fire. I should have told you, sir. I apologize."

Admiral Wesson rose to his feet. "Captain, are you telling me we've lost a chopper with the president's daughter on board?"

"No, sir. The chopper had not arrived at *Emory Land*. Ensign Surber is still on the ship. We just received a FLASH message from

Emory Land that they picked up a signal from an emergency homing beacon in the area where the chopper is believed to have gone down."

Wesson's gray eyes seemed to bore a hole through Draxler.

"Explain to me, Captain, why you used the authority of my office to make this decision and why you did not tell me about ... excuse me" — he held up his right hand as if about to initiate a karate chop — "*tell* is not the right word. *Ask* ... that's the right word. Explain why you did not ask me about it first."

"I apologize, sir. I made the decision in part to protect you from having to make it, because I felt that it was a no-win decision for you, sir."

"To *protect* me? Or were you trying to curry favor with the secretary of the Navy or possibly even the president himself?"

"Well, sir, I had cut orders for her to fly to the carrier to receive some remedial training in the ship's weapons systems. I left open the possibility of flying her back to the ship in case anybody asked. Sir, I was trying to protect you. I was concerned that if something happened to Ensign Surber, you would take the fall because the tender is out there exposed with no cover. You know how it works, Admiral. They're always looking for someone to blame. But I have no excuse for not telling you, sir."

Wesson crossed his arms. "Captain, if this hits the press, the Navy will be accused ... and *I* will be accused ... of giving special treatment to an officer because of who she is. Do you think that's fair to all the other sailors and Marines who put their lives on the line every day?"

Draxler did not answer.

"And do you know what the president's political opponents would do with this if they found out that the Navy was attempting to protect Stephanie Surber?"

"I understand, sir."

"Do you? Well, Captain, if you understand, then are you willing to go to Arlington National Cemetery the next time they're burying a Marine or a soldier who's been killed in Afghanistan? Do you want to look that Marine's mother in the eye and tell her that we would have pulled her boy off the front lines and saved his life if only his daddy had been important enough?"

"Sir, I'll tender my resignation if you'd like and surrender myself to the master-at-arms, if you wish to refer this to a general court-marital."

The admiral stood up, turned his back on Draxler, and walked over to look out his window at the Japanese flower garden just outside. "If I court-martial you, then it comes to light what you've done. If I fire you, same thing." He pivoted around. "All that would hurt the president. All that would undermine the integrity of the armed forces. You technically haven't committed an offense for which I could court-martial you. But you have exercised poor judgment, and that, Captain, will be reflected in your fitness report. You'll never advance to admiral because of this."

"I apologize, sir."

"Do we have any choppers in the area searching for that homing beacon?"

"We have two choppers on the *Vicksburg*, sir. One needs to stay with the ship for defensive purposes. We could send the other out."

"Okay." Wesson turned and faced Draxler. "Get that chopper up. Let me know if we find anything."

"Yes, sir."

"And Captain."

"Yes, sir."

"You betray my trust again, you won't have to worry about resigning or facing a court-martial. And I won't have to worry about you talking." Wesson's eyes flashed glaring anger. "You understand me?"

"Yes, sir."

"Good. Get that chopper up. Now!"

"Yes, Admiral."

Officers Quarters
USS Emory S. Land
South China Sea

Lying alone on her rack in her stateroom, Stephanie twisted, then turned, then twisted again. She could not shake the images—real or imagined—of those officers on board that chopper who had gone down on her account. The fear that must've gripped them in the seconds before the chopper plunged into the water. The faces of their wives, of their girlfriends, of their children, of their mothers and fathers.

She saw them. Surrounding her in a circle like an accusing mob. They pointed their fingers inward, like angry wheel spokes converging on an evil axle.

"Is your life more important than his?" screamed one.

"He was my son! My only son!" a mother sobbed.

"Why should *you* get special treatment!" a man yelled. "Their blood is on *your* hands."

"Dear Jesus, why?" She popped up on the rack.

Thank goodness her roommate, Ensign Elizabeth Ward, had been reassigned to another stateroom closer to the engineering department. Stephanie needed to be alone. That chopper had gone down because of her. She could use a glass of red wine. A liter of pinot noir might just help.

A whistling from the 1MC. "Now hear this. Ensign Surber, report to the bridge. Immediately."

What could that be about? To tell her that another chopper was on its way for her?

Whatever.

She stepped out of her stateroom and, a few minutes later, stepped onto the bridge. The captain, Commander Roddick, several other officers, and a few enlisted men were hovering around instruments on the ship's navigational guidance panel. "Ensign Surber reporting to the bridge as ordered, sir."

Both senior officers turned around.

"Stephanie, I want to talk to you for a second," the XO said.

"Yes, sir."

"Step over here, will you?"

"Of course."

He led her over to one side of the bridge, away from the beeping sweep of radars on the control panel. They stood in a corner by themselves, out of earshot of the other officers.

In a low voice, he offered a reassuring tone. "Stephanie, I know you're taking this hard, but this is *not* your fault."

She looked up into his eyes and, suddenly embarrassed, her eyes began to water.

"It's okay." He put his hand on her back and turned her away from the other officers on the bridge.

"Of course it was my fault, XO." Her index finger flipped a tear off her cheek and onto the deck. "They'd still be alive if it weren't for me."

"First off, we don't know that they aren't alive." He spoke with measured confidence. "And even if they aren't, it's false to say that the crash, if that's what happened, was because of you."

She saw the confident look on his face. "What do you mean, sir?"

"The last distress calls we received from the chopper said that it was having fuel-line problems. Who knows what caused that? Maybe air bubbles in the fuel line. Maybe something the aviation mechanics missed. I don't know. But that chopper, Stephanie, was going to go down no matter what the next time it flew. If it had launched off the *Vicksburg* and flown straight back to the carrier, it still would have gone down. Nothing to do with you." He squeezed her shoulder. "Don't entertain any thoughts of guilt over this."

His words soothed her.

"And there's one other thing I want you to know. Possibly good news."

"Good news, sir?"

"Maybe. Hard to tell. But we've picked up a signal from a homing beacon in the area where the chopper went down. We're steaming straight there at full power. I take this as a positive sign that someone is alive out there."

"Thank God," Stephanie said. "How long until we reach the transmission area?"

"At this rate, maybe two hours."

Stephanie thought for a second. "Sir, could I ask a question?"

"Of course," Roddick said.

"They aren't going to send another chopper for me, are they?"

"I have no clue. I imagine they'll dispatch at least one chopper to the area for search-and-rescue ops. But whether they send it to pick you up is beyond me."

"One other thing?"

"Of course."

"Request permission to complete my target practice on the .50-cal and then assume the forward watch. I'd like to be on the lookout for whatever is in the water out there as we approach the ditching site."

Roddick smiled.

"The first part of the request is denied," he said.

"Sir?"

"You heard me. Flat out denied. I've seen enough of your shooting to know that you don't need any more practice. We need to save on the ammo. The second part of your request is granted. Assume the forward watch. Keep your eyes peeled, and let me know if you see anything."

"Yes, sir."

He started to turn away, then caught himself and turned back. "Stephanie?"

"Yes, sir."

"Just for the record" — a twitch from the corner of his mouth — "I hope they let you stay right here."

"Thank you, sir."

This time he pivoted, turned his back to her, and walked away.

CHAPTER 8

Bridge
M/V **Shemnong**
South China Sea
between Da Nang, Vietnam, and the Paracel Islands
course 180 degrees

First Officer Kenny Chan had stepped back from the wheel and was watching one of the medics insert a needle into the arm of one of the bleeding crew members, who was lying unconscious on a portable cot.

With half a dozen shot-up men on cots, attended to by two medics, *Shemnong's* bridge was more of a triage station, it seemed, than the command center of a major oceangoing freighter.

"To the commanding officer of the M/V *Shemnong!*"

Chan looked up through the shot-out windshield at the hovering helicopter. He stepped to the front of the bridge and fixed his eyes on the enemy chopper.

"This is the commanding officer of the ROCS *Kee Lung!* Marines of the Republic of China are now boarding your ship."

Chan looked around. Nothing. "They must be boarding from the chopper flying over the stern," he said.

"These Marines will make their way to the bridge, where they will take control of your ship. If you resist them, you will be shot, and your ship will be sunk."

A loud thud from behind. "Freeze! Hands up!"

Chan turned around. Two angry-looking intruders, clad in camouflage and helmets, aimed American M-16 automatic rifles at him. Taiwanese. Two more came in. Then two more.

"Who is the captain?" the first one demanded in fluent Mandarin Chinese.

"The captain is dead." Chan held his hands up over his head. "He was killed by the machine-gun fire from your helicopter."

"The same kind of machine-gun fire that your naval forces unleashed on ROC personnel in your murderous assault at Itu Aba."

"I am a civilian sailor. We are not members of the military."

"But you are carrying weapons to support Communist Chinese forces on Itu Aba. Are you not?"

"We are under contract with both governmental entities and private entities to supply materials to several ports of call," Chan said.

"Who is in charge of this ship?" the man demanded.

"I am the first officer. I am now in command."

"We are Marines of the Republic of China. I am Lieutenant Ho. Others are boarding right now. You will order your crew to cooperate and not resist."

"I've already told them that," Chan said.

"Do it again!" The leader jabbed his rifle at Chan.

"Very well," Chan said. He stepped over to the 1MC. "Now hear this. This is the first officer. We have been boarded by Taiwanese Marines."

"Republic of China!" the leader growled, again jabbing his rifle in Chan's direction.

"Excuse me?" Chan said.

"Not Taiwanese Marines. Tell them Republic of China Marines!"

Chan wasn't going to argue with an enemy soldier who was pointing a gun at him nor would he express his true feelings about the so-called Republic of China.

"All hands. Check that. We have been boarded by Marines of the Republic of China." He looked at the leader. "We will cooperate with these Marines while they are on board. We will not resist them in any way. This is the first officer." He looked back at the lieutenant. "Is that satisfactory, Lieutenant Ho?"

"We want to see your cargo. You! Take me to your cargo, both on deck and in your cargo bay! Now!"

"By all means." Chan was certain that when he showed them what was in the cargo bay, he would be shot.

South China Sea
somewhere between USS Vicksburg and USS Emory S. Land

The dolphins had disappeared, their chattering and playful splattering now gone. The only sounds were of the ocean—the wind, the waves—and the *beep ... beep ... beep* of the homing device strapped around his waist.

The dolphins' disappearance had left a feeling of loneliness, as if he now had been abandoned and had no one.

But even if the chattering flippers had hung around to keep him company and stand guard against killer sharks, they could not shade him from the tropical sun, blazing so high overhead and sending down angry waves of heat. Even if the sharks stayed away, the sun and the heat soon would threaten his survival.

Gunner's mind raced through his survival training in the event of a seaborne crash or sinking.

Naval officers lost at sea were taught that their uniforms could be used as a flotation device. By blowing down into the front of his shirt, the shirt would inflate to help keep the officer afloat. But this process was a stopgap measure and had to be repeated over and over again, an exhausting process. He thanked God that wasn't necessary. The life vest was still doing its job.

He could use the second value of the uniform that had been explained. In tropical waters, the uniform pants could be used for cooling and to combat sunburn. Officers were taught to remove their trousers and to wrap them around their neck and head, leaving enough room to breathe, to block the skin from direct exposure to sunlight.

But he had to be careful not to lose the homing device strapped around his waist when he removed his trousers.

He reached down to feel for his belt buckle. As he pulled with his fingers against his belt to unbuckle it, his forearm brushed against the homing device, which was strapped just below his life preserver, just above his belt.

The beeping stopped. Now all he heard was the sound of wind and waves.

"Dear Jesus, help me."

He reached down to feel for the activation button, found it, and pressed it. Nothing. Again. Still nothing. One more time. Silence.

Gunner cursed, then cursed again.

How hypocritical, he thought. Asking Jesus to help in one breath and cursing in the next.

"Forgive me, Lord. Stay focused. One step at a time."

He reached down again, unbuckled his trousers, and unzipped his zipper. Pulling his knees up against his chest, he slipped off his trousers, pulled them up out of the water, and draped them over his head. The cool, wet pants felt soothing to his head, neck, and face.

But now that his homing device had failed, he truly was lost at sea, with no chance of communicating with anyone — except God.

Bridge
USS **Emory S. Land**
South China Sea

Captain, we've lost the signal!"

Commander Bobby Roddick watched as Captain Wilson rushed over to the radio officer's workstation and looked over the officer's shoulder. "You sure it's not just a computer glitch?" the captain asked. "Try shutting it down and re-booting."

"Already tried that, sir," the radio officer said. "Nothing. We're picking up other stuff out there, so our radio's working. Frequency sensors are working. There's no equipment malfunction on our side." The radio officer spun around in his chair and looked at Wilson and Roddick. "I'm convinced that the unit is no longer broadcasting."

"Not good," Captain Wilson said.

"No, sir, it isn't," Roddick agreed.

"We maintain course to the last reported broadcast point," the captain said, "but without that homing beacon, we're looking for a needle in a haystack. And our chances of finding anyone just took a huge hit."

Roddick nodded. "I'm afraid you're right, sir." His thoughts turned to Stephanie. How would she take this?

The best approach, he decided, unless the captain ordered him to do otherwise, was to refrain from telling her that they had lost touch with the beacon. At least not yet.

There was another problem. He sensed a mutual attraction. He had seen the look in her eye. He knew that look. It was the star-struck look of a butter bar ensign enamored with her executive officer. Of course, in this case the butter bar just happened to be the daughter of the president of the United States — the very attractive daughter of the president. But he would never, ever take advantage of that. His duty was first to his country and then to the Navy.

"Did you hear that, XO?" the captain said.

"I'm sorry, Captain, I missed what you said."

"Let's get a FLASH message out to Seventh Fleet. Notify them that we've lost the homing signal. Will continue to search the area looking for any visual ID of wreckage until instructed otherwise."

"Aye, Captain."

CHAPTER 9

Main deck
M/V Shemnong
South China Sea
between Da Nang, Vietnam, and the Paracel Islands
course 180 degrees

With two armed Taiwanese Marines jamming their rifles into his back, and with Lieutenant Ho walking beside him to his left pointing a pistol at his head, First Officer Kenny Chan, sporting sunglasses, stepped out onto the bright sunlit main deck of the *Shemnong.*

"The main cargo deck is this way." Chan pointed to the left. The quartet turned and walked along the edge of the ship.

At least eight Taiwanese Marines with M-16 rifles were posted along the deck. As he walked past, one of the guards glared at him. Chan looked down at the water. Better to drown than be shot.

Would they shoot him for the military equipment on deck or for the atrocious cargo in the bay below? If they didn't shoot him for one, they would shoot him for the other. He looked over the side, only a couple of feet to his right.

Just make a break for it, leap over the side.

"Daddy, come home."

His son's voice, the image of the boy's face, stopped him. He had to live.

"This way." Chan motioned toward the center of the ship, where some of the weapons destined for Itu Aba, including mobile missile launchers, were chained down to the deck. Other weapons were covered with canvas.

"Do you always transport howitzers on the deck of your ship, Mr. Chan?"

"We transport whatever we are paid to transport," Chan replied.

"Mr. Chan, this will be easier if you cooperate. You did not answer my question!" the Marine snapped. "Do you always transport howitzers on the deck of your ship?"

Chan hesitated. "No, sir. We do not normally transport howitzers."

"And what is the destination of these weapons?"

Perhaps he should blame the captain. He could claim that only the dead captain knew the destination for the weapons, that the destination had not yet been revealed to the crew.

"I asked you a question, First Officer!"

Just lie.

"Sergeant, shoot him in the head."

"Wait!" Kenny held up his hand, prompting the lieutenant to make a hand gesture, halting the execution.

"You will answer my question now?" Lieutenant Ho snapped.

"Yes. The captain knew the destination of the weaponry. He was going to reveal the destination to the crew just before we unloaded the weapons."

"Mr. Chan, you did not answer my question. My question was, and is, do *you* know the destination of these weapons? If I discover you are lying, I will have you shot and thrown overboard to the sharks!"

Chan hesitated again. His name wasn't on any of the manifest documents. The captain had signed all those. How would they prove or disprove what he knew? Still, if they found out. His mother's words: "The truth shall set you free."

"At the request of the Chinese government in Beijing, *Shemnong* is under contract to deliver weapons to Itu Aba Island. To maintain our license and to fly under the flag of the PRC, *Shemnong* and the shipping company had no choice but to execute that contract as directed by the government."

The lieutenant re-holstered his pistol. "What weapons are you carrying?"

"The manifest is on the bridge," Chan said. "We are carrying mobile antiaircraft missiles, anti-ship missiles, torpedoes, machine guns, light arms, ammunition, grenades, radar and sonar equipment, rifles, pistols."

Ho looked at him. "So you are carrying weapons for Communist forces on the island to kill my countrymen from the Republic of China."

"Lieutenant," Chan said, "you are a military man and know the purpose of weapons. I am but a sailor. I have no control over how the Chinese Army would put these to use."

Ho barked instructions. Several Marines rushed over and began removing canvas tarps. They began arranging an assortment of weapons and ammunition out on the deck. Ho, his face flashing anger, glared at Chan. "Do you have more weapons in the cargo bay?"

A lump hit Chan's throat. "No. There are no weapons in the cargo bay."

"No? Then what's down there?"

Chan looked away, avoiding Ho's eyes. "Medical materials for a customer in Bangkok."

Ho raised an eyebrow. "Medical materials? Do you mean biological weapons?"

"The cargo is designated as medical materials."

"Very well," Ho said. "Then take me down there. For your own sake, you better be telling me the truth."

"Yes, Lieutenant." Chan's heart thumped as he thought about what was next. "The medical materials are in crates, boarded up with plywood, and some of the plywood will have to be removed for you to examine the cargo."

Ho eyed Chan for a moment. "Sergeant! Corporal!"

Two Taiwanese Marines looked over at Kenny Chan and Lieutenant Ho.

"Come with Mr. Chan and me."

"Yes, sir," one said. They picked up their rifles off the deck and strapped them over their shoulders.

"This way," Chan said as he led the band of armed Taiwanese through the door, into the first deck utility space, then down the ladder leading to the entrance to the cargo bay.

He opened the hatch and stepped into the refrigerated space. He stood there, again feeling sick as the others joined him in the cargo bay. "As you can see," he said, "these crates are marked by the shipper as containing medical supplies. You will need a screwdriver to remove the plywood and examine the contents. There are power screwdrivers in the toolbox attached to the bulkhead."

The two Marines opened the toolbox, and each took out a power screwdriver.

They held the power drivers in front of them, up against the overhead light, eyed them for a second, pushed on the switch, watched them twirl, then flipped them off.

"I will take this one. You take that one," the sergeant said to the corporal.

The Marines inserted their screwdrivers into the Phillips-head screws on one crate. With a high-pitched whine, the screwdrivers spun the screws counterclockwise. The first two screws dropped to the deck.

They then moved to the next set of screws.

Chan could not watch.

"Corporal," the sergeant said, "I am nearly done. Hold off for a second and help me remove this."

"Yes, sir."

Chan breathed heavily, his eyes glued to the floor.

"Oh, my God!"

Headquarters
United States Seventh Fleet
Yokosuka, Japan

His derrière still chapped from the butt-chewing delivered by the admiral, Captain Draxler looked up and saw Walls rushing toward his desk, holding a document in his hand.

"Whatcha got, Wes?"

"FLASH. TOP SECRET. From the *Vicksburg*."

Draxler stood up, took the message, donned his reading glasses, and sat back down.

FROM: Commanding Officer, USS *Vicksburg*
TO: Commander Seventh Fleet
PRECEDENCE: FLASH
CLASSIFICATION: TOP SECRET

1. USS *Vicksburg* received emergency request for medical assistance from ROCS *Kee Lung.*
2. Request for medical assistance on board PRC Freighter *Shemnong,* South China Sea, en route to Itu Aba.
3. *Shemnong* currently under control of ROC Marines.
4. *Shemnong* commandeered for carrying weapons to reinforce Communist forces in Spratly Islands.
5. Commanding Officer ROCS *Kee Lung* advises medical assistance, at least one physician, urgently needed on board PRC Freighter *Shemnong* due to injuries to crew members while boarding and to investigate crimes against humanity.
6. *Kee Lung* advises that situation aboard *Shemnong* is urgent.

> Very respectfully,
> LC Kruger, CAPT, USN
> Commanding Officer

"Crimes against humanity?" Draxler whipped off his glasses. "What's that about?"

"Who knows, Captain," Walls said. "Maybe the Taiwanese Navy shot its way on board this vessel, killed or injured some of her crew members in the process, and found something." He shrugged.

"Where's our nearest Medical Corps officer?"

"On board USS *Vicksburg,*" Walls said. "Lieutenant Commander Fred Jeter."

"On board the *Vicksburg.*" Draxler parroted Walls. "Along with one remaining available chopper within flying distance. How convenient."

"Ain't it though, Captain."

Draxler stood up. "I gotta get this to the admiral."

"Maybe that'll get his mind off the Stephanie Surber rescue attempt," Walls said.

"We'll see. He's gonna have to run this up the flagpole to the Pentagon."

"Agreed," Walls said.

Draxler rushed back to the admiral's office, having called to announce that there was an urgent matter for which he needed to see Admiral Wesson.

"What's urgent, Captain Draxler?" The admiral's voice reflected more curiosity than any of the sharp anger from earlier in the day.

"This just in from USS *Vicksburg*, sir." He handed the message to Admiral Wesson.

The admiral read the message. "Crimes against humanity?"

"Sir, maybe they've got some tortured Taiwanese prisoners on board from Itu Aba or something. But that's just speculation."

Wesson looked up at him. "Is there a medical officer on board *Vicksburg*?"

"Yes, sir. And one chopper still in *Vicksburg*'s hangar bay."

"Hmph," Wesson grunted. "If we do this, I've gotta bring the other chopper back off that search-and-rescue mission. I can't leave *Vicksburg* without one of her choppers for a prolonged period."

"Agreed, sir."

"But a decision to put one of our officers on a Chinese freighter at the request of Taiwan in a time of hostilities needs to be made in Washington." He looked up, as if expecting a reply.

"Agreed, Admiral."

"Very well, Captain. Forward this message FLASH to Washington. Include a cover endorsement that I recommend approving the request on humanitarian grounds. If we get an approval, message *Vicksburg* to call one chopper back to the ship and dispatch the other chopper with the medical officer to the *Shemnong*."

"Aye, sir."

CHAPTER 10

Residence of the Secretary of Defense
Arlington, Virginia

2:00 a.m. local time

The bedroom of the secretary of defense of the United States of America was located in a modest home that Secretary and Mrs. Irwin Lopez had purchased twenty years ago when he had been an undersecretary in another presidential administration.

The secretary's bedroom was also modest, not all that large, considering the power, prestige, and influence of the man who slept in it on nights that he wasn't either traveling or working all night at the Pentagon or the White House.

Three telephones sat on two tables on each side of the king-sized bed, all hotlines to various posts that the secretary of defense could communicate with instantly, in the event of a national emergency. The phones rarely rang. The secured hotlines were for national emergencies or in cases where an urgent military decision was pressing.

Although none of the phones had rung in months, the brewing situation in the South China Sea had kept the secretary of defense on edge. Lopez lay in bed, blinking his eyes in the dark, trying to focus on the red lights of the digital clock beside the bed.

The Pentagon hotline buzzed, igniting a red flashing light.

"I knew it," he mumbled.

"What is it, Irwin?" his wife asked.

"Go back to sleep, baby." Lopez flipped on the bedside lamp and picked up the phone from the Pentagon Communications Center. "Secretary Lopez here."

"Mister Secretary. General McDaniel here. We have an urgent request from the Taiwanese Navy."

"What sort of request?"

"They're requesting a US Navy doctor aboard a PRC freighter that they've commandeered in the South China Sea. They claim they have evidence of crimes against humanity aboard."

"What?" Lopez squinted his eyes. "Let me get this straight. The Taiwanese want a Navy doctor? . . . to board a shot-up Chinese freighter?"

"Yes, sir."

"What crimes against humanity?"

"They didn't say, sir."

Lopez checked his watch. "Okay, email me that message."

"Everything okay, honey?"

"Fine, hon. Go back to sleep." Then, speaking back into the phone, "Hang on a sec." He stepped out of the bedroom, walked a few feet down the hall and turned left into his home office, phone still in hand. Lopez sat down in the chair. He had left the computer on. He typed in his password, moved the mouse to position the arrow over the secure email link, and clicked.

The downloaded message appeared on the screen. After reading it, Lopez asked the duty officer, "Our nearest Navy doc?"

"USS *Vicksburg*, sir."

"What other ships are in the area?"

"*Emory S. Land*, sir."

"Not much firepower on that rust bucket."

"No, sir."

Lopez thought about the situation. "Okay . . . I've gotta wake up the president on this one. Stand by. I'll call you back."

The Lincoln Bedroom
the White House

2:05 a.m. local time

K*nock . . . knock . . . knock . . .*
"Mr. President?"

The president of the United States removed his arms from around the First Lady, pushed himself up in the bed, and squinted his eyes.

"That you, Arnie?" President Douglas Surber thought he had heard the voice of Arnold Brubaker, who had been President Mack Williams' longtime chief of staff and who, along with almost every member of Williams' old national security team, had been retained by Surber when he ascended from the vice presidency to the presidency. Arnie Brubaker was the only man Douglas Surber had ever met who somehow seemed to operate on no sleep.

"Yes, sir, Mr. President," Brubaker said from behind the closed door. "I've got the secretary of defense on the line for you, sir."

"Just a second." Surber reached over and flipped on a night-light, which cast a low subdued light, grabbed the navy bathrobe with the presidential seal embroidered on it and put it on.

When he opened the door, Arnie stood there, disgustingly decked out in a navy pinstripe suit with a white shirt and red tie.

"What time is it?"

"Two in the morning, sir."

"They never woke me up in the middle of the night like this when I was vice president."

"No, sir," Brubaker said.

"SECDEF wants to chat?"

"Got him on the phone right here, sir." He handed the phone to the president.

"Joe, pull that door closed, will you?" Surber nodded at one of the two Secret Service agents, signaling to close the door to the bedroom.

"Yes, sir."

"Irwin. Whatcha got?"

"Mr. President, Taiwan has boarded a PRC freighter in the South China Sea. They claim it was headed to Itu Aba Island and contains evidence of crimes against humanity on board."

"What?" Surber looked at Brubaker. "What do you mean by crimes against humanity?"

"I don't know yet, sir. No other information. But they have an urgent request for you."

"What request?"

"They want us to send a Navy doctor to the freighter."

"What ships do we have in the area?"

"Vicksburg and *Emory S. Land."* Surber's heart pounded at the name *Emory S. Land.* His daughter's ship, her defenseless supply ship, was in the middle of a potential war zone. Against her mother's wishes, Stephanie had followed him into the Navy. No time to dwell on that.

He looked over at Brubaker. "You familiar with this situation, Arnie?"

"Somewhat, sir," Brubaker said. "The secretary of defense briefed me before I woke you."

"Let's step into the office and put this on speaker."

"Yes, sir," Brubaker said.

"Irwin, hang on just a sec. We're going to put you on speaker."

They walked a few feet down the wide hallway, away from the Lincoln bedroom. A Secret Service agent pushed open a door to the right. They stepped into a side office adjoining the bedroom.

"I'll take care of it, Mister President," Arnie said as he punched three buttons on one of the telephones on the desk. "There. Mister Secretary, can you hear us?"

"Loud and clear." Lopez's voice boomed through the speaker.

"Okay, gentlemen." Surber crossed his arms. "What are the pros and cons of our sending one of our doctors out to this Chinese freighter?"

The secretary of defense said, "At a time when China and Taiwan are shooting at each other and we're trying to get them to stand down, if the Chinese find out about it, they'll think we're picking sides in favor of Taiwan."

"That's favoring Taiwan? Sending a doctor to provide care for shot-up Communist sailors?" Brubaker asked.

"Arnie, I see your point," Lopez said. "But we're already sending the fleet into a potential powder keg, and now Taiwan wants a military doctor. That's a naval officer in uniform. If it were a civilian doctor, it might be different."

"We couldn't ask a civilian doctor to step into that situation," the president said.

"Agreed, Mister President," Brubaker said.

"Irwin," Surber said, "how would the Chinese even find out about it?"

"Depends on how it unfolds, sir," the secretary of defense said.

"Why not send the doc in, but limit his time on board the freighter to two hours. Let him render all the aid he can, and then get him the heck out of Dodge," Surber said. "That way we help the injured, reduce the chances of the Chinese finding out about it, and we find out about this 'crimes against humanity' thing they're talking about."

No response from the secretary of defense.

"Irwin, you still there?"

"Yes, sir. Just thinking. We could do that, Mister President, and that would reduce the chances that the Chinese would find out. But what if our doc finds some sort of life-threatening situation among his patients that requires more than two hours' worth of treatment? Are we going to leave patients behind to die?"

Surber thought about that possibility. "We'll cross that bridge when we come to it. But if people are hurting and there's been a request for our help, we need to help. That's the right thing to do." He needed to make a decision. "Besides, if the Chinese find out about it, I'm prepared to defend that decision on humanitarian grounds. We're sending a doctor. Not a SEAL team."

Arnie Brubaker nodded.

"Mr. Secretary, tell Seventh Fleet the request is approved. Unless I extend the time, the doc can stay on board that freighter a maximum of two hours to render aid and to give me a report on these crimes against humanity. I want a report transmitted back to Seventh Fleet while he is on board. I'm headed back to bed, but Irwin, I want you to wake me up when that report is back in."

"Yes, Mister President," Secretary Lopez said. "I'll notify the Pentagon Communications Center to get the message to Seventh Fleet."

"Very well," the president said. "Have a good night, gentlemen. I need some more shut-eye. Unless something else blows up, we'll chat in the morning."

"Yes, sir."

Headquarters
United States Seventh Fleet
Yokosuka, Japan

2:10 p.m. local time

Captain. FLASH message from National Command Authority." Commander Walls strode across the office, paper in hand. "They've approved the request for a doc to the *Shemnong*."

Captain Draxler took the message from Walls. He quickly perused it. "I'll advise the admiral."

Sick Bay
USS Vicksburg
South China Sea

2:15 p.m. local time

Commander Jeter. Report to the bridge."
At the sound of the announcement over the 1MC, Lieutenant Commander Fred Jeter, in the middle of afternoon sick call, stopped his examination of a sailor who had just come in. "What's that all about?" he muttered at his corpsman assistant. "Petty Officer Randall, take over for me, will you?"

"Yes, sir," Randall said.

"Sorry, Seaman Martinez," Jeter said to the patient. "I've gotta run. But you'll be in good hands with the corpsman here. You're going to be fine."

"Thanks, Doc." The young sailor coughed as he spoke.

Jeter handed the stethoscope to the corpsman, then stepped over to the small sink, squirted some soap on his hands, lathered up, then swished his hands under running water and dried off with a paper towel. He stepped out of sick bay, imparting a "Catch ya later, Corpsman" in the direction of his enlisted medical assistant as he stepped out into the passageway.

Whatever the reason, Fred loved avoiding sick bay, the most boring part of his job at sea. The routine of treating headaches, colds, seasickness, and minor cuts and burns could get old. Nothing a good corpsman couldn't handle.

Back out on the main deck in the afternoon sunlight, he stopped just for a second to set down the medical bag and reach into his pocket.

"There you are." His mouth watered when his fingers felt the small plastic-covered cardboard box. Extracting one cancer stick for a much-needed nicotine quickie, he jammed it between his lips, then fiddled in his other pants pocket for a lighter. Relief. Thank God. Actually, he should ask God to help him quit rather than thanking him for another cigarette. As he inhaled, the nicotine brought jolting relief to his body.

He picked up the bag and, with cigarette in mouth, hustled down the deck toward the forward section of the ship, sucking in smoke as fast as he could as he walked.

A moment later, he flipped the cigarette overboard. Climbing the ladder in double-time, he soon stepped onto the bridge, where the captain, the XO, the navigator, the helmsman, the radar and communications officers, and a number of petty officers hovered around the control panel, their backs to him as he entered.

"Doc's on the bridge," the officer of the deck announced, prompting the captain and the XO to turn around.

"Doc, I need you to pack your seabag, get some emergency medical supplies together, and be ready to fly out of here within the next fifteen minutes," Captain Kruger said.

Fred was stunned. "Absolutely, Captain." He hesitated. "Permission to inquire as to my mission and destination?"

"Certainly," Captain Kruger said. He handed Fred a document. "This came in. We sent it to Seventh Fleet. They sent it to Washington. Looks like this order is coming back down from the president himself."

Fred studied the order. "I'm headed to a Chinese freighter?" He kept reading. "Crimes against humanity?"

"Your guess is as good as anybody's, Doc. But whatever that means, you'll be the first to find out. And as you can see from the endorsement, the president wants a report on it."

Fred looked at the captain. "Skipper, I don't know if I can carry out these orders."

Captain Kruger crossed his arms. "What do you mean?"

"Two hours … to render emergency medical assistance and to investigate whatever this other thing is … that's not much time to get the job done."

"What do you suggest?" Kruger asked.

Fred thought for a second. "I'd like to take one of the corpsmen along. The corpsman could render medical assistance while I'm investigating these alleged crimes against humanity."

The captain looked at the XO. "What do you think?"

"Well, the request to Seventh Fleet was only for the doc, sir. And they ran that all the way up the chain to Washington. So that means that Seventh Fleet considers this to be a sensitive matter. The request went to SECDEF, and he considered it to be so sensitive that he ran it up to POTUS. Technically, we have permission to send the doc." The XO nodded at Fred. "I'm not sure it's a great idea to run this back up the chain again. Not sure we have time."

The captain considered his options. "Technically, you're right. But I think one can imply that the doc may need a degree of assistance from a corpsman. It's an urgent matter, and we don't have time to run it back up the chain." He paused. "Okay, Doc. Permission granted. Take one of the corpsmen with you. If we catch any flak, I'll take the heat."

"Thanks, Captain."

"XO, order that chopper into the air ASAP. Order the chopper that's on search and rescue back to the ship. Helmsman. After we launch the chopper, resume course to Itu Aba. All ahead full."

"Aye, Captain. All ahead full."

Bridge
USS Emory S. Land
South China Sea

2:30 p.m. local time

In calm seas and under an afternoon sky punctuated by an occasional cloud, the sun's rays pounded the ship. Because *Emory S. Land*'s bridge was located up toward the front of the vessel, closer to the bow than most US Navy ships, someone perched in the bridge could look down and see everything on the bow area.

At the front of the bridge, Commander Bobby Roddick was finishing off a banana while manning his station alongside the helmsman and was taking advantage of the view.

Down at the ship's forward watch station, her back to the bridge, her face to the sea, her regulation-cropped auburn hair blowing in the breezy afternoon, Stephanie Surber held binoculars to her eyes, scouring waters in front of the ship, hoping, praying for any sign of human life.

Despite the it's-not-your-fault pep talk Commander Roddick had given her, Stephanie was still taking the downed helicopter hard. She was a tough young woman. A fledgling naval officer with unlimited potential. Not a hint of self-entitlement because of who she was. In fact, if one did not know, one would never know.

She lowered her binoculars and turned around. Her back now to the sea, her face to the ship, she looked straight up at the bridge, as if searching for him. For a moment, a brief moment that was all too long, their eyes locked.

Roddick tossed the banana peel in a trash can and brought his binoculars to his eyes. He gazed out to the blue horizon, way above her head.

"XO."

He did an about-face. The senior chief from communications had a message in hand. "Just in from Seventh Fleet, sir. FLASH."

"Thanks, Senior Chief." He took the message from the veteran sea dog and started reading.

FROM: Commander, Seventh Fleet
TO: Commanding Officer, USS *Emory S. Land*
PRECEDENCE: FLASH
CLASSIFICATION: TOP SECRET
SUBJ: South China Sea Search and Rescue for Missing US Navy
      Chopper

1. Be advised Seahawk helicopter from USS *Vicksburg* conducting search-and-rescue efforts in your sector for missing US Navy helicopter is being recalled for another assignment.
2. USS *Emory S. Land* directed to continue search-and-rescue efforts until sundown today unless otherwise directed.

> Respectfully,
> JW Wesson, VADM, USN
> Commander

"Bad news," he said. "They're pulling the chopper off search and rescue."

"Agreed," the senior chief said. "Without a homing beacon, and now without a chopper, it's gonna be hard to find anybody out there."

"Almost impossible." Roddick sighed. "You're excused, Senior Chief. I'll alert the Captain."

"Thank you, sir."

Roddick turned around as the senior chief left the bridge and looked down at the bow. She now was facing forward again, her binoculars scouring the seas.

"Captain's on the bridge!" the officer of the deck announced.

Roddick turned as Captain Wilson stepped back onto the bridge and removed his garrison cap.

"Bad news, Skipper."

"What's up, XO?"

"Just in from Seventh Fleet." He handed the message to the captain. "They're terminating the air search. Pulling the chopper back to the *Vicksburg*."

Wilson studied the message. "Not good." He looked down at Stephanie. "She's wasting her time at this point."

"Probably." Roddick nodded. "She'll take it hard. She's blaming herself for it."

"Helmsman. How much longer until we reach the position of the last transmission?"

"One hour, Skipper."

"Well, for the time being, what she doesn't know won't hurt her," the captain said. "We'll steam out to the position of the last known transmission and see what we can see. It may be a waste of gas, but we'll steam loops in the water until sundown, when Seventh Fleet is ending the search."

CHAPTER 11

South China Sea
somewhere between USS Emory S. Land *and USS* Vicksburg
local time unknown

The whistling breeze, mixed with a rhythmic, hallucinating sound of sloshing water was making him sleepy. With the wet trousers draped over his head and the life jacket holding his head above the water, Gunner closed his eyes. His tongue was parched dry. His mouth tasted cottony. He had already dozed off at least a couple times.

The heat was draining his strength. He tipped his head back, face skyward, his eyes covered by the salty-wet pants. He yawned and closed his eyes, drifting off to a state that was half awake and half asleep.

In his mind, he saw the sun-drenched peanut fields of southeastern Virginia.

The wind grazed over the green leaves, rustling them in the September sunshine along rows spanning the massive acreage surrounding his mother's farm home known as Corbin Hall.

"Gunner! Dinner's ready!" The sound of his mother's voice. A rifle shot cracked the air. Off across the way, at the edge of the field, a twelve-point buck stood. Four hunting dogs charged across the field, sending the buck scampering across the rows.

Another rifle shot. Another miss.

Then splashing.

Chippering.

A bump against his leg.

123

Gunner started unwrapping the pants legs from around his face and was greeted by a splash of water in his eyes.

The peanut fields were gone. The dolphins were back.

Their tailfins splashed around him in a playful fury, raining droplets of seawater on his head.

One of the dolphins bumped against the back of his life preserver, and then bumped again.

He opened his eyes, squinting against the afternoon sunshine, and saw them, all three of them, playing in the water. Two of the dolphins splashed their flippers, spraying water across Gunner's head. The third one, displaying his nose and a broad smile, swam up and began nudging him around to the right, in the direction of the spraying.

Pushed by the nose of the dolphin, Gunner turned around in the water.

There! Off in the distance! The orange pup tent bobbed in the water, perhaps a hundred yards away!

"Thank God! The life raft!" He wasn't alone!

"Lieutenant!" Gunner screamed across the water. "Lieutenant!"

Nothing. He was too far away, he thought.

Gunner kept his eyes focused on the life raft. He reached down and put one leg through his trousers, and then the other. He pulled the trousers up around his waist and began swimming toward the raft.

"God, keep that raft right there!" He swam hard, he wasn't closing the distance. The raft seemed to be moving away as fast as he was swimming.

"Please, God, let me get there!"

He swam harder. Faster. But still was unable to close the distance.

Harder.

Faster.

He looked up.

It was all for naught. The raft was moving farther away. His heart was pounding and he was gasping for breath. He stopped swimming and let himself float. He could see the raft, but he couldn't get to it.

Then the wind picked up again, and the orange tent disappeared behind the waves.

His heart had revved back to a frantic beat. He replayed his survival-school training 101. Conserve energy. Swimming against a current is fruitless. Exhausts you and makes you thirstier.

Treading water, Gunner squinted in the direction where the orange tent had been. He thought the wind might whip into it and blow it back toward him.

He waited. The sloshing of the waves and the whistling of the wind were his only companions. Even his dolphin friends had left him.

"Conserve energy. Never give up. Survive."

He took off his pants and draped them around his head again. He closed his eyes.

CHAPTER 12

The loud roar of the US Navy Seahawk helicopter, combined with the powerful air draft generated by its props as it sat in takeoff position on the ship's helo pad, made conversational speech all but impossible. So as he stepped from the ship's deck into the helo's cargo bay, Lieutenant Commander Fred Jeter shot a thumbs-up to his corpsman assistant, Hospitalman First Class Christian Randall, who was already strapped into the jump seat. Randall responded with a thumbs-up.

As Fred strapped himself into the other jump seat, the copilot handed him a communications headset, mouthing, "Put these on, sir," over the roar of the engines.

The headset cut down on the engine noise and allowed Fred to hear the pilot talking with the controller on the ship about last-second preflight matters.

As the pilot, the copilot, and shipboard controller chatted back and forth, using a litany of strange aviation terms, Fred opened one of the five surgical bags and ran through a mental checklist of the items.

Scalpel. Check. Suture. Check. IV Bags. Check. Needles and tubing. Check. Penicillin. Benson & Hedges. Check ... Zippo lighter ... Check ...

"Ready to take off, Doc?" the pilot's voice cracked over the headset.

"Let's do it, Lieutenant!" Fred said.

The engines revved to a high-pitched whine, and the helicopter lifted off the pad of the ship. The chopper climbed quickly and, moments later, dipped its nose and picked up speed.

Fred looked out the window and watched the *Vicksburg* disappear off in the distance.

"You okay, Doc?" the pilot asked.

"Doing great," Fred lied. He took some slow, deep breaths, breathing out just as slowly to calm himself down.

"Weather looks good this afternoon," the pilot said, as if Fred were interested in the announcement of the flight plan that was about to come. A second later, more unsolicited chatter. "We'll climb to ten thousand, and if all goes well, we'll have you out to that freighter in about twenty minutes or so."

The ominous knotting was twisting his stomach again, that sixth sense of foreboding that never lied.

He had felt it earlier in the morning, and then the first chopper that had taken off from the *Vicksburg*, the one carrying Gunner McCormick, had gone down.

Now what? Was this chopper about to crash too?

No. Whatever it was, it was worse than that.

The knotting tightened. Fred closed his eyes and gritted his teeth.

"You okay, Commander? You look a bit ..."

Fred opened his eyes. "I'm fine, Christian." Perhaps using the corpsman's first name would soothe both their nerves. "Just a twisted feeling that whatever we are getting into, it's a lot bigger than emergency first aid."

Suddenly, the chopper shook. Then dropped. Then smoothed out.

The pilot's voice over the headset. "Little heat inversion, gentlemen. No worries."

Fred did not respond.

"Whatever's out there, Doc," the corpsman said, "I've got your back, sir. And thanks for letting me come along for the ride."

"Appreciate that, Christian," Fred said. "Let's hope you're still thanking me an hour from now."

"Whatever, sir, I've got your back."

"Thanks. Just keep your head in the game, son."

"Will do, Commander."

South China Sea
somewhere between USS Vicksburg *and USS* Emory S. Land

The sun baked the steamy wet pants wrapped around his head. Thirst was now the problem. Drinking saltwater could be deadly.

Conserve energy.

Relax.

Gunner closed his eyes. Soon, he was asleep. When he opened his eyes, he had a strange sense of peace. He wondered how long he had been napping. Looking at the sun, he guessed maybe thirty minutes.

Splashing and chippering. His friends had returned! Gunner smiled as he pulled the wet pants off his head for a look.

They were breaking the surface just a few feet over to his right. Their long mouths under their bulb-nosed snouts were again smiling as they flipped water over his head.

He looked around.

There! Maybe thirty feet behind him! The life raft! Just floating there! No current! No wind!

His body surged with renewed excitement! He cupped his hands and leaned into a breaststroke, pulling himself through the water, quickening his stroke before the wind whipped up again to blow the life raft away.

No sharks. No wind. Please!

He kept swimming, as if pulling water back, drawing himself closer to the floating oasis. His hand finally reached up and felt the edge of the raft.

Thank you, God!

He clutched the raft's life line, then got both arms up over the air-filled rubber tube and just hung there, resting. Gunner had pulled himself against the rubber flotation tube so tight that he felt the hard heartbeat from his chest thumping against it.

He began calculating the consequences of his discovery. The raft could buy him more time. People had survived weeks, some even months on a raft at sea. His legs would be out of the water, no longer obvious shark bait. What a godsend! Now, if he only had fresh water. He would pray for rain and worry about that later.

Gunner started to pull himself into the raft, to get under the protective shade of the water-repellant tent, when he noticed the rope secured to the raft. Like a fishing line going out into the water, the rope drifted out from the raft and curled on the surface behind the raft, the end of it out of view.

Gunner remembered the last time he had seen the rope—uncoiling out of the helicopter at what looked like a thousand RPMs … and then …

"Lieutenant!" he screamed. "Lieutenant!"

Gunner worked his way around to the back of the raft. There, about twenty feet away, he saw the olive-green-clad body floating face down in the water. "Lieutenant!"

Gunner broke into a furious freestyle stroke, kicking and splashing water with his feet as he swam with every ounce of energy out toward the copilot.

His right hand touched something. He jerked his hand away and stopped swimming. Only the back of the copilot's flight jacket was above the surface. Gunner moved closer and pushed up on the lieutenant's shoulder, flipping him over, face up in the water.

"Dear Jesus, no!"

Gunner backed away. The face had been chewed beyond recognition. One leg was gone. The other, or what was left of it, was wrapped in several coils of rope.

"Sharks! I've gotta get out of the water!"

He swam back to the raft, sliding his hand along the rope for security. When he got back, he reached up and grabbed the life line on the rubber tubing. Pulling up and kicking with his legs, he got himself halfway over the rubber tubing, and then, as the raft started tipping up, he tumbled in and moved under the protective shade of the orange tent canopy.

He lay there, looking up at the orange ceiling, listening to the waves and the sound of the breeze whirling outside. Thousands of miles from home, he had found an oasis—for now. He lay there, catching his breath, and gave thanks to God.

All he could do now was wait … and pray.

But first, one more act of duty called. He rolled over on his belly and reached over the air-filled rubber flotation tube at the opening in the tent to find the rope. He gripped the rope and began pulling. The weight of the lieutenant's body offered token resistance as he reeled it in toward the entrance of the raft.

When the body floated into view, leg first, it was again face down in the water, hiding the mutilation.

Gunner didn't know what to do. He was no preacher. He'd never presided over a funeral. But he did know how to pray, to talk to God. Saying a prayer seemed the right thing to do. He held up one hand to the heavens.

"Heavenly Father, take this servant into your arms. And bring comfort to his family in the coming days, as they learn of his death and try to cope with it. Give them comfort and peace. In the name of your Son, Jesus Christ, who died and was resurrected and who lives forever. Amen."

Now what? A sermon? A song? He thought of the Navy Hymn. He knew the words from all those times he'd gone to the Protestant chapel services. Somehow, the words seemed appropriate for the moment. He raised both hands to the heavens and began reciting the words,

Eternal Father, strong to save,
Whose arm has bound the restless wave,
Who bidst the mighty ocean deep,
Its own eternal limits keep,
Oh, hear us as we cry to thee,
for those in peril on the sea.

He lowered his hands, reached down into the water, and carefully unwrapped the rope from the lieutenant's leg.

Then he put his hand on the shoulder and gave the body a huge shove.

He watched as the body drifted away from the raft.

"Good-bye, Lieutenant. God have mercy on your soul."

CHAPTER 13

Okay, Doc, we've sighted the freighter," the pilot said. "I'm gonna do a flyover and see if we can find enough space to set this bird down."

"Excellent, Lieutenant," Fred said. He leaned forward and looked out the front windshield over the two pilots' shoulders. Nothing but blue water and blue sky.

"Doc, I'm banking left," the pilot said. "If you want a good view, look out your left window. It'll be a whole lot easier than trying to look up through the cockpit."

"Thanks, Lieutenant." Fred sat back in the jump seat. The chopper banked hard left. The view out the window at first showed rolling swells cresting with the reflections of the late-afternoon sun. And then, moving across his view, the ship appeared, long and low in the water. Like many freighters, her superstructure, including the flybridge, was built back toward the stern, and out front was flat space the size of a football field for the storage of cargo. The space in front of the bridge contained dozens of wooden boxes and some military equipment that was unboxed.

The freighter looked almost like a military cargo vessel. No wonder it was causing such a hullabaloo with the Taiwanese. The chopper banked again, back into a circular pattern, and the *Shemnong* passed out of view.

"Hey, Doc. Were you a Spiderman fan when you were a kid?"

Fred and Hospitalman Randall exchanged glances. They both knew where this was going.

"Lieutenant, I loved both Spiderman and Superman," Fred said. "But I was never keen on flying through the air like they do, even on the end of a string."

"No worries, sir," the pilot said. "Unfortunately, I don't see enough space to put the bird down. We'll let you gentlemen down real slow. If we get you down too close to the water or something, just give us the thumbs-up, and we'll reel you right back up."

"Roger that, Lieutenant," Fred muttered. "I've done the harness thing before. Doesn't mean I like it."

Now only the roar of the engine. Fred felt the chopper slow down, almost to a hover.

"Okay, Doc," the pilot said. "We're over the back of the ship. I see some smiling Taiwanese Marines down there looking up and waving. I think they're gonna be glad to see you."

"That's good to know." Fred shook his head.

"Chief Perkins will strap you gentlemen in the harness, and we should have you on board the ship in just a few. Okay, Chief. We're ready."

"Roger that, Skipper," the chief said. "Gentlemen, stay strapped in tight until I get to you." The chief's voice was barely audible through the headset.

"No problem," Fred said.

The chief unbuckled his harness. He clipped his belt to a tether line and crouched over and punched a button. Slowly, the chopper's bay door opened. Bright afternoon sunlight and the thunderous roar of the spinning props filled the cabin.

The chief turned a manual lever just above the open bay door, and the steel arm of the winch swung out over the water. He popped open an overhead compartment and retrieved that dreaded harness that Fred had dangled from more times than he cared to remember.

"Okay, Doc, you're first." The chief stood in front of Fred, holding the harness. "Let's get you unbuckled."

"Got it, Chief." Fred unlatched his seat buckles.

"Okay, please stand and hold your arms out."

Fred stood while the chief strapped him into the transfer harness.

"There, that should do it. Ready, sir?"

"Ready, Chief."

"I'm gonna clip the line to the back of the harness, and you'll be on your way."

"I just love bungee cords," Fred quipped.

"I hear you, sir." A click in the midsection of his back. Another click just behind his collar. "You're secured, sir. You know the drill. I want you to sit on the floor and slide toward the opening of the hangar bay. Just dangle your legs over the side."

"Got it." Fred hated this part. Even though he was attached to a secure line, he still hated it. A moment later, with his butt on the chopper floor and the chief's hands on his shoulders, his legs dangled over the side. The freighter was about a hundred feet below, but his instinct told him to look straight out, not down.

"Okay, sir, I'm going to tighten the cord a little with the winch so you don't swing too much."

"Got it."

The electronic winch hummed. The cord tightened, pulling up against Fred's back.

"Ready, sir?"

"Ready." Fred lied. He wasn't ready. He never was.

"Okay, I'm just going to give you a little shove out the chopper. Ready?"

"Sure."

"Here we go!"

Fred felt the crew chief's hands on the back of both of his shoulders. Then, a hard shove pushed his butt off the security of the platform. He dangled outside the chopper, suspended in the air high above the ship, swinging back and forth like a ball on a string under the down blast of the chopper's propellers.

Yes, he hated this dangerous bungee-cord exercise. Yet, at the same time, he loved it! Moments like these were the reason he had snubbed his father's lucrative practice in Hattiesburg at the Jeter Medical Clinic. How many other physicians in the world got opportunities like this to live on the edge, all in the name of defending the Hippocratic Oath?

He tipped his head back and looked up at the chief. Then, remembering the hand-signal sequence, he gave a thumbs-down.

The winch started unwinding, and Fred descended—a bit too quickly.

Thumbs-up. The winch stopped. He looked down. A group of armed Marines, looking very Chinese, stood in a circle on deck. They motioned him down, rather excitedly, as if they were in a rush. Fred looked up again. The thumbs-down signal. Another descent, still a bit too fast, but this time he would not stop it.

He looked down. The deck rushed up. This was no parachute drop, but still, too fast for comfort. The Marines stepped back, widening the circle on deck as if expecting a crash landing. He extended his legs, bracing for impact. A second later, the rope jerked up and swung there, less than a foot off the deck. Then another brief descent. Contact. Not a bad landing.

"You doctor? You doctor?" The question was shouted in broken but understandable English even as a couple Marines were unstrapping him. Fred didn't know who had spoken.

"I'm Lieutenant Commander Fred Jeter, Medical Corps, United States Navy. And yes, I'm a doctor!" he shouted at them. The harness, now off, was being reeled quickly back up to the Seahawk.

"I am Lieutenant Ho! Marine Corps of the Republic of China." The speaker identified himself with a quick, sharp salute shot Fred's way. Fred returned the salute. "Come, Doctor. There are many things to show you."

"I have an assistant and medical supplies coming down from the chopper." He looked up and saw Petty Officer Randall already dangling in the air just outside the Seahawk.

"No time to wait, Doctor!" Lieutenant Ho protested. "Many things to see! My Marines will bring your assistant and supplies to the bridge. Also we have some medics on board to help."

"Okay, let's go," Fred said.

Ho turned, motioning Fred to follow. The deck was crowded with large wooden crates, and they walked around them, making their way to the side deck, then headed toward the stern, jogging down the side deck.

Lieutenant Ho opened the door to the entrance of the superstructure, ready to head up to the bridge. Just then the Seahawk peeled away from over the ship and headed back toward the *Vicksburg*. That meant Hospitalman Randall was now on board.

Stepping into the superstructure, the stark contrast between the late-afternoon sunshine and the indoor shade was blinding.

Ho stepped onto a steel ladder leading to the upper decks. Fred started up the ladder right after him.

"Do any of your medics speak English, Lieutenant?"

"They not our medics. Communist Chinese medics were assigned to the ship. And no," he said, continuing up the steel ladder in a quick double-time, "they do not speak English. But our officers do. We will translate."

"Excellent."

They continued climbing past a third deck, then a fourth. Fred's slight shortness of breath underscored what he already knew—time to quit the cancer sticks.

Reaching the fifth deck, they approached two closed double doors, guarded by two Taiwanese Marines.

"This is the bridge," Lieutenant Ho said. "It was shot up bad. Two dead, including the captain of the ship. Lots of blood."

"I'm a doctor, Lieutenant. I'm used to blood."

Ho nodded, then opened the doors.

Shattered glass lay all over the deck from the shot-out windshield. Off to the right, two bodies on the floor were covered in white sheets. Six men were on cots along the perimeter of the bridge. Their heads were wrapped in bandages. Each man had an IV stuck in an arm.

The ship's navigational systems seemed intact. The radar screen appeared functional. Several men were seated at the instrument panels, and a man, perhaps the ship's XO or first officer, was looking over their shoulders as if in a supervisory capacity. A helmsman was at the wheel. And standing at attention, imposing a commanding presence, were two rifle-bearing Taiwanese Marines.

Three other men, apparently medics, were attending to the wounded. One held a stethoscope to a wounded man's chest, another adjusted an IV bag. A third was checking a patient's eyes.

What a surrealistic montage! Fred thought. A morgue, a ship's bridge, a hospital, and a bloody war zone—all wrapped into one.

"Who's in charge of the medical treatment?" Fred's question brought looks from every man on the bridge, followed by a rapid-fire translation into Mandarin by Lieutenant Ho.

The man adjusting the IV spoke in Mandarin.

"He says he has been in charge," Ho said.

"Tell him that I am a United States Navy doctor. Tell him now I am in charge."

Translation followed. First Ho. Then the medic's response. "He says he will obey your instructions, Doctor."

Petty Officer Randall arrived on the bridge, accompanied by two more Taiwanese Marines carrying the surgical bags that they brought from the *Vicksburg*.

"What's the condition of these men?"

Response in Chinese. Translation. "All shot by bullets from helicopter. Some in stomach. Some in arms and legs. We have some antibiotics, but short on everything else. We have no blood. This man bleeding badly. Shot in stomach. Will die with no blood." The medic pointed at the man he was standing beside. "They all die with no blood."

"Is he the most serious?" Fred asked.

"All serious. He the most."

Fred walked over to the man. His face was pale, his breathing slow, his mental state delirious. The bandages around his abdomen were soaked with fresh blood. Fred looked back at his corpsman. "Christian, come over here, please."

"Yes, sir."

"Stay with this man. Keep pressure on wounds to try to reduce the blood loss. That's the only thing that might save him."

"Yes, sir."

Fred walked to the next cot. The patient looked up at him, grimacing. The bullet hole was high in the front of the right leg, just below his pelvic region. The blood-soaked makeshift tourniquet, which consisted of a ripped sheet, was tied above the wound, and a second bandage held down gauze on the wound.

"Help me!" the man cried in a raspy voice in Chinese-accented English.

"Lieutenant Ho, bring me that medical bag right beside you."

"Yes, Doctor."

Fred kneeled on the deck and zipped open the bag. Removing a syringe, he drew a small dose of morphine into it.

"Somebody cut this man's sleeve off."

A quick translation. Then, one of the Chinese medics cut the sleeve with a pair of scissors. Fred reached back into the bag for a cotton ball, soaked it in alcohol, and then swabbed an area high up on the man's upper arm.

"Hang tight for me, my friend." He slid the hypodermic needle into the man's arm and depressed the plunger. "This will make you feel better." He removed the needle and put it back in the bag. Fred noted that the man's leg would need amputation.

He started a brief examination of the four other men on cots around the bridge.

"Who is in command of this ship?"

The man in the center of the bridge turned around. "I am Chan. The First Officer. I am in command." The man spoke in better English than Ho. "Subject, of course, to the orders at the moment of the armed occupiers we have on board."

"Well, Mr. Chan," Fred said, "your medics have done a good job considering what little they have to work with. But without blood transfusion—and soon—your men will die."

"We have no blood on board, Doctor."

"I understand," Fred said. "That's why they must be medevaced off the ship immediately. I recommend that they be airlifted to the USS *Carl Vinson*, an American aircraft carrier. The *Vinson* is en route to the South China Sea. She has surgical facilities and enough blood to save their lives if we can get them there in time."

"Very well, Doctor," the Chinese seaman said. "Do what you must to save them."

"Lieutenant. Radio the *Kee Lung*. Relay message to USS *Vicksburg*. Request emergency transport of six men, critically wounded, to USS *Carl Vinson* for blood transfusions and treatment."

"Yes, Doctor," Lieutenant Ho said. He barked orders in Chinese to another Marine, who nodded and saluted. "My assistant will relay request for emergency air transport to USS *Carl Vinson* of six PRC nationals for emergency treatment and blood transfusions."

"Excellent," Fred said. "I believe you had something else you wanted to show me?"

Lieutenant Ho's eyes locked with the first officer's. It was a tense and mutual stare down.

"Mr. Chan here showed this evidence to me. He claims no foreknowledge of this cargo."

"What do you mean by evidence?" Fred asked.

"You must see for yourself, Doctor. No discussion. Mr. Chan will escort us to the cargo bay."

"Is that necessary, Lieutenant?" Chan asked.

"Necessary for you to come? Yes! You are to look again, Mr. Chan. You are carrying this ... this disgusting cargo for money!"

"I told you I knew nothing about it!"

"Yes," Ho snapped. "So you have said. You better pray that the evidence supports your claim."

"Okay, gentlemen," Fred said, "I'm not staying on board this freighter all day while the two of you argue. Whatever it is, let's get to it. I have a job to do on my own ship."

"Let's go, Mr. Chan." Ho opened the door. "After you."

They fell in behind the Chinese first officer. Two ROC Marines followed them. When they reached the main deck and stepped out into the sunshine, Fred decided at that moment that he was done smoking. He pulled the pack from his pocket and tossed it overboard.

"This way," Chan said.

They stepped through another door and were back inside the ship. They descended another ladder and at the bottom, just down the passageway, was another double door.

"This is the cargo bay," Chan said.

"Open it," Ho said.

Chan opened the doors, and a rush of cold air hit them.

"Feels like an icebox," Fred said.

"The cargo bay is refrigerated," Chan said.

"Let's go, Mr. Chan," Ho snapped. "Get it over with."

Chan stepped in. Fred followed him. Lieutenant Ho and the two Taiwanese Marines followed Fred.

Fluorescent lights illuminated the long, narrow passageway that stretched back away from the entrance perhaps twenty yards. Plywoodcrated boxes were stacked up along the bulkheads on each side, from the deck to the overhead.

Ho just stood there, saying nothing. Doing nothing. It was as if both Ho and Chan had been stopped in their tracks by some magnetic force. Fred broke the silence. "What's in these crates?"

The question stirred Ho from his trance. "Mr. Chan, unscrew the plywood from the center crate. Sergeant, Corporal. Unscrew a plywood side on the crates to the left and the right.

The three men walked over to a wall-mounted toolbox, grabbed three power screwdrivers, and began to remove the plywood.

The center plywood sheet, the one Chan had unscrewed earlier, fell to the floor. Chan turned away, bent over, and started heaving.

Fred walked over to examine the large glass container that was inside the crate. The container resembled a large aquarium.

"Am I seeing what I think I'm seeing?" He squinted his eyes to get a better look. "Oh, my God. Please, no," he said, almost in a whisper.

Just then the sergeant and the corporal both removed the plywood from their containers and slid them onto the deck. They too turned away as if suddenly sick.

Fred stepped back. Even the strong stomach of steel that all doctors have to possess, the callous resistance to the grotesque, a product of his medical training, had been weakened.

Fred looked around the cargo bay, from one side to the other and to both ends of the long passageway. No one was looking at what was in the glass-covered containers. Not Lieutenant Ho. Not Mr. Chan. Not the tough rifle-bearing Marines. Over in a corner, Chan was puking.

Fred knew he had to take control. He was the doctor. Whatever had to be done was up to him.

He turned back to the large aquarium-like glass tank in front of him. Miniature hands were plastered up against the glass. The faces and eyes stared out at him in a frozen look of terror, the agony of a painful death, screaming in silence for help that never came.

Others had no faces. For one, the skull had been crushed. Another's face was unrecognizable, like an obscure picture on a folded napkin. Locks of black hair floated like a halo in the clear liquid in which they were entombed. Some had no hair.

They were infants. Some were late-term fetuses, fully formed, their umbilical cords dangling in the liquid.

Fred stepped closer. Between the three tanks that were now uncovered, perhaps eighteen to twenty dead babies and small children floated in clear liquid—probably formaldehyde. Some were turned away from him—only their backs and buttocks visible.

From the ones he could see—and he checked all three tanks to make sure—all were girls.

Fred stood there in the cold floating dungeon, in a secret world kept hidden—until now.

Then, as his eyes moved to the temple of one little girl, the shock that had initially gripped his body morphed into rage. How had he not noticed this before? He looked again at her temple, just under the lock of black hair.

A puncture wound. Perhaps the result of an ice pick through the brain. Or a long nail or narrow spike.

The baby packed just under her had no hair, and so the mortal puncture wound to her head was visible and easy to see.

The infant jammed just under the bald girl had black curly hair and no puncture wound to her head. Instead, her neck had been slit. Fred stepped back.

That's when he saw them all: puncture wounds to temples, slit throats, crushed skulls. He walked over to the other two tanks. All the same.

Fred turned around. "Lieutenant Ho. Mr. Chan. What's going on here? Why are these babies in these tanks? Where are you taking them? Why?"

Silence.

"I want an answer!"

"Tell him, Chan!" Ho said.

"They were sold to a medical company in Bangkok," Chan said.

"A medical company." Fred shook his head. "Okay. First, I want all the plywood removed from these crates." He thought about that for a second. "No, belay that." He glanced at his watch. "We don't have enough time. Just remove the rest of the plywood from these three tanks. Then set out three or four big tables in here. Stretch the tables out in a line, end to end.

"Take these babies out of the tanks and lay them on the tables. I want to examine them. We'll need gloves."

Fred looked at Ho. Ho nodded and looked at the sergeant and corporal. "You men, do as the doctor said. Take the plywood off. Sergeant Lu, you are in charge of the setup."

"Yes, Lieutenant."

"Mister Chan," Ho said.

"Yes, Lieutenant."

"Get tables from the ship's galley. Have them brought in here to serve as examination tables."

"Yes," Chan said. "In the galley. In the lounge. We have tables."

"Very well," Lieutenant Ho said. "We will all go topside. I will assign a couple of my Marines to accompany you and some of your crew members to bring tables back down here and set them up."

"Yes, of course." Chan's voice sounded both defeated and dejected.

"Doctor, do you have any other instructions before we go topside?" Ho asked.

Fred felt his shirt pocket for a cigarette. Then he remembered he had thrown his only pack overboard.

"Yes. We'll need plastic sheets to cover the tables. Lay the babies out on the plastic. I will also need digital cameras along with a pen and a legal pad ... some paper. This will need to be documented photographically. You got that, Mr. Chan?"

"Yes," Chan said. "We have all that. I knew nothing of this, Doctor. Please tell your superiors that I knew nothing of this."

Fred looked Chan in the eye. Usually he knew when a patient was lying to him. Shifting, nervous eyes marked a liar. Sincere eyes, slow to blink, slow to glance left and right or up and down, these eyes marked a truth-teller.

Usually.

Chan's eyes neither danced with deception nor reflected the peaceful gaze of sincerity. In Chan, Fred saw only fear. Probably fear of execution by firing squad. Perhaps worse.

Still, somehow, Fred believed Chan. The spontaneous puking all over the deck could not have been contrived.

Or could it?

"Tell you what, Mr. Chan. When we get back up on deck, if you can spare a cigarette and a light, I just might have something in my medical bag that can soothe that stomach of yours."

"Thank you, Doctor. I have many cigarettes. I be happy to share."

"Lead the way, Mr. Chan," Ho said.

Chan pushed open the door, and Fred was grateful to step from that dungeon, that refrigerated tomb.

They headed back up the ladder and stepped back out onto the deck—back into the light of the late-afternoon sun, now nearing the horizon.

Fred stopped and just looked out to sea. He closed his eyes, his face soothed in the warm caress of sunshine. This was better medicine than he could prescribe on even his finest day as a doctor.

"How about that cigarette, Mr. Chan?"

"I have it here, Doctor. Here is cigarette and a lighter."

Fred lit the cancer stick. And then, in desperate need of a nicotine fix after what he had just seen, he inhaled as deeply as he ever had. He exhaled, then flipped the cigarette overboard.

"Thank you, Mr. Chan. I just quit smoking. Now let's get to work."

USS Emory S. Land
South China Sea

late afternoon

The wind whipped out of the northeast, and with it, the steady footing at the forward watch station had given way to alternating thirty-second intervals of up ... and then down ... as the *Emory S. Land* plowed into the five-foot swells that were still building.

The stream of sunshine that had baked the mid-afternoon temperatures into a hot inferno had yielded to recurrent shadows from high-forming rain clouds sweeping the seascape, blocking the sun for longer periods, bringing cooler breezes mixed with the warm weather.

Off in the distance, boiling clouds rose into the heavens. Under them, black vertical streaks connected the clouds and the water.

Although Stephanie was a young, green ensign, she had already learned the summer weather patterns in the tropics. Showers, often thunder boomers, rolled in during the late afternoons.

The seascape was graying, and she worried that the weather would threaten visibility. In a rainstorm, they could steam within a hundred yards of that downed chopper and never see a thing.

The first raindrop splattered on the steel deck a few feet from where she stood.

Then another off to her right.

Then three more fell at her feet.

Out in the water in front of the ship, maybe three hundred yards out, a hundred thousand angry raindrops pelted the cresting waves, beating down the foam of the whitecaps. This great shower wall rolled inbound, like a giant wall stretching for miles from left to right, its furious path marked by the splashing line. "You'll need this if you stay out here."

She turned around at the sound of his voice. He had already donned a black rain poncho, one with the silver oak leaves of a Navy commander on his shoulders. In his hand he held out another black rain poncho for her.

She took it from him. "Thank you, sir." She smiled at the thought of him thinking about her. As he helped her slip it over her shoulders, the ship collided with the rain wall.

She pulled the hood over her head, just seconds before her hair would have been drenched.

"You know, Stephanie, there's no point in staying out here right now," he said in that rugged South Carolina accent of his, raising his voice just enough to be heard above the sound of thousands of drops of rain pelting the steel deck around them. "You've got no visibility."

"Thank you, sir. But if it's okay, I'd rather stay here. This weather will clear. And when it does, I'd like to be here to make sure that our visibility is maximized at the moment it clears. If there's even a slight window to find these guys, I don't want to be anywhere other than right here."

He looked at her. The rain intensified. His face turned serious. "There's something you should know."

"Yes, sir?"

He looked off into the stormy horizon. "Seventh Fleet has pulled off the helicopter conducting the aerial search."

"I don't understand. Is it the weather?"

"No. Not the weather." He looked back at her. "This China-Taiwan war is heating up. Taiwan requested assistance from one of our Navy choppers. The request was approved."

"I'm stunned," she said.

"Even worse," the XO continued, "Seventh Fleet has ordered us to end our search at sundown."

She struggled for words. "So who … who would pick up the search after that?"

The XO shook his head. He looked at his watch. Hard rain splattered off the glass face.

"Stephanie, we've got an hour and a half." He looked at her. "Maybe two hours at most. Even less than that when you consider that our visibility is zero because of this rainstorm."

"That's it?"

"That's it."

Silence. Except for the steady drumming of the rain. Her emotions almost took over, but she steeled herself.

"All the more reason to stay at my post, sir. With your permission, I'll stick this out until the end." With that, she pulled herself to sharp attention and snapped a sharp Navy salute to her superior.

He returned the salute and disappeared into the rain.

US Navy life raft
South China Sea
somewhere between USS Vicksburg and USS Emory S. Land

The whipping late-afternoon wind lit into the waves, and the small orange raft rolled up and down along the elongated swells that had come to life in the sea.

Gunner poked his head out the entrance of the waterproof orange tent. The sky had turned a menacing gray. A few sunbeams still broke through the clouds out on the horizon, but for the most part, the sun had surrendered to darkening clouds. Off in the distance, black vertical streaks fell from the clouds.

He ducked back into the raft and zipped up the door of the tent. He lay down on the floor of the raft and looked up at the orange ceiling, now dimly translucent with a faint orangish color, but fading darker with the heavy cloud cover and setting sun.

"God, please bring rain. But not too much wind."

Gunner closed his eyes. Trying to sleep. Up ... Down ... Up ... Down ...

Swish ... swish ...

Phat ...

Phat ...

Phat-Phat-Phat ... Phat ... Phat-Phat-Phat ...

The sound of a thousand driving rain pellets pounded the roof of the tent.

Gunner opened his eyes. He reached up and started unzipping the flap. Rainwater poured through the crack and started flooding the canvas floor inside the raft.

Gunner raised his face to the sky, soaking in the cool of the glorious rain. He opened his mouth, and cool raindrops splashed on his parched lips and tongue. He swallowed them, as best as he could, as small as they were, soothing his dried-out throat.

He looked down. About an eighth-inch of water was covering the bottom of the raft.

Like a dog about to lap his parched tongue into a fresh stream, Gunner bent over, touched the canvas deck, and drew a stream of fresh rainwater into his mouth. He sloshed the water around his tongue for a few wonderful seconds. Then he swallowed.

Liquid manna from heaven! Praise God!

"Woohoo! Keep raining! Keep raining!"

The Lincoln Bedroom
the White House

5:00 a.m. local time

K*nock ... knock ... knock ...*
"Mr. President?"

Douglas Surber glanced at the digital clock beside his bed: 05:00.

"Be right there, Arnie."

"Yes, sir!"

The president swung his legs out of bed, grabbed his bathrobe, slipped it on, and walked over to open the door.

"Don't you ever sleep?"

"Wish I could, sir."

"What's up?"

"Sorry to bother you so early, sir," the pinstripe-suited Brubaker said, "but both the secretary of defense and the secretary of state have requested an emergency meeting of the National Security Council. The council is convening right now in the Situation Room."

"At this hour? What's going on?"

"Taiwan and China, sir. We've got a report back from the *Shemnong*. It needs your immediate attention."

"Okay, Arnie. Be right out."

Five minutes later, the president, accompanied by his chief of staff and two armed black-suited Secret Service agents, stepped into the 5,000-square-foot White House Situation Room in the basement of the West Wing.

Everyone in the room rose to their feet.

"Sit down. Please."

Not all the members of the NSC had arrived, but the main power players were present: Vice President William O. "Rock" Morgan, the Chairman of the Joint-Chiefs-of-Staff Admiral Roscoe Jones, National Security Adviser Cynthia Hewitt, Secretary of Defense Irwin Lopez, and Secretary of State Robert Mauney.

"Okay. What's the justification for dragging me out of bed thirty minutes early?" He glanced at his secretary of state and then at his secretary of defense. "Who wants to start?"

Mauney and Lopez looked at each other.

"It's early, gentlemen," the president snapped. "Let's get moving here."

"I'll start," the secretary of defense said. "Sir, two things. Earlier this morning you authorized dispatch of a Navy doctor, via a Navy chopper, to the Chinese freighter *Shemnong*, which had been commandeered by Taiwanese Marines."

"Yes, at my two a.m. wakeup call," he snorted.

"Well, there are two items for immediate attention. One, our doctor on the *Shemnong* has requested an emergency medevac of some of the Chinese crew members. The other involves evidence that our doctor gathered on this crimes-against-humanity issue."

"Sounds like a fine way to start the day, Mister Secretary. Why don't you start with the emergency request first."

"Yes, sir," Lopez said. "Six members of the Chinese crew were shot up pretty bad and are critical, sir. Our doctor says they need blood transfusions or they'll die. Problem is the nearest facility for treatment is on board USS *Carl Vinson*, and the doctor is requesting these men be airlifted to the *Vinson* for emergency blood transfusions, which is the only means of saving their lives."

"Let me get this straight. The doctor is asking for helicopter transport of six civilian Chinese sailors, who've been shot up by the Taiwanese, to a US Navy ship for emergency treatment?"

"That's correct, sir," Lopez responded.

Secretary of State Robert Mauney said, "Mister President, I don't think the doctor is thinking about the diplomatic ramifications of his request. He's just thinking about saving lives."

The president poured himself a cup of black coffee from one of the heated pitchers that had been set out for every attendee prior to the meeting. "Okay, Bobby." He eyed his old friend. "You're my secretary of state. You've never held back your thoughts, even when you used to clean my clock on the tennis courts at Providence Country Club. So let's hear your thoughts."

Mauney screwed the cap back on the bottled water he was drinking. "Sir, the phrase 'political hot button' hits the nail on the head. We do have a longstanding history of using our military to help render humanitarian aid whenever possible. But if we medevac these guys, the Chinese might find out that we've got a US officer on board a Chinese civilian freighter that has been attacked by and is now under the control of the Taiwanese. Their enemy."

Brief silence.

Mauney continued, "This could be spun against us a dozen different ways. A Navy doctor becomes an American military adviser to Taiwanese Marines — or an intelligence officer rendering assistance to the enemy."

"Bobby, you're right," the president said. "This thing could blow up. But if I do nothing, these men will die. We could always grant the medevac request and tell the Chinese the truth, that we responded to a humanitarian request from the Taiwanese to save Chinese sailors, their own citizens."

"We admit that," Mauney said, "and we admit that we've been in contact with Taiwan during this shooting war. You know how paranoid the Chinese are. I mean, we're sending the Seventh Fleet to try to quell this whole thing, to keep the two Chinas from going to war against each other. If we lose even the appearance of impartiality, we lose whatever influence we have to keep this thing from blowing up. This thing blows up, we've got both a military and an economic disaster."

"So we just let these guys die?" the president said. "Let's face it. Eventually, the Chinese will find out anyway. There will be crew members of that ship who will have seen our doc and talk about it."

Another pause.

Vice President Rock Morgan said, "Mister President."

"Mister Vice President."

"Sir, you may wish to consider the evidence for the second issue on the table—the issue of crimes against humanity—before you make a decision on the medevac request. You may decide that your decisions are linked."

The president took a deep breath. "Thank you, Mister Vice President. Okay, who wants to address this one?"

The secretaries of defense and state again exchanged glances.

The president waited, then said, "Let me make this easy. Secretary Lopez, let's hear it."

The secretary of defense looked up. "Mister President, our Navy medical officer on board the freighter, Lieutenant Commander Fred Jeter, has investigated this claim. There's a large refrigerated cargo bay on that ship. In the cargo bay, Dr. Jeter discovered dead babies. Perhaps up to a thousand."

"What?"

"That's right, Mister President. Ranging from late-term fetuses to … the doc estimates up to two years old. Maybe a little older. All the children so far are girls. What's more, every one that he has examined appears to have been murdered. He's opened only a few of the containers, so these are estimates."

"Am I hearing this right?" The president struggled for words. "Little girls? Murdered? I don't understand. How?"

"We've got photos. They are horrible, sir. Some have had their skulls crushed. These appear to have been killed during late-term abortions. The older ones, the doc notes, were killed in other ways—ice pick to the brain, slit throat."

The president tried to process what he had just heard. "And you say we've got photos of this?"

"We have some photos right here, Mr. President," Lopez said. "And, sir, as a reminder, these shots are graphic."

"Give 'em here, Irwin." Douglas held his hand out to the defense secretary. As he took the yellow envelope, Joint Chiefs Chairman Admiral Roscoe Jones grimaced. National Security Adviser Cynthia Hewitt looked down at her feet. Vice President Rock Morgan tightened his lips. "You've all seen these?"

"Yes, sir," the vice president said. "We have. And the secretary of defense is correct." Surber glanced over at Lopez, then back at Morgan. "Except frankly, the word used by Irwin, that these are 'graphic,' is an understatement."

The president reached into the large manila envelope and felt a stack of eight-by-ten photos. Carefully, he slid them out.

The top one was a close-up shot of two small infants that froze him in his seat. He could not pry his eyes from the sickening photograph.

"Dear God. How did this happen?"

"There are a lot more, Mister President," someone said.

One by one, he studied them all. More of the same. All girls. The Navy doctor had documented the gruesome evidence abundantly. Close-up shots of puncture wounds to the temple. In some cases, a slit to the throat. Some of the very smallest ones had crushed skulls.

How? How could this be? He thought of Stephanie, of how much she had meant to him and to Hope-Caroline over the years. Of how much he loved his only daughter with all his heart.

He and Hope-Caroline once had a son.

Even before he was born, they had already started loving him, and seeing him active on the ultra-sound, they could even sense his personality. They knew that he would be an athlete. Hope-Caroline played classical music close to her abdomen. He enjoyed Beethoven and would slow down and not kick so much when she played Beethoven's Ninth. But when the music ended, he would wake up and start kicking again.

The boy was very active in his mother's womb up until three days before he was born.

Then he stopped moving. The baby arrived stillborn.

They named him Alexander Manning Surber. They gave him a Christian funeral, then buried him in a casket the size of a shoebox. Three people had gone to the grave that sunny afternoon—his father, his mother, and the minister.

Douglas Surber could think of nothing else that had ever ripped his heart in such a cruel coldness. Hope-Caroline cried every day for a solid month. Finally, he sent her to Palm Springs for a week to try to recuperate in the warm desert sunshine.

Though they'd never seen their son in life, they loved him even in death. On the day of his burial, they'd joined hands and prayed to be reunited with him in heaven someday. But still, only Stephanie's birth the next year stopped the awful grieving.

As he stared at the photos, the old knife, once again, jabbed pain straight through his heart. He had hoped never again to feel that pain. But the photos triggered flashbacks of Hope-Caroline's uncontrolled sobbing during the long days alone after Alexander's burial.

"Does no one value the gift of life anymore?" he asked. "Is there no innate sense of decency? Wasn't there enough shock from photos of Nazi death camps liberated by our troops?" No one answered. "And now this. How could someone be so callous to human life? Just to kill little babies in such a brutal and cold way. And to kill because they are girls."

He held the final photo, studied it, and then laid them all facedown on the conference table.

"Okay, someone tell me. I want to know who did this. Because if I find out, it's not going to be pretty."

The secretary of defense said, "Mister President, we've retrieved copies of the ship's log. She was in transit from Qinzhou, China, to Bangkok, Thailand, with an interim stop at Itu Aba, in the Spratlys, to drop off military equipment."

"All right." The president could not contain the anger in his voice.

"Will someone please explain this to me. What were they going to do with these little girls?"

"To sell them, sir," Secretary Lopez said.

"Sell them?"

"Yes, sir."

"Why? Who would buy them?"

Lopez looked at Mauney. "I'll defer to the secretary of state."

President Surber looked at Bobby Mauney. "Bobby, what's this about?"

"Well, sir, the ship's manifest lists them as medical supplies."

"Medical supplies?" Surber slammed his fist on the table. "These are babies! They are not medical supplies!"

"Of course, Mister President. This is a situation the State Department's human rights section has been following. I'm talking about the sale of the corpses of Chinese babies on the black market. There is a shortage of baby corpses for medical research and for other purposes, and baby corpses and parts command a high price on the international black market."

"Medical research," the president parroted Mauney. "What other purposes?"

"We hear they're for some sick cultish type of sacrifices and rituals in India and Southeast Asia."

The president wanted to vomit. "And so someone is murdering babies to feed this black market?"

"We've heard this is the case. But we haven't had solid proof" — Mauney looked down at the photographs, then met the president's eyes — "until now, sir."

Douglas pounded his fist on the table. "Who did this? How could this happen?"

"Sir, who did it remains to be seen. But how it happened ... it happened, I'm sure, because of China's one-child sterilization policy."

"Wait a minute," Douglas said. "I knew Mao had instituted this forced-sterilization policy. But this goes way beyond forced sterilizations."

"Correct, Mister President. We've heard that the Communists' forced sterilization exceeds forced sterilization — that babies born beyond the first child have been killed, sold on the black market, and that the Communists have targeted little girls because they complain about having an overpopulation of girls in China."

Douglas leaned back in his chair and folded his arms. "How widespread is this problem?"

"Well, sir, put it this way. Our Asian human rights officials in the State Department have monitored the situation, along with other situations in Asia like slave-trafficking and sexual exploitation of minors.

"Part of the problem is that we've had a lot of hearsay on all these matters. Back in March of 2010, the *Economist* magazine ran an article entitled, as I recall, 'The Worldwide War on Baby Girls.' At that time the *Economist*, which is one of the world's most respected international periodicals, estimated that over 100 million baby girls had been murdered by or with the assent of governments aimed at curbing perceived overpopulation of women. The magazine reported that the largest percentage of those took place in China."

"One hundred million killed." The president was trying to control his emotions. He'd gone from shock, to anger, to sorrow, back to anger, and now to shock again.

"It's a good thing I wasn't born in China," Cynthia Hewitt said, breaking the stunned silence. Hewitt had been President Mack Williams' longtime national security adviser when Williams' term had expired two months ago and had been asked to stay on by President Surber.

"Bobby, you seem to be up to speed on this issue."

"Yes, sir," the secretary of state responded. "There's a huge market out there for the sale of baby cadaver parts. This, plus an innate disdain for girls in certain parts of the world, has resulted in this sort of thing."

"So they either abort or kill the babies and then sell the babies for profit," the president said.

"That's one way of putting it, sir. It's a regular profit mill."

President Surber shook his head. "How long have we known about this, Bobby?"

Mauney leaned back, exhaled, and crossed his arms. "Well, Mister President, the State Department has monitored this situation ever since the first Bush administration. But the problem, as I've mentioned, is that it's been largely hearsay, based on word-of-mouth reports. Because of that, it's hard to monitor."

"We've had abortions going on in this country legally since 1973,"

Cynthia Hewitt said. "And we've known for some time that there's a big market for the sale of those baby parts."

"I understand your feelings, Cyndi," Mauney said. "And maybe there's no distinction between killing a baby in the womb versus after birth. But whether we like it or not, abortion is allowed under the law in this country. But it's against the law to kill a baby after birth." Mauney's eyes shifted from the national security adviser to the president. "In this case, it looks like we finally have evidence of someone killing babies after birth just because they're girls."

The president looked over at the secretary of state. "Bobby, why haven't you brought this to my attention earlier?"

"As I said, Mr. President, we've never seen solid physical evidence of mass murder of babies. It's all been hearsay." The secretary of state picked up his packet of photographs and waved them in the air. "Until now." He set the horrible images back down on the table. "Now ... now we've got the smoking gun."

That statement resonated throughout the room, as if the secretary of state had proclaimed the advent of a significant historical moment.

The president nodded. "Okay, so now on this ship, in the middle of this warlike atmosphere between the two Chinas that we're trying to stop, because our country's economy depends on it, now ... suddenly ... we've got smoking-gun evidence that the State Department has been searching for. So tell me. What do I do about it?"

Secretaries Mauney and Lopez exchanged contorted glances.

"Irwin, Secretary Mauney has had the floor. What are your thoughts?" the president said.

"Sir, you've already touched on this, but I remind you of our mission's original purpose — to deter war. I think we can get away with rendering emergency medical aid. But, sir, if you're thinking about doing anything about these babies, as horrid at these photos are, then in my judgment the original purpose of our mission is compromised."

"So I'm to do nothing about the apparent mass-murder of baby girls?"

"Sir, you're the president," the secretary of defense said. "I won't second-guess you either way, but I respectfully remind you of our original mission to deter war between the two Chinas. We can't deter a war if we interfere with the passage of this ship, in my opinion. We might even find ourselves in it. Remember, sir. We need China economically. They are funding our debt."

"I understand, Irwin," the president said. "But I got run out of bed for the *second* time in the last four hours for an emergency meeting of my National Security Council to deal with two pressing, late-breaking issues. One," he held up an index finger, "this request for an emergency medevac of the Chinese guys shot up by the Taiwanese, and two"— holding up two fingers—"what to do with this gruesome discovery. And some of you think these issues are related and my decision on one ought to be linked to the other. Am I right?"

"Yes, sir, Mister President."

Heads nodding.

"Yes, sir."

"I'm going to simplify this," the president said. "Admiral Jones"— he looked at his joint chiefs chairman—"the medevac request is granted. Get on the horn right now and get a chopper out to that ship. Let's save life if we can. I know that might be spun against us, but it's the right thing to do."

"Yes, sir," Jones said. He picked up the secure telephone. "This is Admiral Jones. The president approved. Get a chopper out there now." He hung up the phone. "Done, Mister President."

"Very well. Now let's focus on the second issue and our options. The floor is open."

Vice President Morgan raised a finger.

"Mister Vice President?"

"We start with two basic choices. Either we ignore these atrocities, which best serves our short-term military and political objective of quelling this dispute, or we move in some way to preserve the evidence, which in my judgment would destroy our military-political objective and drag us into something with China."

"I agree, Rock," the president said. "Preserving the evidence could make things dicey with the Chinese. Maybe even jeopardize our economy or risk war." He thought about that for a second. "But let's put the international political ramifications on the back burner just for a second and talk logistics. How could we preserve the evidence? If that's what I were to decide?"

"Well, Mister President," Secretary Mauney said, "if I may?"

"Go ahead, Bobby."

"I'm a diplomat and not a logistics guy. So I'd defer to my friend the secretary of defense on specific logistics. But it seems that we have three options to consider."

"Let's hear 'em."

"Well, first, we could take pictures of the babies and then let the ship go. Second, we could find a way to remove the babies and let the ship go. Third—and this is the option I would favor if you decide to take action to preserve evidence—we could seize the ship itself, preserving the evidence exactly as it is."

"Seize the ship?" President Surber said. "Aside from the fact that the Chinese are not going to like us just seizing a civilian freighter flying under their flag, what legal basis would we have for seizing it?"

"That's easy, Mister President," Mauney said. "Same legal theory used in places like Nuremberg, Tokyo, and Darfur. You would seize the ship on the grounds that it contains evidence of crimes against humanity."

"But seize the evidence and preserve it for what?" Secretary Lopez interjected. "Are we just going to report to the world that we've found this and demand that China stop it? It's not like we've not heard of these rumors before."

"That's true," Secretary Mauney responded. "But until now, that's all we've had. Rumor and innuendo. Now ... now we have something of a smoking gun. For the first time." Mauney jabbed a finger in the air. "This is significant. Historically and politically. Just look at these pictures!" Mauney's voice rung throughout the room. "And now we know that this is happening in the country that we're most economically dependent on! How can we ignore it? To ignore this is the same as ignoring Auschwitz or ..."

With all eyes glued upon him, a shocked look crossed Mauney's face, a stunned look of apparent realization that he was coming across like a pulpit-pounding Southern Baptist preacher unleashing a sermon of fire and brimstone. "Please accept my apologies, Mister President. I was out of line. I am supposed to be a diplomat."

"Apologies unnecessary, Bobby," the president said. "We're all enraged about this." He was determined to control the shaking in his own voice. "Secretary Lopez."

"Sir."

"Usually, it's Secretary Mauney calling for restraint, as I'd expect from a diplomat, and you calling for action, as I'd expect from a warrior. But this time, you seem to have switched sides, with you advocating restraint and the secretary of state advocating military action of some sort."

"Mister President," Lopez said, "I share everyone's anger." Nods all around the table. "But this proposal undermines our role as a neutral party and undercuts our leverage to persuade Beijing to come to the negotiating table and stop their military aggression. A decision to seize that ship, if that's what you order our Navy to do, changes the dynamic of the whole situation. With all due respect, think about it, sir.

"First, the *Shemnong* is flying the flag of the People's Republic of China. Seizing it could be considered an act of war against China. On top of that, it's a ship carrying military supplies to Itu Aba. So if we seize it, that makes us appear to be siding with Taiwan in the military conflict. Also, sir, it isn't like the national security interests of the United States are at stake here. This isn't May Day 2011, the day our SEALs took out Osama bin Laden, a terrorist threatening American security. These atrocities are despicable, but they don't threaten the United States."

Cynthia Hewitt, her green eyes darting back and forth, blazed with fury.

"You wanted to say something, Cyndi?" Surber said.

"Yes, sir. China might have a big army. But what are they going to do? March across Siberia and then across the frozen Bering Strait and invade us? This ship is carrying evidence of mass murder. Is it always about an immediate threat to our national security? President Obama launched a hundred Tomahawk cruise missiles against Libya because he claimed, on shaky evidence, that he wanted to stop the slaughter of innocent civilians. This evidence is anything but shaky. We've all seen the photos.

"President Clinton bombed Bosnia because of ethnic cleansing when the Bosnian Serb Army was targeting Bosnian Muslims and Croats.

"This" — she stopped and wiped her eyes — "this is not only a crime against humanity but it's also a crime against women. Are we going to let them get away with it just because it's China? Are we as a nation going to say that the lives of innocent Chinese baby girls are not as important to us as the lives of Bosnian Muslims? Are we going to stand against gendercide in the world? President Franklin Roosevelt, when he loaned American destroyers to the British in World War II, said that if your neighbor's house is burning down, you lend him a fire hose. Isn't the murder of innocent, helpless baby girls, and then selling their body parts for profit, just as despicable as what the Nazis did to the Jews at Auschwitz? Don't these babies deserve a decent burial before their body parts are carved up and sold on the black market? Have we no dignity when it comes to life?"

Electric tension flooded the room. Several NSC members stared at their laptop screens. Admiral Jones looked at the secretary of defense. The vice president and the secretary of defense and the secretary of state looked at the president.

The president looked at Cyndi. Her words reminded him of Margaret Thatcher's eloquence after Sadaam Hussein invaded Kuwait in 1990. The first President Bush had decided to take no action until Mrs. Thatcher bent his ear with a passionate plea to stop the dictator.

"Assuming that I ordered this ship seized, where would we take it?"

Secretary Mauney looked up.

"Bobby? You have thoughts on that?"

"Yokosuka is our nearest base, but that would place our Japanese allies in a predicament with China. The Philippines is a possibility. But once again, we're placing an ally in an awkward position they haven't asked to be in. So I'd recommend taking it to Guam, which of course is United States territory."

"I agree with that, Mister President," Secretary Lopez said.

The president looked around the table, then at Secretary of State Robert Mauney. "Secretary Mauney, I'm directing you to expedite a range of diplomatic and legal options for me to act upon in dealing with the evidence we've found on the *Shemnong*, anywhere from calling a UN Security Council meeting, to pressing the Chinese to crack down, to prosecuting the crew members of the ship, to finding these murderers ourselves. I want a range of proposals on my desk by"—he glanced at his watch—"ten this morning."

"Yes, Mister President."

Members of the Security Council fidgeted. NSC Adviser Cynthia Hewitt drummed her fingers on the table. Vice President Morgan chomped on a wad of gum. The secretary of defense pursed his lips.

But regardless of the nervous movements of their lips, or their mouths, or their fingers, it was their eyes that brought them together in a common silent bond. With the intensity of a dozen laser guns, they shot at the president with a montage of looks, each with a huge dose of nervous anticipation.

But even under the intensity of their stares, the president still could not shake the image that had been triggered from all those photographs.

"Admiral Jones."

"Yes, Mister President."

"If I order the Navy to seize this ship, do we have any warships in the area yet that could do that in short order? Say in the next few hours?"

"Mister President, Seventh Fleet is on the way, but we don't have a lot of firepower in the area yet. Right now, USS *Vicksburg* is closest. The USS *Shiloh* is just a few miles behind *Vicksburg*. But both *Vicksburg* and *Shiloh* are heavy cruisers.

"I'd hate to waste that kind of firepower on escort duty. Because if this thing blows up, we're going to need all the firepower in the area that we can get. And of course the cruisers provide maximum protection for our carrier."

The president thought about that. "Any destroyers or fast frigates approaching the area behind the cruisers?"

"Yes, sir." The admiral leaned back and crossed his arms. "Right now we've got one *Arleigh Burke*–class destroyer about two hours behind the *Shiloh* and a couple of smaller *Perry*–class fast frigates an hour or so behind the destroyer. They're all steaming full speed to the South China Sea."

"All right," the president said. "What if we have the *Vicksburg* seize the *Shemnong*, start escorting it back toward Guam, then pass it off to one of the smaller ships and return to station in the South China Sea?"

"Mister President, that would be a whole lot better than having the cruiser escort her all the way back to Guam, if this is what you decide."

"Let me think about that."

"Yes, sir."

The president swiveled around in his large black leather chair, turning his back on the members of the NSC gathered around the oblong conference table.

It had been a warm, breezy afternoon in that cemetery outside of Omaha. The funeral home had dug the small grave. After the minister said the last prayer, the next part was something he had to do himself. He took the shovel and slowly, lovingly began to drop dirt into his son's grave onto the small casket. And when he had finished, he looked down on it and said, "Daddy will see you in heaven, Alex. I promise."

In the years since that last shovelful of dirt, his life had been a life of adventure and now great political power. This was a life millions could only dream about.

But despite all of it, after all the unmerited blessings, he knew he would give it all up, in fact would give it all back, the presidency included, if he had never had to drop that dirt in his boy's grave.

Now, what to do? Most of the military actions of his predecessor, Mack Williams, had been against militant Islamic terror groups. But this? This would involve military action against the world's largest country, a country that had become a raging economic power that many countries, including the United States, had become dependent on.

Through it all, after all the successes and failures, Douglas Surber had never left his Christian roots, never forgotten the One who had saved him. Each day, he took a call in the Oval Office from his best friend, a Baptist pastor in San Diego he met all those years ago when he was a young naval officer and heard these words: "Douglas, remember Deuteronomy 6:18. Do the right thing."

Those last words rang in his head as he swiveled his chair back around to command position at the head of the table and looked into the eyes of his secretary of defense. He would do this for Alex. He had to.

"Secretary Lopez."

"Yes, sir."

"If this country does not stand for life, if we cannot stare down atrocities, no matter who the perpetrator is, then we've lost everything that once made us great."

"Agreed, sir."

"Pass the orders to the Navy. Seize the *Shemnong*. Escort her to Guam, pending further orders from me. Secretary Mauney."

"Yes, sir."

"Be prepared to open a diplomatic channel to China on this. Let's give Tang an opportunity to cooperate and save face. That would mean China arrests and prosecutes the perpetrators and avows to stop this policy. But contact them only after we've seized the ship and removed it from the area. I don't want them interfering with our military ops. Contact Taiwan as a courtesy, but wait until about an hour before our ship arrives on station."

"Yes, sir."

CHAPTER 14

Long orange rays from the late-afternoon sun streamed across the darkening blue sky in a direction that was now more horizontal than vertical. Daylight over the sea had dwindled down to ninety minutes at most before sundown.

The heavy cruiser *Vicksburg*, the tip of the dagger of the *Carl Vinson* Strike Group, bore down full speed through calm seas on a course of two-two-zero degrees toward the waters surrounding Itu Aba Island. By daybreak, she would be patrolling eight miles off the coast, the first American man-o'-war to arrive in a dangerous naval hornet's nest, made more dangerous by the presence, somewhere, of the new Chinese aircraft carrier.

Captain Leonard Kruger, the *Vicksburg*'s commanding officer, sipped a hot tea and scanned the horizon. For the mariner, nothing rivaled the peaceful calm of a late-afternoon summer seascape, as the fading rays of the sun triumphed over a driving tropical rain.

Kruger checked his watch, then glanced at his executive officer, Commander Hugh Bennett, who was scanning the seas through the windows to starboard.

"XO, I'm stepping outside for some air before dinner. You've got the conn."

161

"Aye, Captain, I have the conn."

Captain Kruger headed toward the hatch leading out of the bridge.

"Captain, FLASH message just received from Washington," the radioman said.

"Washington?" Kruger said as he stopped and turned around. "Whatcha got, Lieutenant?"

"New orders, sir."

Kruger walked to the front of the bridge as the lieutenant ripped the orders from the printer.

FROM: National Command Authority
TO: Commanding Officer, USS *Vicksburg*
VIA: Commander, Seventh Fleet
  Commander, *Carl Vinson* Strike Group
  Commander, CRUSDESGRU 10
PRECEDENCE: FLASH
CLASSIFICATION: TOP SECRET
SUBJ: Orders for Seizing PRC Freighter M/V *Shemnong*

"XO, check this out," Kruger said. "Orders from National Command Authority, which probably means they were authorized by the president himself."

The XO peered over his shoulder as Kruger laid the orders on the navigation table.

1. Current orders to proceed to waters surrounding Itu Aba Island, Spratly chain, canceled until further notice.
2. Proceed immediately to location of PRC freighter M/V *Shemnong*, now in the custody of ROCS destroyer *Kee Lung*, 100 nautical miles due east of Da Nang, Vietnam.
3. Your new orders are to seize the M/V *Shemnong*, then set course, along with M/V *Shemnong*, for US Naval Base, Guam, Mariana Islands, western Pacific.
4. You will escort *Shemnong* on a course to Naval Base, Guam, resisting by force any attempts to interfere with escort of M/V *Shemnong*, until relieved by other United States warships. Upon completion of your mission under these orders, you will return to

your station in the littoral waters surrounding Itu Aba Island for completion of original orders in deterring shooting war between PRC and ROC.

5. ROC Navy will be informed of US intentions through diplomatic channels.

6. Expect full cooperation from ROCS *Kee Lung*.

7. However, despite full expectation of cooperation from ROC, bear in mind that you are proceeding into a volatile situation.

8. It is impossible to fully ascertain or predict the reaction of either the ROC or the PRC in response to the execution of your orders.

9. Therefore, you are authorized to use full force short of nuclear weapons in self-defense if fired upon or threatened by any possible belligerent.

10. Proceed immediately to 15.749963N Latitude, 111.873779E Longitude.

> Respectfully,
> Irwin Lopez
> Secretary of Defense

"Wow!" The XO rubbed his hand through his wavy red hair. "Talk about a detour, Skipper."

Kruger re-read the FLASH message. "Something hot's going on out there."

"Could be, sir. But it looks like they are ordering us away from the action."

"Or right into the teeth of it. Helmsman!"

"Aye, Captain."

"Set the *Vicksburg* on a new course to latitude 15.749963, longitude 111.873779. All ahead full!"

"All ahead full! Aye, Captain!"

"XO, open the 1MC."

The XO flipped a switch on the control panel and handed the captain a microphone.

"Now hear this. This is the captain. USS *Vicksburg* has just received new orders." He paused as his voice reverberated throughout the ship. "We are changing course to two-seven-niner degrees, where our destination will be the PRC civilian freighter *Shemnong*.

"*Shemnong* is in the custody of the ROC Navy. We've been ordered to commandeer *Shemnong* and to accompany her to US Naval Station, Guam, unless relieved by other US naval warships." Another pause. "We don't know how China or Taiwan will react. But we know that this situation is a powder keg, and we've been authorized to use full force short of nukes to defend ourselves.

"We will intercept the *Shemnong* around midnight. Boarding party, prepare to board. All hands, be ready to go to Battle Stations at my direction. This is the captain."

CHAPTER 15

Forward watch station
USS Emory S. Land
South China Sea

Emory *Land* plowed through the late-afternoon chill in a sea of a dozen splendid colors, lit by the deep-orange glow of sunset. Purplish clouds and a deepening blue sky surrendered to the dusk above the aqua hue of the sea. Off to the eastern horizon, patches of blue sky were breaking through the remnants of the thick, dark clouds now drifting off toward the Philippines whose driving showers earlier had blinded search efforts.

A magnificent seascape!

But the grandeur of the nautical colors at dusk was dimmed by fear. For the sight of the setting sun was a clock ticking down—an hourglass draining its last granules of hope for finding life on the sea.

She had tried to absorb and enjoy the great array of colors, as she had on other days on this voyage before this day arrived. Surely a God magnificent enough to display his handiwork in the heavens held the power to save the lives of this helicopter crew.

But the hope of finding anyone alive faded as the bottom of the sun kissed the edge of the sea.

Off in the distance, a buzzing sound disturbed the peace. The buzzing got louder, giving way to a mechanical roar.

The sound of an aircraft! Perhaps a rescue chopper to help in the search! Or perhaps the missing Seahawk itself had gotten disoriented and was now coming in for a safe landing on the *Emory Land.*

Excitement flooded her body. She rushed to the port gunwale and searched the skies in the direction of the noise.

The rotor noise grew louder as the light faded. Still nothing. She searched the skies with her binoculars ... sweeping ... sweeping ... still nothing. No sign of the approaching chopper. Just deepening blue skies and the darkening edge of the sea.

Or was there more than one plane? Now it sounded like multiple engines slicing through the air.

There! Coming from behind the ship! She held her binoculars still and her heart sank. Four turbo-jet engines stretched across the wings. The fuselage hung under the wings. The plane looked like a large seaplane. Most likely a military plane.

But whose?

She gripped her binoculars, arms against her body, to stabilize the view. The roaring grew louder.

The plane had nearly caught up with the stern of the ship, and now the sight of the single orange star painted on the fuselage jumpstarted her pulse!

Stephanie picked up the deck phone, opening a line to the bridge. "Bridge! Forward lookout! Aircraft approaching portside appears to be PRC military!"

"We see it, Ensign Surber," the XO's voice came over the dedicated line. "We've been tracking it on radar for a few miles now. Looks like a Chinese Navy plane. Looks like we've been spotted." Static. She heard the XO saying something to someone else on the bridge, but couldn't make out what he was saying. "Stephanie, the skipper wants to know if you've seen any sign of wreckage or anything out on the water that could be from the missing chopper."

"No, sir." Sobering reality of failure. "Nothing yet, sir."

"Okay, we've got about fifteen minutes of daylight. Keep an eye on that plane, and we'll call off the search in another twenty minutes."

"Aye, sir. Twenty more minutes."

The four-engine seaplane flew out in front of the ship, then turned, banking in a large circle to the right. Now the Communist orange star was visible as the plane cut a path in front of the ship's bow. Turning wide right, it flew back toward the stern, and then made another right turn, making one complete circle around the ship. Then the plane turned away from *Emory Land* and headed to the north, toward the Chinese mainland.

A late-afternoon rainbow stretched to the west, falling into the water out beyond the horizon. High in the sky, lit by the fading rays of the sun, the colors of the rainbow were brightest. The plane crossed high in front of the broad tapestry of the rainbow in a slight left-right angle.

The rainbow's beauty distracted her eyes from the seaplane, and she noticed that the colors faded as they cascaded down to the water.

She blinked her eyes hard for a double-take.

Down on the surface, partially camouflaged by the orange of the rainbow, was something—something orange—bobbing on the water. Something orange!

She picked up the telephone and yelled into it, "Forward Watch to Bridge!"

Harbin SH-5 maritime bomber
People's Liberation Naval Air Force
altitude 3,000 feet
en route to Yantian Naval Base in Shenzhen
Guangdong Provence
South China Sea

Senior Lieutenant Jung Hai, in his drab-olive flight suit, had been selected to the prestigious position of senior pilot of one of only six SH-5 maritime bombers of the air fleet of the People's Liberation Naval Air Force. He looked back over his shoulder, away from the setting sun, and took a final look at the ship cutting a path in the darkening waters.

Long-range reconnaissance was one of the principle roles of the SH-5, and Jung Hai knew that this discovery would please his superiors.

He turned his plane to a course of three-five-four degrees, almost due north, on a route back to Yantian Naval Base in Shenzhen, China.

"Yantian Control. Air Ostrich One. Final coordinates of US Navy warship are as follows: 15 degrees, 18 minutes, 57 seconds north latitude; 112 degrees, 7 minutes, 35 seconds east longitude. Course bearing one-zero-four degrees.

"Ship is believed to be a US Navy submarine tender. Possibly USS *Emory S. Land*. Returning to base. Over."

"Feel like celebrating, boss?" the copilot asked.

Jung Hai grinned. "Put it this way, Lieutenant. We will capture the admiral's attention. Perhaps I will take you out for a shot of baijiu when we get back to base."

"Great idea, sir. But I think it's my turn to buy."

A burst of static over the radio. "Air Ostrich One. Yantian Control. Roger that. Copy last known coordinates of American warship at 15 degrees, 18 minutes, 57 seconds north latitude; 112 degrees, 7 minutes, 35 seconds east longitude." More static. "Belay return to base. Repeat. Belay return to base. Stand by for new orders."

Senior Lieutenant Jung Hai looked at his copilot. "Stand by for new orders?"

"Perhaps they want us to follow the American ship for a while longer. That would seem logical," the copilot said.

"Perhaps it would make sense had we discovered a carrier or a cruiser. But a sub tender?"

Static. "Air Ostrich One. Yantian Control. Itu Aba has lost contact with the PRC freighter M/V *Shemnong*, which was en route to Itu Aba with military supplies. At last contact, *Shemnong* was in the vicinity of the Paracel Islands. Your orders are to change course to Paracel Islands to begin aerial search for the *Shemnong*. Land at Yŏngxīng Dǎo, Paracel Islands, to refuel. Resume search at dawn."

"How does a freighter disappear?" the copilot asked.

"Good question, Lieutenant," Jung Hai said. He pressed the broadcast button. "Roger that, Yantian Control. Altering course for Yŏngxīng Dǎo, Paracel Islands, to refuel and commence search for M/V *Shemnong*."

US Navy life raft
South China Sea
somewhere between USS Vicksburg and USS Emory S. Land

Gunner had thanked the Creator for the fresh water from the heavens, for the floating refuge, and for calm seas. Then, feeling drowsy and remembering the maxim to conserve energy and with dusk falling over the sea, he had zipped up the raft and decided to settle in for an evening of rest.

The khaki uniform pants he had wrapped over his head to avoid debilitating sunburn now served another purpose. Lying flat on his back, the makeshift balled-up pants-turned-pillow under his neck kept the back of his head out of the thin covering of rainwater in the bottom of the raft.

His thoughts became blurred somewhere on the road between consciousness and unconsciousness, and the sound of water sloshing morphed into the sounds of rural Virginia — wind whipping over green peanut crops, the roar of the green John Deere tractor crossing a field as it headed toward the house.

His brother Gorman is driving the tractor, its engine chugging and roaring as he pulls up to the edge of the field, turns it off, and gets off. Gunner embraces him with a bear hug befitting a long-lost brother, and they go into the house, greeted by the smell of the luscious roast in the electric roaster their mother has been cooking all day.

Gunner hears the horn of the tractor ...

The second long blast on the tractor's horn pops open his eyes. It's almost dark inside the orange raft-tent and, heart racing, he realizes that the long rapping blast is no tractor!

Gunner pushes himself up and unzips the tent. The dim light of dusk lit the inside of his tent-raft. Outside, perhaps a hundred yards away, a great steel ship, its massive gray bow rising from the water, towers into the darkening skies. The ship's horn goes silent, and from off to the right, a spotlight splashes his face, then moves away to focus on the orange tent. He squints at the light. A small boat, the silhouettes of two figures seated in it, is puttering toward the raft. He hears the click of a loudspeaker echo across the water.

"Ahoy in the life raft! This is the USS *Emory Land!*"

CHAPTER 16

Bridge
USS Vicksburg
South China Sea
100 miles east of Da Nang, Vietnam

ten minutes before midnight

The bridge of a US Navy warship, the nucleus of activity in times of war and peace, was, in the early twenty-first century, an electronic command center capable of obliterating any major population center on the planet. But despite the great destructive power matched by few other instruments of war and surpassed only by God himself, the level of activity on the bridge varied.

Routine missions with low alert levels permitted a more relaxed atmosphere on the bridge, often with a skeleton crew left to the charge of the officer of the deck, while the captain and executive officer were off attending to other duties on the ship or even in their wardrooms sleeping, depending on the watch.

But tonight, as the long sweeping hand of the clock on the bulkhead crept to within ten minutes before twelve local time, the routine on the bridge of the *Vicksburg* was anything but routine.

As midnight approached some one hundred miles off the Vietnamese coast, the bridge of the USS *Vicksburg* was a bustling panorama of flashing lights, gadgets, and the rhythmic beep of sweeping radar screens. With crew members glued to monitors, many with their ears covered with headsets, the tension aboard *Vicksburg* rose like the mercury in a thermometer in Death Valley.

Captain Leonard Kruger, perched in the captain's chair at the center of the bridge, focused his binoculars on the lights of two ships in the distance.

His crew was on edge, he knew, not so much because of the Taiwanese destroyer and Chinese freighter out in front of his ship, neither of which would be any match for the firepower of the *Vicksburg*, but rather because of what was unseen beyond the dark horizon.

Out there, somewhere, still, was the elusive and deadly Chinese aircraft carrier *Shi Lang*.

Actually, it wasn't the *Shi Lang* that worried Kruger. What worried him were the warplanes stationed aboard her. The power of an aircraft carrier rests in her air wing, in the ability to launch aircraft to fly out hundreds of miles and then launch deadly anti-ship missiles that can fly hundreds of miles more to a target, strike the target, set it ablaze, and sink it almost in the blink of an eye.

Kruger remembered the history of the attacks by anti-ship missiles against NATO warships. French-made Exocet missiles had wreaked havoc on the British destroyer HMS *Sheffield* during the Falklands War, sending her to the bottom of the Atlantic. Two British frigates, HMS *Ardent* and HMS *Antelope*, were attacked and sunk by Argentinean aircraft.

In 1987, two Exocet missiles fired by an Iraqi warplane struck the frigate USS *Stark* in the Persian Gulf. *Stark* survived the attack, but thirty-seven Americans died. The captain of the *Stark* could have faced a court-martial for dereliction of duty. Instead he was reprimanded, relieved of his command, and forced into early retirement.

Kruger remained confident the *Vicksburg* could defend herself against missiles better than the British ships sunk in the Falklands War and better than the *Stark*. But he worried about the prospect of facing multiple missiles launched from multiple aircraft at the same time. This was a cruiser commander's nightmare.

"XO, sound General Quarters. Lieutenant, after we go to General Quarters, open a frequency to the Taiwanese destroyer."

"Aye, Captain," the XO said.

"Yes, sir," the communications officer said.

Bells rang out all over the *Vicksburg*, as the XO flipped on the 1MC. "General Quarters! General Quarters! General Quarters! All hands to Battle Stations!"

Sailors scrambled to man missiles, radar screens, antiaircraft guns, and medical stations. These were the positions they manned in the event of actual hostilities, ready in a hair-trigger instant to carry out any battle orders issued by the captain.

A moment later, the XO reported, "General Quarters executed, sir. The *Vicksburg* is at Battle Stations, awaiting your orders."

Kruger checked his watch. Execution of his General Quarters command was still thirty seconds too long! Any other time and he'd tear the XO a new one, as he had tasked the XO with the job of improving the ship's General Quarters execution time. "Very well, XO." Kruger fumed. "Lieutenant Morrison. Open frequency to the *Kee Lung*."

"Aye, Captain."

Kruger waited as his communications officer punched several buttons on the control panel.

"Frequency open, sir." He handed the captain a headset with microphone. "At your pleasure, Captain."

Kruger put on the headset. "To the captain of the ROC destroyer *Kee Lung*. This is the captain of the USS *Vicksburg*. We are one thousand yards off your starboard. Please acknowledge."

Five seconds passed. No word. Kruger was about to rebroadcast, and then —

"Good evening, USS *Vicksburg*." The voice spoke understandable English with a dose of a Chinese accent. "This is Captain Won Lee of the ROCS *Kee Lung*." Static crackled. "It is a pleasure to make your acquaintance, Captain."

The XO, Commander Bennett, shook his head nervously. "Sounds friendly enough," he mumbled.

Kruger held the microphone back up to his mouth and said, "Likewise, it is a pleasure, Captain. Greetings to you and your crew on behalf of the president of the United States, who has sent us here on a mission which will require your cooperation."

Static. "And how may we be of assistance to President Surber tonight, Captain?"

More static. Kruger said, "We are ordered to seize the PRC freighter that you have commandeered and to escort it to a location under the control of the United States Navy. We would appreciate your full cooperation."

Another pause. The second hand on the bridge clock swept off seven seconds. "Captain, are you aware of the cargo being carried by this freighter?"

Kruger replied, "We are somewhat aware, Captain. The US Navy doctor aboard the freighter is from this ship. Again, we ask for your cooperation."

"It is not only the medical atrocities that concern the Republic of China. *Shemnong* carries sophisticated weaponry destined for Itu Aba Island ... to reinforce the illegal invasion by Communist forces against ROC territory." Transmission static. "Those weapons would become problematic for Republic of China forces attempting to retake the island. My government intends to prevent those weapons from falling into Communist hands."

Captain Kruger thought for a second. Would the Taiwanese skipper pose a problem? The last thing Kruger wanted was to sink the ROC destroyer to get access to the *Shemnong*. But if he had to, he would blow the *Kee Lung* out of the water if the Taiwanese captain gave him even the slightest reason to do so. "Captain, I'm a naval officer, not a diplomat. I can assure you that the weapons on board the freighter will not wind up in Communist hands. The US Navy will remove the *Shemnong*, along with all of its contents, from the area."

Twenty seconds ran off the clock. "Please stand by, Captain," the ROC captain said. Then thirty seconds more passed.

Kruger looked at Bennett, who stood there with his arms crossed. "My patience is running thin, XO," Kruger said as he waited.

"We'll improve the speed on the General Quarters execution, Captain."

"We do need to shave it down another thirty seconds." Kruger glanced at his watch. Then the thought struck him. What if the Taiwanese destroyer decided to take a shot, point-blank, at his ship? That seemed inconceivable. But then, both *Vicksburg* and *Kee Lung* were vying for the same trophy, the *Shemnong*, and were in the middle of a shooting war between China and Taiwan. That changed the dynamic.

The skipper of USS *Stark*, Captain Glenn Brindle, had believed there was no danger to his ship, rationalizing that an Iraqi warplane, which had been seen, would not dare fire on an American warship. In 1987, that seemed to be a reasonable assumption. That was three years before the first Persian Gulf War broke out, before Sadaam Hussein invaded Kuwait, and before the first George Bush, speaking about that Iraqi invasion, declared, "This will not stand."

That miscalculation left the *Stark* defenseless in the attack. Two missiles were fired by the plane from twenty-two and fifteen miles away that weren't detected until seconds before the first hit the ship, giving the *Stark* no time to respond. Only a miracle kept the *Stark* from sinking. But the loss of American life was significant.

A captain is responsible for the protection of his ship and the safety of his crew.

What if the *Kee Lung* tried a quick strike to take out the *Vicksburg* and blame it on the Chinese?

What if this delay in response was an opportunity for the *Kee Lung* to bring her guns down on the *Vicksburg*? What if the next message from the *Kee Lung* was a lethal salvo from her cannon? Or an anti-ship missile?

In an even fight on the high seas, *Vicksburg* would win, hands down. But even David felled Goliath with a lucky shot to the head.

Vicksburg was at General Quarters, her crew ready for combat at a moment's notice. But her guns were not trained on a specific target.

"Weapons Officer."

"Yes, Captain."

"Target both Mark 45 cannons right at the *Kee Lung*. Aim one on the bridge and one on the rear magazine rack. Order the gun crews to be ready to fire at my direction."

"Aye, Captain."

Presidential Palace
Zhongzheng District
Taipei City, Republic of China (Taiwan)

approaching midnight

From a distance, to an American visiting the island of Formosa for the first time, the ornate Renaissance-baroque building located at the heart of Taipei City's bustling Zhongzheng District, the Presidential Palace of the Republic of China, might bear an odd resemblance to the main Smithsonian building located on the National Mall in Washington, DC. Both buildings feature an old tower rising into the air at the center of the building. Both towers are of similar height, about 200 feet high. Both buildings are flanked by horizontal wings stretching to left and to right from the central tower.

When bright spotlights flood the Presidential Palace in the evening, an American familiar with Washington, when approaching the palace from Chongqing South Road, might think that the palace and the Smithsonian were built from the same blueprints.

But in daylight, the sun reveals that the Presidential Palace, once known as the Governor General's Palace and also as the Presidential Office Building, is larger and more ornate than the Smithsonian in Washington, its wings spreading twice as far on each side of the 196-foot central tower. The Japanese designed and built the building, with an ornate baroque flair, over a seven-year period, from 1912 to 1919, at a time when Japan still exercised colonial rule over Taiwan. Taiwan renamed it the "Presidential Palace" in 1950, when Chiang Kai-shek became president in exile of China and made his headquarters there.

Unlike the Zhongnanhai Compound in Beijing, which is surrounded by secrecy and by walls, here in Taipei City's vibrant Zhongzheng District, there were no secrets about where the president of the republic lives and works. Anyone could drive straight up Chongqing South Road almost to the gates of the Presidential Palace, within a few feet of the president's workspace. Such was the difference between a constitutional republic and a Communist dictatorship.

Although the Presidential Palace in Taipei City normally was far more open and visible than the secret buildings behind the walls of Zhongnanhai, for the last three nights, the streets and grounds surrounding the palace had been a virtual armed camp.

War fever now swept this island nation, which is about the size of Maryland and Delaware combined—245 miles long and 89 miles at its widest point. The attack on Itu Aba had become the most dangerous crisis threatening Taiwan since the Chinese Civil War, when in 1950 the ROC government was forced off the mainland and relocated on Taiwan.

President Lu Yen-hsun, as commander in chief of the armed forces of the Republic of China on Taiwan, was preparing for a possible invasion by Communist forces from the mainland. He had raised the military readiness to the highest alert level.

For Lu and for a number of senior members in the Legislative Yuan—the ROC Parliament—and for most of the nationalist Chinese living on Taiwan, the Communist government in Beijing, by attacking sovereign ROC territory on Itu Aba, had committed an act of war. Taiwan's main newspaper, the *Taipei Times*, called the attack "Taiwan's Pearl Harbor" and, in an obvious attempt to garner British sympathies, likened it to Argentina's attack against the British-controlled Falkland Islands.

Taiwan's war cabinet, a term used by Lu to refer to the group, was meeting for the third consecutive night in emergency session in the long ornate cabinet conference room. An hour ago, Taiwan had received a back-channel communiqué from the United States notifying it, as a "courtesy," of America's intentions to seize the PRC freighter *Shemnong*.

The president was refereeing a sharp disagreement between his minister of national defense, Shen Tao-Ming, and his minister of foreign affairs, Mark Huang, on the proposed response to America's request or, as Shen called it, the Americans' "demand" for the *Shemnong*.

Exhausted, Lu turned his back on his colleagues and looked out on the flashing collage of white, red, and green lights, of lit skyscrapers, of bustling Taipei traffic even this late, just before midnight. He squinted, hoping that the blur of lights would breathe vitality into his tired eyes. So far, no luck.

Defense Minister Shen said, "Mister President, that freighter carries arms headed for Itu Aba that would prove deadly when we try to retake the island. Our Navy has its hands full worrying about the Communist aircraft carrier. We cannot risk those weapons falling into the hands of the Communists. We must maintain control of the freighter ourselves."

"I disagree!" In the reflection of the glass, Lu saw the minister of foreign affairs throw up his hands. "Mister President, it is important, in a crisis like this, to maintain close diplomatic ties with the Americans."

"Diplomatic ties?" the defense minister said. "May I remind my colleague that the Americans do not even maintain an embassy here in Taipei. Even Belize and Nicaragua have embassies here. But not America! They don't wish to offend the Communists in Beijing."

Defense Minister Shen had touched on a sensitive area. America's decision to move its embassy from Taipei to Beijing in the 1970s remained a hot-button issue.

The president turned around just as Foreign Minister Mark Huang shot back with, "And you can also remember, Minister, that the same Americans sold our Air Force those F-16 fighter jets and sold our Navy those *Oliver Hazard Perry*–class frigates that keep the Communists from crossing the Taiwan Strait! In fact, the very ship that captured the freighter *Shemnong*, the *Kee Lung*, was sold to our Navy by the United States Navy!"

"Colleague," the defense minister said, "no one disputes that America was helpful in the past. But beginning in 2008, they became progressively unreliable with their allies. After helping Britain in the Falklands War in the 1980s, in 2011 they reversed themselves and joined the Organization of American States, the OAS, in opposing the British for their occupation of the Falklands. President Obama even removed a bust of Churchill from the White House, yet another slap to the British. In 2011, they agreed to give the Russians sensitive information about British Trident nuclear submarines without the Brits' knowledge or permission. Twice they stabbed their best ally in the back. And they've tried ramming a Palestinian state right down Israel's throat, on sovereign Israeli territory. And Israel was their most loyal ally in the Middle East. Can we trust them that these weapons will not wind up in the hands of PRC forces?"

The president scratched his chin. His defense minister did have a point. Vice President Feng Zongren and General Lien Chan, two of the other three participants in this midnight meeting, sat at opposite ends of the long table, exchanging glances and taking notes on legal pads.

The fifth and final participant in the meeting, Admiral Wong Lu-Chen, commander in chief of the ROC Navy, sat at the other end of the table in summer dress white uniform, not saying anything, but nodding his head in agreement with the comments of his immediate boss, the minister of defense.

President Lu raised a finger, just as Foreign Minister Huang flashed a contorted expression to signal that he had another word for the group. The president hesitated. "Minister Huang? You have something else to add?"

"Yes, Mister President." This time, Huang spoke in softer tones.

"Gentlemen, my colleague the defense minister makes some points on which we can all agree. First, it would be disastrous for the armaments on board the *Shemnong* to fall into the hands of the Communists on Itu Aba. Surely, more of our Marines would die trying to retake the island if that happens.

"Second, it is true that the US administration took some diplomatic positions that seemed contrary to the best interests of Great Britain and Israel, as the defense minister suggests. But I would remind everyone that these aberrations occurred under a different administration. There is no reason to believe that President Surber would take a similar approach by turning his back on American allies. I say we let the Americans have the *Shemnong*."

All eyes shifted back to the president. Except the defense minister, who was grimacing and shaking his head. "Defense Minister, is there anything you wish to add?" the president said.

The defense minister stood up. "It is true that the US shift in position on Britain occurred in the Obama administration, as the foreign minister said. However, the shift against Israel started under George W. Bush, and both Obama and Bush were pushing this Palestinian state idea on America's closest ally in the region.

"Now," he said, "they're stepping in and demanding that we turn over this freighter full of weapons that were to be used against us. I don't trust them to keep the weapons out of PRC hands. What happens if the PRC threatens to dump all those American Treasury bonds they've bought? And they could. Think of the financial crisis that would create. Does anyone think that Douglas Surber would not buckle under that type of pressure?"

The president realized they were no closer to a decision on the *Shemnong* than they were when they started. "Very well, Defense Minister Shen. The foreign minister has made his recommendation." Lu glanced over at Mark Huang, then back at Shen. "What recommendations would you have for me, Defense Minister Shen?"

Shen sat down. "The first recommendation I have, Mister President," he continued in a softer tone, "is that we protect the *Kee Lung* and give her the ability to defend herself."

"Of course the *Kee Lung* has the authorization to defend herself."

The president felt defensive, as if the defense minister had taken an underhanded shot at his performance as commander in chief. "She's been ordered, on my orders as a matter of fact, to sink any PRC vessel that threatens her. My orders also are for the *Kee Lung* and all ROC warships in the region to intercept PRC warships and supply ships headed to Itu Aba. But you already know this. If you are insinuating that I have not issued adequate orders as commander in chief for our fleet to protect itself, just let me say that I am not happy about such an insinuation."

The defense minister nodded. "I meant no disrespect by the comment, nor do I in any way call into question your orders to the fleet. But I wasn't talking about the ability to defend herself from the PRC. Of course she has that ability."

The president scratched the back of his head. "You leave me confused, Minister. Do you believe the Vietnamese may attempt to take advantage of the situation and get involved? Perhaps while we are distracted with the Chinese, Vietnam may try to seize ROC territory in the Spratlys?"

Shen shook his head. "Sir, I meant that we should give *Kee Lung* the authority to defend herself against the Americans."

"The Americans?" the foreign affairs minister shouted. "Minister, are you suggesting that the Americans might be a threat to ROC naval forces operating in the area?"

"Hmph," Shen snorted. "Remember this, my friend. The US Navy has sent one of its most powerful cruisers, the USS *Vicksburg*, to seize the *Shemnong*. But it was our warship, the *Kee Lung*, that captured the *Shemnong*. If we decide that we do not wish to turn over the *Shemnong* as the Americans have demanded, then you can bet that the *Vicksburg* is not going to play a simple little game of patty-cake."

Nods of agreement from Vice President Feng, General Lien, and Admiral Wong. The consensus appeared to be four against one, with the vice president, the two high-ranking military officers, and the defense minister pitted against the diplomat.

The president looked at the head nodders. "I take it you all think the Americans would actually attack our ship?" His eyes bored into the chief of staff. "General?"

"Permission to speak frankly, Mister President?"

"Of course, General."

"I agree with the defense minister. This could be a dangerous situation for the *Kee Lung*." He exchanged glances with the admiral. "That is, sir, unless you accede to the Americans' demands, at which point, our worries would shift from having the Americans attack our ship, to having those weapons fall into Communist hands to be used against our Marines retaking the island. I share the defense minister's concerns that while Douglas Surber may mean well, he may succumb to economic blackmail by the Communists if they threaten to unload bonds."

President Lu looked at Admiral Wong. "Admiral, the *Kee Lung* is under your command. Do you believe that she is in danger, not just from the PLA Navy but also from the US Navy?"

The admiral nodded. "Mister President, as a flag officer of the ROC Navy, I must always put myself in the position of my opponent. That is what we do during war games as we conduct military exercises to anticipate the moves of our opponents." The admiral stopped for a moment. "As you know, like most of us here, I also have a background with the Americans, having studied as a foreign officer for one year at their Naval War College in Newport, Rhode Island. I have studied their wartime commanders, their naval commanders, and I know their doctrine. They are diplomatic on one hand, yet forceful on the other.

"Do I believe their captain has been instructed to take out the *Kee Lung* if we do not cooperate?" He paused. "Absolutely. Therefore, Mister President, if your orders are to resist turning over the *Shemnong*, and I would urge you to resist turning her over, then I recommend, reluctantly, that we must order the captain of the *Kee Lung* to take out the *Vicksburg*."

"Admiral!" the foreign minister snapped.

"Foreign minister, sir," Admiral Wong replied, "I am certain that this order has already been given to the captain of the *Vicksburg*. If we do not act, we will either lose the *Kee Lung* and her crew or more Marines will die if the Americans turn those weapons over to the PRC forces. And remember, sir, with respect, the Americans are interested in the dead babies on board that ship. They aren't interested in the weapons. And why should they care who controls the Spratlys? The Spratlys are important to us. They are not important to the Americans and not part of America's strategic interest. Not when the PRC could pull the plug on bonds it has bought to finance America's debt." He paused and looked at everyone in the room, then said, "That is my recommendation, Mister President."

The Taiwanese president looked around the table and felt the hot stares boring into his soul. The time for discussion was over. The weight of the office had settled on his shoulders. Never had he felt so lonely.

He rose again, hoping, somehow, to delay the moment of decision, for this was a decision that could forever change Taiwan's relationship with the country that had supported it most for all of its years, the United States of America.

Lu again walked to the window and looked out at the Taipei skyline.

In the years since the nationalist government had come in exile from the mainland, the vibrant Taiwanese capital had flourished, earning the proud nickname "Skyscraper City."

Off in the distance, amidst a seabed of spotlights and street lights and window lights and streaking white car lights rushing along wide boulevards, the crown jewel of free Chinese engineering, the skyscraper known as "Taipei 101," loomed as a tower of proud independence into the star-spangled midnight sky.

Reaching upward over 1,600 feet into the heavens, Taipei 101 claimed the title of the "world's tallest building" for a six-year period from 2004 to 2010, when it was eclipsed by the immediately bankrupt 2,700-foot monstrosity in Dubai known as Burj Khalifa.

Still, Taipei 101 loomed higher than anything either in the People's Republic or the United States, a thought which, in a strange way, reassured the president that his small country had the wherewithal to go toe-to-toe with either of these two military giants in this escalating crisis in the South China Sea.

Still, it seemed odd and almost surreal that in such a modern age, Taiwan, which, along with South Korea, Singapore, and Hong Kong, had been branded one of the "Four Asian Tigers" for her highly developed economic prowess, was now poised on the verge of war.

Lu turned and faced his immediate underlings.

"Gentlemen, this crisis was thrust upon us. We did not ask for it. But if we do nothing and allow Itu Aba to remain in Communist hands, then all of our careers are over." He glanced at his minister of defense and saw heads nodding in agreement. "All of us, gentlemen"—he shook his fist in the air—"we are the heirs to the dream of restoring the great

Republic of China to her true territorial home on the mainland. We are the sons of Chiang Kai-shek, and the dream will either live with us or it will die, here … with us." Lu paused. "As for me, I will not allow myself to become Taiwan's Neville Chamberlain."

The president exhaled and rested his hands on the back of his large leather swivel chair.

"Here are my instructions. Minister Sheng, Admiral Wong, the *Kee Lung*'s rules of engagement shall give the captain authority to defend his ship against all warships, including United States warships. The captain shall have authority to fire upon the USS *Vicksburg* and to sink and destroy that ship at will. If the captain in his judgment senses even the slightest danger to his ship, he may fire upon the *Vicksburg* and sink her." A sick feeling blanketed the president's stomach. "Do you understand my instructions?"

"Yes, Mister President."

"Foreign Minister Huang."

"Yes, sir, Mister President."

"Contact the director of the American Institute here. See if an acceptable diplomatic solution can be reached which would guarantee that the weapons aboard *Shemnong* do not fall into Communist hands. But hurry. If we cannot resolve this in very short order, we have no other choice but to sink the *Vicksburg* and blame the sinking on the PRC. This goes against my conscience, but as of this moment, it is the Republic of China against the rest of the world. Are my instructions clear?"

"Yes, Mr. President."

Bridge
ROCS Kee Lung
South China Sea

approaching midnight

Captain Won Lee, the commanding officer of ROCS *Kee Lung*, stood on the bridge and, peering through his high-powered binoculars, gazed out over the dark waters of the South China Sea.

The three ships swirling at the heart of this military-diplomatic standoff, two warships and a freighter, were all positioned in a floating triangle, all spaced a thousand yards apart.

From his position in the middle of the bridge, at an angle of ten o'clock, he saw the lights of the American warship, the USS *Vicksburg*. Then shifting his view to an angle of two o'clock, and just as visible against the black of the star-filled night, were the lights of the PRC freighter M/V *Shemnong*.

He swept the binoculars back from right to left, from two o'clock to ten o'clock, again studying the navigational lights of the powerful guided-missile cruiser *Vicksburg*. Somewhere on the bridge of the ship, the American captain, sitting on enough firepower to single-handedly wipe out any city on the planet, was staring right back at him.

"Captain! FLASH message in from Taipei, sir! It is urgent."

"Thank you, Lieutenant." Captain Won Lee took the communiqué from the officer and read it. "Oh, dear!" He folded the message and stuffed it into his pocket.

"Weapons officer!"

"Yes, Captain!"

"Target USS *Vicksburg*. Aim all weapons and missiles at the American warship. Prepare to fire on my orders!"

The weapons officer looked around with a perplexed look on his face.

"You did not understand my orders, Lieutenant?"

"Understand, Captain," the weapons officer barked. "Targeting all weapons on new target—USS *Vicksburg*—preparing to fire on your orders, sir."

"XO!"

"Aye, Captain."

"Take the *Kee Lung* to General Quarters. All hands to Battle Stations!"

"Aye, Captain. Take *Kee Lung* to General Quarters. All hands to Battle Stations!"

Presidential Palace
Zhongnanhai Compound
Beijing, People's Republic of China

The ornamental sound of plucked musical strings flooded the dark of the presidential bedroom, and the tranquil and hypnotic chords of the great Chinese classical masterpiece "Return of the Fishing Boat" filled every corner of the room.

Each night, whether he was in bed alone or with any number of a half dozen mistresses who had been pleased to entertain him at various times over the last year, the ambitious new president of the People's Republic closed his day, in the dark of his bedroom, with the same music.

Tonight, he was alone by design. Only the peaceful harp-like strains of "Return of the Fishing Boat" could minister to his soul. The melody evoked images of one man, alone on a single skiff on the Yangtze River, returning home with a great harvest of fish to a single pier at the end of the day, to a dock where there was no one.

Tonight, even in the wake of today's glorious events and before tomorrow would bring more basking in the glory of the Chinese sun, a tomorrow in which the glory would be spread among many, tonight was about one man. And he was that man. For the events of today, and the events of tomorrow, were about him and him alone.

Tang lay in bed, smiling, absorbing the placid sounds of the solo harpsichord, his eyes closed ... imagining the wide-flowing river ... the reeds along the way ...

The electric buzzing from the hotline beside his bed aroused a short barrage of Chinese profanity. His meditative state had been ruined. He reached over, flipped on the lamp, and picked up the phone.

"What is it?" he blurted out.

"I am sorry to bother you, Mister President." Tang recognized the gruff voice of his minister of defense, General Shang. "But we have a situation about which you may wish to be briefed."

Tang raised up in the bed. "Has Taiwan counterattacked against our forces on the island?"

"Not yet, Mister President," the defense minister said. "This situation involves one of our ships in the area."

"One of our ships?" The thought sent the president's heart pounding. "Dear God," he said, then remembered the state's official position that there was no God. His mind raced. Had an enemy submarine gotten through to his flag warship? "Please do not tell me, General, that anything has happened to the *Shi Lang!*"

"No, Mister President," the general answered. "The *Shi Lang* remains on station in the South China Sea, north of Itu Aba, prepared and ready to intercept the anticipated Taiwanese counterattack."

"Then which ship?" the president demanded. "One of our frigates or destroyers?"

"Not a Navy warship, sir. It involves the civilian freighter *Shemnong.*"

"The *Shemnong?*" Tang's eyes shot to the eight-by-ten photograph of an attractive thirty-eight-year-old Chinese woman, whose smiling face seemed to look back at him from the desk across the room. "What about the *Shemnong?*"

"We have lost all contact with her."

"Lost contact? When? How?"

"Earlier today. She disappeared from all ship-to-ship frequencies, all ship-to-shore frequencies. She no longer broadcasts her position to any GPS satellites."

"That sounds odd." Tang's eyes lingered on the photograph of the woman. "It would be understandable if we had lost her on one of those three. But all three going silent raises serious questions."

"Yes, Mr. President. Either she has had a total power failure, which seems unlikely because she has backup generators, or something else has happened."

Tang sat up and swung his feet over the side of the bed, resting them on the ornate Oriental rug. He feared this war was about to become personal, but not in a way he had expected. "What was the ship's last known position?"

"One hundred miles off the coast of Da Nang, in the South China Sea, on a course to Itu Aba."

"When was that?" the president asked.

"Earlier today, sir."

"Have we dispatched search planes?"

"Mr. President, it wasn't until dusk that we discovered the ship was missing. Because of nightfall, our planes have not yet been able to conduct a meaningful search. However, we will have several planes out searching the area at daybreak, sir."

Tang stood up, put the phone on speaker, and walked across the room to the desk with the photograph. He was gritting his teeth together. "Of course, by morning the ship may no longer be anywhere in the vicinity, that is, assuming that she is steaming at full power and further assuming she is still on the surface."

"True, Mister President," the general said. "On the other hand, it is possible that by tomorrow morning she will show up off the coast of Itu Aba with a reasonable explanation."

"Somehow, your words are not providing much assurance, Minister."

"My apologies, Mister President. I wish that I could offer you more. But at the moment, the darkness works against us."

Tang ran his hands through his hair and looked at the photo. He dismissed the thought of calling her tonight.

"General, are our plans still running smoothly for our National Day of Victory tomorrow?"

"Yes, Mister President. Workers labor around the clock, even at this hour, decorating Tiananmen Square with hundreds of flags and streamers bearing the colors of the People's Republic. Prior to your speech, the Beijing Symphony will perform military marches for one hour, live, on national television, broadcast on every station in China. School children will be given thousands of red and yellow roses to cast upon the parade route. Lieutenant Wang Ju, our helicopter pilot who led the aerial assault on Itu Aba, is in flight to Beijing from the South China Sea at this very moment."

The president thought for a moment. "Very well. We must remain focused on the task at hand. There is no point in having the disappearance of the *Shemnong* detract from the important national celebration of victory that our nation needs."

"Yes, sir. Of course, Mister President."

"Very well," the president said. "Make certain that the situation with the *Shemnong* is kept under wraps until after tomorrow's ceremony."

"Yes, Mister President."

CHAPTER 17

Bridge
USS Vicksburg
South China Sea
100 miles east of Da Nang, Vietnam

three minutes after midnight

From the skipper's chair in the middle of the bridge, Captain Kruger peered out at the running lights of the ROCS *Kee Lung*.

Something wasn't right. Somehow, he felt danger rolling in as a dark storm cloud across the waters.

He lowered his binoculars, letting them drape around his neck. Kruger glanced up at the clock on the bulkhead. Ten minutes after midnight.

Lennie Kruger was a patient guy. But he'd had enough. Every lapsed second increased the level of danger.

Washington was a long way away. Washington had given its orders, and he would follow those orders.

But out here, half a world away from the Pentagon, all the weight of the world rested on his shoulders. As the captain, he was responsible for the lives of all 400 members of his crew. Should something go wrong, it was he, and only he, who would have to look square into the eyes of grieving relatives and explain why he let their loved ones die.

"Lieutenant," he snapped at his communications officer. How long since our last communication with the *Kee Lung*?"

"Thirteen minutes, Captain."

Kruger cursed under his breath and locked eyes with his XO, Commander Hugh Bennett, who now looked nervous. Not the look of confidence expected from an officer one step removed from command. Kruger would be hard-pressed to recommend Bennett for command, although luckily for Bennett, he still had time to prove himself.

But in fairness to the XO, there was plenty of reason to be nervous. Thirteen minutes of silence from the *Kee Lung*. More than enough time for the Taiwanese captain to lock his weapons on the *Vicksburg*. Just as *Vicksburg* had her guns trained on *Kee Lung*, Kruger was now certain that *Kee Lung* was taking point-blank aim of her own.

Enough was enough. "Lieutenant Morrison, prepare to re-open that frequency to the *Kee Lung*."

"Aye, Captain," the lieutenant said. "Frequency open, sir. Ready to broadcast at your discretion, sir."

Kruger glanced at his weapons officer. "WEPS, be ready with the Mark 45 cannons. Remember. He might have his guns trained on us just like we've got our guns trained on him. So it could be that the first to fire stays afloat, and everyone else gets to be shark bait."

Tension flooded the bridge, as two ships in the middle of the night faced each other in a Mexican standoff, like two hungry, sharp-clawed predators circling the lone juicy kill—a kill without enough meat to feed both dinner. If one captain blinked, ball game over.

Kruger picked up the microphone and depressed the broadcast button. "To the ROCS *Kee Lung*. This is the USS *Vicksburg*. It has been fifteen minutes since your last broadcast. As you know, we are under orders to seize the freighter *Shemnong* and escort it out of the area. I have been ordered by the president of the United States to carry out those orders, either with your cooperation or without it. Because of the longstanding history of goodwill between the United States and the Republic of China, and because of longstanding American support of the Republic of China on the Island of Taiwan, we seek your cooperation. However, we intend to take that ship whether you cooperate or not. Please respond."

Kruger waited. He wasn't accustomed to playing diplomat, and the diplomatic mumbo-jumbo he'd just spewed over the airways reminded him of some of the State Department and United Nations beanie-heads he had been around, occasionally, over the years. That made him want to puke.

Every eye on the bridge bore into the ship-to-ship speakers, like Cardinals' fans from the forties, hanging over the radio, awaiting the next word from the legendary broadcaster Harry Carey that would bring news of a strikeout or a home run.

Nothing.

Enough was enough.

"WEPS officer. Prepare to fire. On my command."

"Aye, Captain, fire on command." The WEPS officer punched several buttons. A second later, an infrared live television view of the *Kee Lung* appeared on the screens, with target markings on her bridge and magazine rack.

Bridge
ROCS **Kee Lung**
South China Sea

five minutes past midnight

Although the ship's air-conditioning had not malfunctioned, the bridge of the *Kee Lung* felt like an oven. From Won Lee's brow, sweat slid down to the tip of his nose, then splatted on the deck.

"Are you going to answer the American captain, sir?"

Captain Won Lee wiped his forehead. He heard his executive officer's voice. Yet, it was as if he did not hear him at all.

"Captain! Sir!" the XO persisted. "Will you answer the American captain?"

"No, XO," he said. "There is nothing left to say. The moment calls for action. Weapons officer."

"Yes, Captain."

"Enter firing coordinates for two Harpoon anti-ship missiles. Target ... the American warship USS *Vicksburg*. Target ship's superstructure just under the bridge and target amidships."

"Aye, Captain. Entering firing coordinates." The weapons officer began punching numbers into the fire-control computer. Digital numbers whirled on the screen in front of the weapons officer, rolling and flashing so fast that the eye could not follow.

The numbers stopped, reflecting precise lat-lon coordinates. "Firing coordinates entered, Captain. Two Harpoon missiles locked on the American warship USS *Vicksburg*."

"Very well. Arm missiles."

"Arming missiles. Aye, Captain." The weapons officer punched several other buttons. More numbers whirled across the screen, then stopped. "Harpoon missiles locked on target and armed, Captain. Ready to fire on your order."

Captain Won Lee glanced at his watch.

"On my mark. Prepare to fire in thirty seconds."

"Aye, Captain. Preparing to fire on your order."

"Start countdown. Alert the crew."

"Aye, sir."

Won Lee eyed the digital clock countdown from thirty seconds. Then twenty. Then ten seconds. "Five ... four ... three ... two ..."

"Captain! FLASH message from Taipei. Hold fire!"

Bridge
USS Vicksburg
South China Sea
100 miles east of Da Nang, Vietnam

seven minutes after midnight

Weapons officer. Prepare to fire!" Kruger ordered.

"Aye, Captain. Ready to fire on your command!" The weapons officer, Lieutenant John Klifton, announced.

"Four ... three ... two ..."

"To the captain of the USS *Vicksburg*!"

"Hold fire!" Kruger threw his hand up.

"This is the captain of the ROCS *Kee Lung*!"

Kruger's heart was a jackhammer pounding inside his chest. He glanced at his men. Their eyes screamed for his leadership. Their lives depended on him making the correct decision.

"WEPS, remain on standby to fire at my command."

"Aye, Skipper."

Kruger wasn't much of a praying man. But he uttered a quick prayer under his breath, then depressed the transmit button on the ship-to-ship circuit.

"This is the captain of the USS *Vicksburg*. It's been a while since we've heard from you. What can I do for you, Captain?"

No response. Static on the loudspeakers.

Was this a trick?

More static. More posturing by the Taiwanese? Perhaps a delay tactic to buy time to fire their weapons.

No more game-playing.

"Weapons officer. Prepare to fire."

Loud static blasted over the loudspeaker. "Captain Kruger!" The Taiwanese captain had spoken Kruger's name, which took him aback.

"This is Captain Kruger."

"Forgive me, Captain. I obtained your name from your ship's official website."

"Captain, over half an hour ago, I told you my orders regarding the freighter *Shemnong*. With all due respect, I can wait no longer. What is your answer?"

"It appears that our respective governments have reached a solution to solve this dilemma concerning the PRC freighter that is captivating our mutual interests."

Kruger looked around at the officers on the bridge. Some shook their heads. Others nodded. Still others looked blank.

"I think he's blowing smoke, Skipper," the weapons officer said. "Ready to fire on your command, sir."

"With all due respect, Captain, I think I'd follow up with this," the XO volunteered.

Fire or talk. This was the question. Another quick prayer under his breath — "God give me wisdom."

"Captain, we've received nothing from our government confirming that," Kruger said. "What are the terms of this agreement you claim our governments have reached?"

Another static burst. "Our government tells us that we are to release the *Shemnong* to the custody of the United States Navy, with one caveat."

"An obvious trick, Captain," the weapons officer said. "We've received *nothing* from Washington verifying any agreement."

"I don't know, Captain," the XO said. "He said they're willing to turn over the *Shemnong*. That's what we came for."

"Yes, sir, but he said there's a caveat," the weapons officer insisted.

Kruger held up his hand in a "don't talk" gesture. He depressed the transmit button again. "Captain, what is this caveat?"

The transmission static over the speaker was nothing short of maddening.

"This is the captain of the *Kee Lung*. Under the agreement hammered out by our governments, we shall relinquish the *Shemnong*, but you shall—"

"Dangit!" Kruger screamed. "To the captain of the *Kee Lung*! You are breaking up!"

"My apologies, Captain. We were forced to institute electronic jamming to prevent the *Shemnong* from alerting the PRC that we have captured her."

"Sounds fishy," the weapons officer said.

Kruger held up his hand to quiet Klifton. "You were saying, Captain, that there is a caveat to our taking control of the *Shemnong*."

Static. "Under the terms of the agreement, you are permitted to take the *Shemnong*, with one caveat." More static.

Kruger cursed.

"He's stalling," the weapons officer said.

Kruger pressed the transmit button. "What is the caveat, Captain? My patience is running thin."

Static. Crackling. "Our government has a vested interest in preventing weapons on board the *Shemnong* from falling into enemy hands. Therefore, a contingent of ROC Marines shall stay aboard the vessel to ensure that no one delivers these weapons into the hands of the Communist PRC military forces. Our Marines shall be authorized to use deadly force against anyone who attempts to dispose of these weapons in any manner not authorized by our government."

Kruger winced. "Did I hear that right? Did he just threaten us?"

"Yes, he did, sir," the weapons officer said.

"Sounds like a reasonable proposal, Skipper," the XO said. "Sounds like the perfect solution. We take the ship. Their Marines stay aboard with the weapons. No harm, no foul."

"Maybe, XO, but if that's true, why haven't we heard from Washington?"

"Maybe because they're stalling, sir," the weapons officer said.

"Please elaborate, Mister Klifton."

The weapons officer pivoted around, his back to the fire-control panel, so he was now facing both the CO and the XO. "Think about it, sir. First off, he claims that he's still jamming the *Shemnong* so they can't radio a distress signal to the Commies. I can understand that he'd have to maybe jam them at first, but now they control the ship. And they're still jamming?"

"Captain," the communications officer spoke up.

"Lieutenant Morrison."

"Sir, it *does* make sense that they'd keep jamming. It's possible that someone could be deep in the bowels of the *Shemnong* with a transmission device. So they have to jam to prevent that."

"Or perhaps," Lieutenant Klifton said, "they're jamming so that we can't get off a distress signal if they attack us. They attack us, take us out, and then blame it on the Commies. Remember. We've heard nothing from Washington. That's the problem with this whole thing. They come up with a story that on its face sounds reasonable enough ... just reasonable enough to fool us into thinking it's true, giving them time to program the missile codes for their Harpoons into their fire-control computers."

Silence on the bridge.

"Captain," the XO said, "it makes no sense that the *Kee Lung* would attack us. After all, it was this very ship, the *Kee Lung*, that requested that we send a US Navy doctor to the *Shemnong*. And the president approved sending Commander Jeter out there. So why would they, on the one hand, request a US Navy doctor, and on the other hand, attack the very ship that sent the doctor?"

"Good point, XO," Kruger said, "except they requested the Navy doctor before they knew we were going to demand their ship. My guess is they wanted Dr. Jeter to come aboard and photograph the atrocities and document them so they would have a third-party witness against the Chinese. Now the dynamics have changed."

"But, sir," the XO continued, "why don't we just send a message to Washington asking them to verify?"

"Lieutenant Morrison?" Kruger directed the question to his communications officer. "How long would that take?"

Morrison shrugged. "Hard to say, sir. Part of the problem is the Taiwanese are jamming the area. We might be able to get a message off, we might not. Right now it's spotty. Like waiting for an opening in the clouds, and then waiting for another opening in the clouds for the response. They'd have to cut off their jamming, or we'd have to move out of the area to get a reliable signal off."

Kruger shook his head. "We don't have time for that."

"Skipper, may I add one other thing?"

"Yes, Lieutenant Klifton."

"Sir, you ordered me to ready the Mark 45 cannons. And we're ready to fire those. But you didn't order that we arm the Harpoons. The Mark 45 is a great naval gun, sir, and we might disable the *Kee Lung* on the first shot, and we could do a lot of damage if we hit their magazine rack. But Captain, our Harpoons aren't targeted on the *Kee Lung*. And if they hit us broadside with even one Harpoon, it's all over. No one would know what hit us. They're jamming the signals. They pop us with a Harpoon and we're toast. Remember what those two Iraqi Exocets did to the USS *Stark*, sir."

The weapons officer spoke wisdom far beyond his years. And young Lieutenant Klifton was right. Kruger had indeed neglected to order the arming of the *Vicksburg*'s Harpoons. When he ordered that the less-powerful Mark 45 cannons be trained on the *Kee Lung*, he had envisioned using just enough firepower to coerce the Taiwanese into complying with the American demand to release the *Shemnong*.

He had hoped to avoid sinking *Kee Lung*.

What if Lieutenant Klifton was right? What if this was a stall game? The proposal sounded reasonable enough, so why nothing from Washington? A point-blank hit from a Harpoon missile at this range, and the *Vicksburg* was history.

"Captain?"

"Yes, Lieutenant Klifton."

"Permission to speak freely."

"Absolutely."

"Sir, in 1987 more than forty American sailors died on the USS *Stark* from that Iraqi missile attack. And we are way too close for any of our anti-missile defenses to work. If they fire first, Captain"—he nodded in the direction of the *Kee Lung*—"we won't survive a close-in Harpoon attack."

Kruger let that sink in for a second. "And if we fire first ..."

"Correct, sir. At this range, only the first to fire a Harpoon would survive."

Kruger paced across the bridge and wiped his forehead. Lieutenant John Klifton was the sharpest of his young officers on board. He had command written all over him. He was right. "Very well, Lieutenant Klifton. Enter firing coordinates for two Harpoon anti-ship missiles. Target, ROCS *Kee Lung*. Arm missiles. Prepare to fire on my command."

"Captain!" the XO blurted out.

"XO, I've got four hundred lives I'm responsible for, including yours. Unless I hear from Washington, we are going to take out the *Kee Lung*."

"But, sir." This was the XO again.

"Lieutenant Klifton, do you understand your orders?"

"Aye, sir," the weapons officer spun back around and began punching buttons. "Entering firing coordinates now, Captain. Stand by to arm Harpoons."

Bridge
ROCS **Kee Lung**
South China Sea

twelve minutes past midnight

How long since last contact with the Americans?" Captain Won Lee asked.

"Five minutes, Captain."

Won Lee checked his watch.

His ship remained at Battle Stations, on highest alert, ready to destroy a warship that he had never believed would become a target of a Taiwanese missile. An attack against an American vessel was never contemplated during his time as a midshipman at the ROC Naval Academy at Kaohsiung City. In fact, many ROC Naval Academy grads wind up doing post-graduate work at the US Naval War College, with a focus on potential enemy navies: Russia, Vietnam, Cambodia, and Laos.

But now ...

The American silence was a warning.

Won Lee could wait no longer. He had his orders from Taipei. He had to protect his ship from a first strike by the *Vicksburg*. He had to act—now.

"Weapons officer. Reset countdown. Launch Harpoon missiles in T minus thirty seconds. On my mark. XO, announce missile launch."

"Aye, Captain," the XO said. "Now hear this. This is the executive officer. By order of the captain, stand by for missile launch in T minus thirty seconds ..." He looked at Won Lee.

"Mark it," Won Lee said.

"T minus twenty-nine, T minus twenty-eight ..."

Bridge
USS Vicksburg
South China Sea
100 miles east of Da Nang, Vietnam

twelve minutes after midnight

Captain, Harpoon missiles targeted and armed!" the weapons officer announced.

"Very well!" Kruger said. "XO, on the 1MC. Announce missile launch in ten seconds. On my mark!"

"Aye, Captain." The XO opened the 1MC. "Now hear this. This is the executive officer. Stand by for missile launch in ten seconds. This is not a drill!"

"On my mark," Kruger said, "launch Harpoons in nine ... eight ... seven ..."

"Captain! FLASH message from National Command Authority!" the communications officer said.

Kruger snatched the message from Morrison's hand.

FROM: National Command Authority
TO: Commanding Officer, USS *Vicksburg*
VIA: Commander, Seventh Fleet
          Commander, *Carl Vinson* Strike Group
          Commander, CRUSDESGRU 10

PRECEDENCE: FLASH
CLASSIFICATION: TOP SECRET
SUBJ: Negotiated Terms with ROC Navy for Seizing PRC Freighter
M/V *Shemnong*

"Belay missile launch!" Kruger yelled, having read only the subject line.

"Belaying missile launch! Aye, sir!" Lieutenant Klifton said. He began hitting switches to override the computerized launch command.

Kruger's heart pounded as he prayed that his override command wasn't too late.

"Missile launch belayed, sir! Countdown at T minus one second and holding, sir. Awaiting further instructions."

Kruger exhaled. If the captain of the *Kee Lung* knew that he had just come within one second of being blown to smithereens ...

"Very well, stand by, Lieutenant Klifton."

"Standing by, sir! Aye, sir!"

Kruger started at the top of the message.

FROM: National Command Authority
TO: Commanding Officer, USS *Vicksburg*
VIA: Commander, Seventh Fleet
       Commander, *Carl Vinson* Strike Group
       Commander, CRUSDESGRU 10
PRECEDENCE: FLASH
CLASSIFICATION: TOP SECRET
SUBJ: Negotiated Terms with ROC Navy for Seizing PRC Freighter
       M/V *Shemnong*

1. Be advised that the United States of America and the Republic of China (Taiwan) have negotiated terms for naval forces of each nation to transition custody of PRC freighter M/V *Shemnong*.

2. Under the terms negotiated, boarding party from USS *Vicksburg*, including navigational personnel and master-at-arms personnel, shall board *Shemnong* and take command from ROC (Taiwanese) forces currently controlling the vessel.

3. Armed Marines from the Republic of China (Taiwan) shall remain aboard *Shemnong* until further notice to carry out their mission of

guarding certain weapons and weapons systems which ROC forces have captured and which are stored on the deck of the ship.

4. ROC Marines shall not interfere with US Navy transport of *Shemnong* to Naval Station Guam. US Naval forces shall not interfere with ROC Marines' mission on board M/V *Shemnong*.

5. ROC Marines shall remain aboard M/V *Shemnong* until further notice, pending continued negotiations between the United States of America and the Republic of China (Taiwan) concerning disposition of weapons captured by the Republic of China (Taiwan) currently aboard M/V *Shemnong*.

6. Upon receipt of this FLASH message, the Commanding Officers of USS *Vicksburg* and ROCS *Kee Lung* shall begin to arrange for expedited immediate transfer of control of M/V *Shemnong* to USS *Vicksburg*.

7. Time is of the essence, and transfer of control of M/V *Shemnong* shall be complete no later than one hour after receipt of this directive.

8. Upon assumption of custody of M/V *Shemnong*, USS *Vicksburg* shall immediately begin escort of M/V *Shemnong* to Naval Station Guam, cruising at the freighter's maximum speed, until relieved by other US Navy warships.

9. The Commanding Officer, USS *Vicksburg*, shall proceed with execution of these orders immediately.

END OF MSG.

"Unbelievable." Kruger handed the message to the XO. "Reopen hailing frequency."

"Aye, sir. Hailing frequency open, Captain."

Kruger depressed the transmit button. "This is the captain of USS *Vicksburg*. We've just received orders from Washington, which are consistent with your proposal. We've got a deal, Captain!"

USS Emory S. Land
South China Sea

fifteen minutes past midnight

Amazing what a hot shower, a shampoo, a clean set of khakis, and discrete sprinkling of baby powder down the neck and back could do to restore energy from the depths of fatigue.

As her workday had come to a grinding end, fatigue had given way to adrenaline, which had given way to fatigue again, all of which had been blanketed with alternating emotions of anxiety, sorrow, anger, bitterness, and hope.

Of course, as they had taught her at the academy, no one expected a naval officer to be void of emotion. Facing situations involving life, death, and danger, as naval officers would be required to face, would invoke emotional responses in anyone.

But the only emotion that an officer should ever show in public was cool-handed professionalism, which had been a difficult challenge for her during this day.

Through it all, for the most part, she had kept a cool hand except for one stupid moment with the XO.

Now, at a quarter after midnight, she was about to face her final test of the day. And after that, she could retire to her stateroom and shelve her professionalism.

As she walked down the passageway, a hospital corpsman, a second-class petty officer, came to attention. "Good evening, ma'am," the corpsman said.

"At ease, Hospitalman Collins," Stephanie replied, still unaccustomed to guys old enough to be her big brother—and sometimes old enough to be her father—calling her ma'am.

"Yes, ma'am." The petty officer transitioned from full attention posture to parade rest.

"How's he doing?"

"Doc was by earlier, ma'am. He was dehydrated, but should be fine soon. Doc says we need to keep him confined for several days, keep the IVs going. He should be up and about in a few."

"Has he been responsive?"

"Oh, yes, ma'am. In fact he argued with the doc about ordering him to sick bay. He's as feisty as his reputation."

She tried suppressing a snicker. Another crazy emotional response in a day of crazy emotions. "You think it would be okay if I just step in for a moment to see him?"

"Yes, ma'am. He was awake just a minute ago."

"Hmm," she mused. "Check and see if he's still awake."

"Yes, ma'am." Collins opened the door to sick bay and went in.

Stephanie checked her watch. Almost twenty after midnight. Zero-five-hundred was coming soon. She needed to hit the rack. Otherwise she would be no good to the commander tomorrow.

Petty Officer Collins stepped back out into the passageway. "He's awake and he'd be happy to see you, ma'am." Collins pushed open the door.

"Thank you." Sick bay was a brightly lit utilitarian space with six medical cots, three on each side of a narrow passageway running down the middle. Five of the cots were unoccupied, their white sheets and pillows unwrinkled. The man in the sixth cot smiled at her. He had a sunburned tan and salt-and-pepper hair. An IV hung on each side of his cot, each feeding a plastic tube and needle sticking into an arm.

"Behold, the lady who saved my life," he said, his hazel eyes looking up at her.

"Good evening, sir. Or perhaps I should now say good morning." She felt a sudden nervousness. "I'm Ensign Stephanie Surber."

"Yes, I know who you are. I once met your father."

"I recognize you too, Commander. I saw you on television with President Williams when you got back from North Korea."

Gunner grinned. "I'm lucky I wasn't court-martialed for that."

She smiled. Even sunburned, blistered, and stuck with tubes in his arms, the man had a certain charm. "Sir, I hardly think that anyone who goes behind enemy lines like you did in North Korea and brings back American prisoners who had been there more than sixty years should be court-martialed."

He chuckled. "You'd have done the same thing. I got lucky."

"You're too modest, sir. Anyway, I know you need to rest. But wanted to stop by and check on you. How do you feel?"

"Ready to go back to work. Doc says he wants me to lay up here for three days. But that's ridiculous. We're in a war zone. This is no time for an intelligence officer to be holed up in the sick bay of a sub tender."

"Sorry you came all the way out here just to pick me up. I feel responsible that good men died."

Gunner nodded. "You're right. This was a stupid mission, but that's not your fault. That chopper was going down anyway and would have gone down even if we'd flown straight back to the *Carl Vinson*. You saved my life, and I owe you one. The XO told me they had called off the search, but you remained on post. If you hadn't stayed and kept looking, I might never have been found." He reached for her hand. "If I ever see your father again, I'm going to tell him exactly that."

"You're kind, sir." She felt embarrassed and let go of his hand. "Anyway, is there anything I can do for you?"

He rolled to his right. "Ohhh!" He grimaced.

"Careful, sir."

"Over there. On the deck to the right of the rack. Oh!"

"Please lay back, sir. Just let me know what you want."

"They ... aah ... maybe the doc was right ..."

"Here." She took a pillow off another cot and brought it over to him. "Maybe this will give you some more support." She slipped it under his head, giving him a second pillow to rest on.

"Thanks, Stephanie ... Uh ... over there ... they put together a sea-bag for me. It's right over there. It's got my uniform they washed and dried and some other stuff I had on me from the crash. Would you move it over here under my rack? I've got a feeling I'm going to need that stuff sooner rather than later."

"Certainly, Commander." She moved the seabag under his cot.

"Thanks, Stephanie."

"My pleasure, sir. It's been a long day, and it seems like we both could use some shuteye. I'll check on you tomorrow."

"I'd like that." He smiled.

"Sir." She nodded, then stepped back out into the passageway and started a quick walk back through the decks to her stateroom. There was something unique about this Lieutenant Commander McCormick. But what? She could not put her finger on it. Yes, he was one of the Navy's best-known officers, but that wasn't it.

Maybe the thing that made him unique at the moment was the fact that he was alive. And he was alive, in large part, because of her. As that realization hit her, flooding her with emotions she feared not even her professional naval officer's poker face could mask, she quickened the pace, for she was now fighting hard to keep from losing control.

Finally, she stepped into her stateroom, kicked off her shoes, killed the lamp, and, still in full uniform, crashed onto the rack. She buried her head in the pillow to muffle her sobbing. Then, catching her breath, she gave thanks to God for the miracle of life, that Gunner McCormick was alive, and that she had been used to save him.

CHAPTER 18

Harbin SH-5 maritime bomber
People's Liberation Naval Air Force
altitude 2,000 feet
South China Sea
250 miles east of Da Nang, Vietnam
100 miles south of Paracel Islands (Xisha Qundao)

5:14 a.m. local time

Were it not for the adrenaline flowing in Senior Lieutenant Jung Hai's veins, the roaring hum of the four turbojet engines hanging under the wings of the SH-5 could almost lull him to sleep.

But there would be no sleep this morning.

With his hands gripping the yoke in the cockpit and his plane flying due east over open water, all eyes were fixed on the ghastly green of the pre-dawn sea below in search of a missing freighter.

"Any sign of anything yet, sir?" His crew chief had stepped into the cockpit from the back of the plane.

"Not yet. Just miles of greenish open water. But my guess is one of three things."

"You think the Taiwanese Navy, Skipper?"

"Either that or a total engine failure or rogue wave. Take your pick, Chief."

"Sounds logical, sir."

"But if they sent her to the bottom, that makes our job harder. It's hard to spot isolated floating debris from this altitude. And if they took a civilian freighter out, you can bet they would fire their antiaircraft missiles at us too. Times like this? I wish I'd become a fighter pilot. At least we would stand a better chance if we get shot at." He looked out the left side of the plane, out to an empty expanse of water, water that was now coming to light with the imminent appearance of the rising sun. "The enemy's down there somewhere, Chief. I can feel it."

Bridge
USS **Vicksburg**
South China Sea
108 miles south of Paracel Islands (Xisha Qundao)
course 094 degrees

5:28 a.m. local time

Skipper!" the radar officer shouted. "We've got a bogie. Unidentified aircraft. Approaching from two-seven-zero. Range ten miles! Airspeed two-five-zero! Altitude two thousand. Appears to be a heavy, sir."

"Dang!" Captain Kruger grunted. "At that altitude and speed, likely a search plane."

"I agree, sir," the XO said.

"Lieutenant Morrison."

"Aye, Captain."

"Send an IFF signal."

"Aye, sir. Transmitting Identify-Friend-or-Foe signal now."

"Very well. XO! On the 1MC. Sound General Quarters."

"Aye, Captain." The XO flipped a switch on the control panel. Bells and alarms sounded all over the ship. "General Quarters! General Quarters! General Quarters! Unidentified aircraft approaching at two-seven-zero. General Quarters! General Quarters!"

"WEPS!"

"Ready for your orders, sir!"

"Ready antiaircraft weapons. Lock onto approaching aircraft. Be prepared to fire on my command."

"Aye, sir. Readying AA weapons, sir! Preparing to lock on. Preparing to fire on your command, sir!"

Harbin SH-5 maritime bomber
People's Liberation Naval Air Force
altitude 2,000 feet
South China Sea
258 miles east of Da Nang, Vietnam
104 miles south of Paracel Islands (Xisha Qundao)

5:30 a.m. local time

The huge orange sun had slipped halfway above the watery horizon, like half of a bright orange pumpkin in the path of the SH-5.

Squinting at the orange light of the sunrise streaming into the cockpit, Jung Hai slipped on a pair of aviator's glasses to block the glare.

"Lieutenant! Warship below! American *Ticonderoga*-class!" Ensign Wo Ju, the copilot, said.

"Where?"

"Three o'clock, Lieutenant! One thousand yards off."

Jung Hai looked out. Nothing but blue water lit by the orange morning sun.

"Lieutenant! There's a freighter! Cutting a parallel course with the cruiser!"

"Where?"

"There!" The copilot pointed out the right cockpit window.

This time, Jung Hai saw the sleek gray lines of the *Ticonderoga*-class cruiser sitting low in the water. Just behind her, only a hundred yards off her port side, was the long black-hulled freighter.

"How did I miss that?" Jung Hai said. "I think we've found our missing freighter. But if that is in fact the *Shemnong*, why would she be sailing alongside an American warship?"

"Perhaps it is Taiwanese, not American."

"Impossible," Jung Hai said. "Only the US Navy operates *Ticonderoga*-class cruisers."

"Shall we go in for a closer look?"

"Yes," Jung Hai said. "Ensign Wo Ju, begin a circular pattern. Fly a moving circumference of five hundred yards around the ships."

"Yes, sir," the copilot said.

Bridge
USS **Vicksburg**
South China Sea
108 miles south of Paracel Islands (Xisha Qundao)
course 094 degrees

5:32 a.m. local time

Skipper!" Lieutenant Morrison shouted. "No response to our IFF transmittal. Based on radar imagery, the plane appears to be a heavy bomber. Probably PRC, not Taiwanese. It's cutting a course toward us, sir."

"Very well, Lieutenant. Open a radio frequency to unidentified aircraft. Lieutenant Klifton, lock on fire-control radar at my command."

"Aye, sir," both Morrison and Klifton said.

"Captain. Hailing frequency open."

"Thank you, Lieutenant." Kruger picked up the microphone for shortwave transmissions. "To approaching aircraft. This is the captain of the American warship USS *Vicksburg*. State your identity and intentions. Over."

Five seconds passed. Then another five. "Lieutenant Klifton. Light 'em up with fire-control radar!"

"Aye, Captain. Activating fire-control radar."

"If this bird starts acting too funny, we're gonna take her out."

Harbin SH-5 maritime bomber
People's Liberation Naval Air Force
altitude 2,000 feet
South China Sea

5:33 a.m. local time

Lieutenant," Copilot Ensign Wo Ju said. "They've lit us up with fire-control radar!"

"They're gonna take us out," Jung Hai said. He had to think. "Ensign, open an emergency frequency to Beijing. Report our coordinates, and report that we think we've found the *Shemnong* and that she's headed zero-nine-four degrees under the escort of the American cruiser USS *Vicksburg*."

"Yes, Lieutenant. Opening emergency frequency now."

Bridge
USS **Vicksburg**
South China Sea
108 miles south of Paracel Islands (Xisha Qundao)
course 094 degrees

5:34 a.m. local time

Still no response, Captain," the XO, Commander Bennett, said. Kruger depressed the transmit button again. "Attention unidentified aircraft. This is the captain of the USS *Vicksburg*. State your intentions now. If you refuse to answer, and if you continue to approach, you will be shot down."

Squawking. "This is the commander of the Harbin SH-5 warplane of the People's Liberation Army-Navy. Be advised that our intentions are peaceful. We are on a search-and-rescue mission for a missing civilian freighter, the M/V *Shemnong*, which is flying under the flag of the People's Republic of China. We have no intentions of making any low-altitude flights over your ship, Captain. We have detected your weapons system's lock-on with fire-control radar. Please be advised that your fire-control radar will not be necessary. Over."

The radio went silent.

"What would you like me to do about the fire-control radar, sir?" the weapons officer asked.

Captain Kruger stood up and folded his arms. "Would you trust a Communist, Lieutenant?"

"Sir. No, sir."

"Well, I know it's been a long, hard night, but does your captain look suddenly stupid?"

"Sir. No, sir."

"Then stay locked onto that plane until I instruct otherwise, and be prepared to fire on my command."

Harbin SH-5 maritime bomber
People's Liberation Naval Air Force
altitude 1,000 feet
South China Sea

5:38 a.m. local time

Make a sweeping bank out to the left and in front of the ships. No maneuvers to make it appear that we are plotting direct overflight," the pilot, Lieutenant Jung Hai, said to his copilot, Ensign Wo Ju.

"Yes, Lieutenant."

"Then bring our altitude to five hundred feet. I want as close a look as possible without making anyone trigger-happy."

"Yes, sir."

Jung Hai had given Wo Ju control of the cockpit so that he could free his hands and study the two ships through his binoculars. And as his plane executed a wide loop out in front of the two ships, Jung Hai looked out from the left cockpit window. The ships were steaming straight at him, with the sleek gray cruiser about a hundred yards to the left of the wide black freighter.

"To the pilot of the PRC SH-5 maritime bomber."

Ju Hai dropped the binoculars to respond to the radio call. "This is the PRC. Go ahead, US warship."

"This is the captain of the USS *Vicksburg*. We note your intentions of avoiding low-altitude overflight of this ship. That statement is helpful and we expect you to abide by it. However, because we are operating in hostile waters involving armed conflict between the military forces of the People's Republic of China and Taiwan, our current rules of engagement do not permit us to disengage fire-control radar from either party. Just last night, we were forced to lock our missiles on a Taiwanese warship for the same reason. As long as you maintain your stated position of avoiding direct low overflight and demonstrate no hostile intentions, we would anticipate no action other than fire-control radar."

"Bank wide and left," Jung Hai said to the copilot. "No closer than five hundred yards."

"Yes, sir."

Lieutenant Jung Hai depressed the transmit button. "US Navy warship. This is PRC maritime bomber. Confirm again our intentions of no low-level flights over your ship. Please be advised of our intentions to maintain a circumference of no closer than five hundred yards around you. Over."

Mild static in Jung Hai's headset, and then, "PRC maritime bomber, this is US Navy warship. Confirm your intentions to maintain minimal five-hundred-yard distance. We will maintain fire-control radar lock until you break off. Over."

"US Navy warship. PRC maritime bomber. Roger that."

The plane banked farther to the left, this time out on the side next to the freighter. "Bring us in to about six hundred yards and hold there," Jung Hai said.

"Yes, Lieutenant," the copilot said.

Lieutenant Jung Hai picked up the digital camera with the telephoto lens and pointed it out to the left. Now he saw the black-hulled freighter churning low in the water and moving from right to left. *Snap.* From this distance, the lines of the ship looked identical to that of M/V *Shemnong*.

Snap . . . snap . . . snap . . .

"I think we have found our missing freighter, Ensign Wo."

"That would appear to be the case, Lieutenant."

The SH-5 continued its wide aerial sweep, rounding at an angle approaching five hundred yards off the stern of the two ships.

The vessels were cutting a course of zero-nine-four degrees, just south of due east. This course would take them toward the Philippines and north of Itu Aba.

The reflection of the rising sun swept across the top of the rolling swells. Jung Hai again brought the camera with its powerful telephoto lens to his eye. Propeller wash gushed behind the freighter, her engines pushing the ship through the water to the east, away from the plane.

Off to the right, more propeller wash churned behind the warship. He raised the camera, giving him a view of the cruiser's gray stern. In the center of the stern, painted in black letters, was the word VICKS-BURG.

Snap . . . snap . . .

Raising the camera again revealed the red, white, and blue of the flag of the United States of America flapping in the wind.

Snap ... snap ... snap ...

Tilting the camera to the left showed the gulf of water between the two ships and then the stern of the freighter. Flying off the stern and flapping just as vigorously as the American flag was a red flag with a large golden star within an arc of four smaller golden stars in one corner.

The "Five-Star Red Flag" of the People's Republic of China. *Snap ... snap ...*

He pointed the camera down below the flag, onto the black-painted stern of the ship. In the center of the stern, painted in white, was the ship's name:

SHEMNONG

Below the name of the ship, painted in white, was the name of her home port:

QINZHOU, CHINA

"We've found our freighter!" Lieutenant Jung Hai exclaimed, depressing the shutter.

Snap ... snap ... snap ... snap ...

"Ensign Wo, open a frequency to the freighter."

"Yes, Lieutenant." The copilot switched the front panel radio to the frequency used by civilian freighters on the high seas. "Frequency open, Lieutenant."

"To the M/V *Shemnong*. This is PRC warplane. Acknowledge. Over."

Bridge
USS Vicksburg
South China Sea
course 094 degrees

5:40 a.m. local time

Captain, the bomber is attempting radio contact with the *Shemnong*," Lieutenant Morrison said.

"I hear that, Lieutenant," Captain Kruger said. "Okay, not that I'm worried about the *Shemnong* talking back, since our people are over there driving her. But I'm not crazy about the idea of that plane signaling our coordinates to Beijing."

A second passed. "Electronic jamming, Captain?"

"Absolutely, Lieutenant. Do it now."

"Aye, sir." Morrison flipped a series of switches on the panel at his workstation.

Harbin SH-5 maritime bomber
People's Liberation Naval Air Force
altitude 1,000 feet
South China Sea

5:40 a.m. local time

Lieutenant! We've got jamming on our circuits! Powerful shortwave interference!"

"From the American warship," the pilot, Lieutenant Jung Hai, said.

"No question, sir." The copilot's voice sounded nervous.

"I do not like the behavior of the American cruiser, nor do I trust its captain. Something is not right."

"Agreed, sir," Ensign Wo Ju said. "They may have started jamming to prevent us from broadcasting a distress signal if they open fire on us, sir."

Jung Hai felt his stomach knotting. "Good point, Wo Ju. Break off from the American ship. Go to ten thousand feet and ten miles down-range. Let's get out from under the umbrella of this jamming signal and radio in our coordinates. I'm sure Beijing is going to want to follow up with this."

"Yes, sir, Lieutenant." The copilot pulled up on the stick and increased the throttle. The SH-5 climbed, pulling away from the freighter and cruiser, and headed back to the west.

Bridge
USS Vicksburg
South China Sea
course 094 degrees

5:40 a.m. local time

Captain, the bomber's breaking off. She's climbing ... looks like to ten thousand. Turning west."

"Very well," Kruger said. He exhaled in relief. "Well, the cat's out of the bag, gentlemen. We've been spotted. Stand down on fire-control radar. Disengage jamming."

"Aye, Captain."

"Enjoy the respite while you can, gentlemen," Kruger said. "They will be back. And in full force."

Presidential Palace
Zhongnanhai Compound
Beijing, People's Republic of China

7:55 a.m.

President Tang Qhichen looked in the mirror and finished adjusting his red tie. There. Excellent.

He checked his watch. 7:55 a.m. Five minutes until his morning military briefing with General Shang and Admiral Zou, and then, at 9:30 a.m., his appearance before the nation at Tiananmen Square to announce the greatest military conquest since the expulsion of the capitalist nationals.

He threw on the navy blue pinstripe jacket of his suit, tailored in Hong Kong.

A knock on the door.

Ah, the perks of presidential power! Tang thought. That knock would be from Captain Lo, the low-level, starry-eyed, and well-intentioned military attaché whose sole duties at the moment involved escorting the president from the presidential bedroom to the morning military briefing, or to the next meeting in the Presidential Palace at Zhongnanhai, or whatever else he, as president, ordered him to do.

He smiled, but then that smile was doused by the sobering thought that the *Shemnong* was missing, and with it ...

"Focus, Tang," he said to himself.

The president opened the door of the bedroom. In the ornate hallway, two junior officers snapped to attention, as did the young Army officer Captain Lo. "Good morning, Mister President," Captain Lo said. "General Shang and Admiral Zou are in the briefing room, sir. Also, Foreign Minister Liu is present this morning as well."

"Foreign Minister Liu?"

"Yes, Mister President. Apparently there were overnight developments that may require diplomatic coordination."

"What kind of diplomatic coordination?"

"I am uncertain, Mister President. I am passing along only bits and pieces that I overheard when I was in the briefing room earlier, preparing your oolong, which is awaiting you as well."

"Excellent." But why would Liu Tanchong, the foreign minister, attend the military briefing? "And after that, I would like you to accompany me to Tiananmen Square for my speech to the nation."

"It will be an honor, Mister President!" The young officer's eyes ignited with excitement.

"Very well," Tang said. "Let us proceed."

They walked down several long hallways on the second floor and then took the elevator to the first floor of the palace and walked into the military briefing room.

"Sit down, gentlemen," the president said as he sat down in the plush leather presidential swivel chair. "Let us get down to business. The first thing I want to know is about the *Shemnong*." He picked up the cup of hot, steaming oolong and took a sip.

"Mister President, we have found the *Shemnong*," General Shang said.

The president put down his tea. "Found it? Where?"

"One hundred fifty miles east of her previous location. She is steaming just south of due east. Toward the Philippines. And she seems to be under forced escort by an American warship."

Tang wondered if he had heard that right. "Did you say the *Shemnong* is being escorted by an American warship?"

"Admiral?" General Shang deferred to his naval colleague.

"*Shemnong* is under escort by the cruiser USS *Vicksburg*," Admiral Zou said. "When our long-range bomber flew close to investigate, it was warned not to fly a low-altitude overpass over the top of the American ship. The American captain even locked his fire-control radar onto our plane."

"He locked on?"

"Yes, Mister President. The American captain claimed that his rules of engagement required him to lock on because of the dangerous military situation in the South China Sea. When our pilot tried to radio the *Shemnong*, he was hit by powerful electronic jamming from the American warship."

Tang leaned back in the chair, then leaned forward and slammed his fist on the table. "Where did this take place?"

"About one hundred miles south of the Paracel Islands, sir. And well north of the Spratlys."

"Where is the *Shi Lang*? Is she in the area?"

"Yes, Mister President," the admiral said. The *Shi Lang* is about one hundred nautical miles to the south of this location, which is well within striking distance for her aircraft if needed."

"The Americans are siding with Taiwan." Tang slammed his fist on the conference table again, this time so hard that hot oolong tea sloshed out of his cup. He stood, gritted his teeth, removed the pinstripe jacket, and flung it across the other end of the long table. "The Americans are asserting themselves in the midst of Operation Lightning Bolt, gentlemen, which as you know, is my brainchild! And they are doing so for one reason only."

He stared into the faces of his senior military officers, who stared back but said nothing.

Tang said, "They are doing this because they do not wish for the People's Republic to become the world's dominant military superpower!"

He caught himself before he said more. He knew he had to calm down, show control in front of his subordinates. He looked at his foreign minister. "Well, Liu Tanchong, now I see why you are here. You are hoping to propose a diplomatic solution with the Americans?"

The slender, wrinkled diplomat nodded. "My services are available, should you so choose," the foreign minister said.

"Thank you, Liu Tanchong. We go back a long way, from my days in the diplomatic corps. And I have a feeling we shall have to exert both diplomatic and military pressure on the Americans." He turned to Admiral Zou.

"Admiral, can you show me where this occurred on a nautical chart, along with the current position of the *Shi Lang*?"

"Yes, Mister President." The admiral tapped several keys on a laptop computer. A map of the South China Sea appeared on a large computer screen at the end of the table.

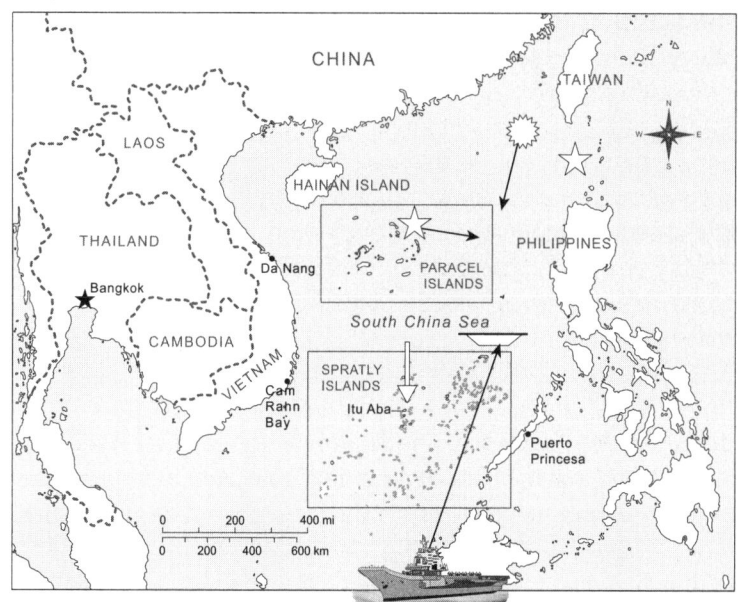

Ships' positions in South China Sea

"Very well, Mister President. The star in the center of the screen is where we spotted the *Vicksburg* and the *Shemnong*. The arrow from the star shows the course heading, toward the Philippines. The sunburst at the top of the screen represents the Taiwanese naval task force heading toward Itu Aba.

"At the tip of the white arrow is Itu Aba Island. Our carrier, the *Shi Lang*, as you can see, is operating to the northeast of Itu Aba and to the southeast of the current position of the *Shemnong* and *Vicksburg*." The admiral paused.

"And our carrier-based aircraft are now within striking distance of the *Shemnong*?" the president asked.

"Yes, sir. That is correct. We positioned the *Shi Lang* in this sector following our assault on Itu Aba so that she could be ready to ambush and destroy the Taiwanese naval task force sailing south. The remarkable flexibility from having our first aircraft carrier gives our fleet a tremendous array of military options."

"Are there other American ships in the area?"

The admiral nodded. "We believe that the *Vicksburg*'s sister ship, the *Shiloh*, is in the area, although we have not spotted her. *Shiloh* would be the only other ship with significant firepower in the sector that would concern us at the moment. However, the same plane that found the *Shemnong* also discovered the American sub tender *Emory S. Land* steaming in the vicinity last night at dusk. The *Emory Land* carries light weapons and is not much of a threat. But her presence suggests that American attack submarines are nearby, which is a concern for any of our surface ships, including the *Shi Lang*."

Tang thought for a moment. "Admiral, do we have coordinates on the *Emory Land*?"

"We have coordinates as of twelve hours ago, Mister President. Noting her speed and course, it would be simple to find her. The *Shi Lang*'s planes could track her down. The *Emory Land* is not that fast."

Tang stood, walked to the end of the table, and picked up his pin-striped jacket. He stopped to study the faces of his subordinates—the general, the admiral, the foreign minister, and a handful of junior officer aides, including Captain Lo—all looking to him for leadership.

He could not dismiss the historical significance of this day ... not only of the historical speech that he would make at Tiananmen but also the historical decision that he was about to make on dealing with Americans at the zenith of a power struggle between the world's old superpower and its new emerging one. This could become the defining moment of his presidency.

He put his left arm through the jacket, and then Captain Lo, seeing what he was doing, rushed forward to help him with the right.

"Thank you, Captain," he said. He lowered the tone of his voice as he began to deliver what he considered to be historic orders. "Foreign Minister Liu."

"Yes, Mister President."

"Open a channel to the Americans. Demand an explanation as to why one of their warships is escorting a freighter on the high seas that is flying the flag of the People's Republic."

"Yes, sir."

"Tell them that the PLA Navy will board that freighter and take control of it, and that we expect no interference from the US Navy or anyone else when we do."

"Yes, Mister President."

"General Shang. Admiral Zou."

"Yes, sir."

"Your instructions are twofold. First, I want the Navy to find that sub tender"—he held up a finger—"which ship is that?"

Admiral Zou said, "The USS *Emory Land*, sir."

"Yes, of course. Find the *Emory Land* and keep track of it. Do not let it out of our sight. And I want the PLA Navy to keep track of every American warship in the South China Sea."

"Yes, sir."

"In fact, I am issuing a new mandate from this day forward that the South China Sea shall become a naval mandate for the People's Republic. As our Navy continues to grow, we shall dominate that sea, just as the US has done with the Gulf of Mexico."

"An excellent idea, Mister President," General Shang said.

"Finally, Admiral Zou, you will dispatch a platoon of PRC Marines from the *Shi Lang* by attack helicopter to seize control of the *Shemnong*, and then we will steer her to Itu Aba."

Admiral Zou nodded. "Yes, sir, Mister President."

"Today is the dawn of a new era," he said. "Today, we shall witness the birth of the People's Republic as a military superpower! And no one, and no nation, shall stop us. If necessary, we shall bring all our diplomacy to bear, and all our weapons to bear, to bring this about." He shook his fist. "Any questions about my orders?"

"No, sir."

"Very well," he said. "Now, I have a speech to make. Captain Lo, is my motorcade ready?"

"Yes, sir," the young eager-beaver said.

"Very well. Alert my security detail. Let us head toward Tiananmen Square."

Presidential Palace
Zhongnanhai Compound
Beijing, People's Republic of China

8:15 a.m.

Surrounded by a cadre of bodyguards and with his personal aide, Captain Lo Chen, beside him, President Tang Qhichen stood inside the front foyer of the Presidential Palace.

"Ready, Mister President?" Lo asked.

"More than ready," Tang said.

"Follow me, sir."

Lo pushed open the front doors, letting in a stream of morning sunlight and warm air. A small sea of humanity, including military personnel and state-appointed journalists from Xinhua, the official Chinese news agency, had gathered to record the beginning of this historic day.

"Attent-chun!" The booming voice of the honor guard commander was followed by the sharp clicking of leather boots echoing off the marbled entryway to the Presidential Palace.

"Preezent arms!"

Pop ... pop ... slap ... slap ... echoed as the twirling rifles were slapped in place into the hands of the twelve-man honor guard of the People's Liberation Army.

Now at strict attention, the honor guard formed two human walls of soldiers facing each other on each side of the red carpet that led from the front door of the mansion down to the circular driveway, where a long black limousine, a Chinese-designed Hong Qi HQE with the five-star red flag of the People's Republic mounted above each headlight, waited at the other end.

In front and in back of the HQE, two other limousines were parked with their engines running. In front of the first limousine was a squad car from the Beijing police department with its blue roof lights twirling. In front of the squad car, at the vanguard of the motorcade, three police officers in blue uniforms waited on motorcycles. At the end of the motorcade, behind the last limousine, nine more officers on motorcycles were positioned in three groups of three.

Two helicopters of the People's Liberation Naval Air Force hovered above.

Tang was not concerned about security. Beijing was not as dangerous as Western capitals. But the mob assault on the Rolls-Royce of Prince Charles and Lady Camilla in the streets of London in December of 2010 had gotten Beijing's security personnel on edge permanently.

But security was the last thing on Tang's mind. Not even his speech in Tiananmen Square concerned him. He needed to make a telephone call.

"Are you ready, Mister President?" Captain Lo asked.

"Let's go," Tang said.

The president stepped forward and, at the request of the public information minister, who had informed him that his departure from the Presidential Palace would be a cut-in live national broadcast, strolled slowly down the red carpet, through a tunnel of flashing strobe lights and Xinhua news cameras.

He stopped at the limousine's right rear door and waited as a PLA major in service dress green uniform opened the door for him. He turned and gave a final wave into the sea of flashing lights and television cameras, then got into the limousine.

"Good morning, Mister President," the driver said.

"Good morning, Sergeant."

Captain Lo got in the front seat and turned to look back at Tang.

"Are you ready to roll, Mister President?"

"Yes. Let's move."

"Yes, sir."

The three lead motorcycles moved out first, followed by the police cruiser, then the first armored limousine, and then the presidential limousine.

"Captain Lo."

"Yes, Mister President."

"Put through a secure call to my sister."

"Yes, sir."

The Zhongnanhai Compound had within it two large placid lakes, known as the "Central Sea" and "Southern Sea." These lakes were part of a series of irrigation projects carried out during the construction of the adjacent Forbidden City.

From the lakes, Tang had learned to draw strength. Although official Communist Party doctrine embraced atheism, the party tolerated the somewhat peaceful and nonthreatening movements of Buddhism and Taoism.

All places of worship, whether a temple or a church, had to be approved under a tightly controlled state licensing procedure. All religions were superficially tolerated in one form or another, with the exception of evangelical Christianity. The Christians worshiped in so-called "underground churches," which the state considered an official threat and found reasons to punish them.

Tang agreed with the American Ted Turner and the great Karl Marx, who had said, "Religion is the opium of the people." Turner was just as negative: "Christianity is a religion for losers." Tang had found his personal tranquility in the placid lakes of Zhongnanhai. In recent days he had more than once walked to the lakes, trailed in the distance by a handful of armed security guards. He would walk down to the water's edge, alone, where he would gaze and meditate, drawing strength from whatever force was there. Standing by the lakes, he would at times reflect on his rapid rise from a boy in an orphanage in Harbin, adopted by a Communist Party couple that did not have any children, to the presidency of China. It was almost enough to make him believe in God, if there was a God.

Now, as he rode along the road headed to the southern gate, Tang looked over at Nanhal, the Southern Sea. A flock of graceful swans floated near the shoreline, their images replicated on the water as clear as if they were resting on a mirror.

Tang's innermost core was twisted with anxiety. He wanted to call out for help. But who could help? A higher being? Tang wondered how he could be wrestling with such a feeling. He was the highest of all beings.

His thoughts were broken by the sound of Captain Lo's voice on the secure cell phone in the front seat of the limousine. "Tang Lenlin? This is Captain Lo, the president's military attaché ... Yes, ma'am, the president wishes to speak with you." Lo handed the cell phone to Tang. "Your sister, Mister President."

"Tang Lenlin. How is my wonderful sister?"

"I am watching on television. Are you at Tiananmen yet?" she asked with excitement in her voice.

"Not yet. My motorcade is en route now. We are about to leave Zhongnanhai."

Tang held the phone from his ear as his sister continued babbling with the excitement of a school girl. "Tang Lenlin, listen to me! There is something I must tell you. It is about Fu Cheuk-Yan."

"What about Fu Cheuk-Yan?"

"His ship is missing."

"What do you mean?"

"We lost communication with it yesterday. It stopped responding to our radio calls. One of our planes discovered it this morning at sunrise in the South China Sea headed east toward the Philippines. It was under the escort of an American warship."

"What?" The schoolgirl excitement was gone. "Why? What has happened? An American ship?"

"I don't know yet. Perhaps the Americans are aiding their puppets in Taiwan, as they have since the Great Revolution."

"Tang Qhichen, please do not let them harm Cheuk-Yan!"

"I have no reason to believe that anything has happened to Fu Cheuk-Yan ... but yes ... I am concerned about it."

"Tang Qhichen! Please—"

"Sister, I must go. I will call you when I know something."

"Qhichen! Please."

"Good-bye, my sister. I love you."

Tang gave the phone back to Captain Lo as the motorcade approached the exit at the southern gate, known as the Xinhua Gate, or "Gate of New China." The motorcade slowed again, and Tang looked up at the inscription engraved over the gate in the handwriting of Mao Zedong. "The immortal Mao Zedong," he murmured. The inscription could only be read by those inside Zhongnanhai as they were about to leave. Tang read the words: "Serve the People."

The limousine rolled to a stop, just under the Xinhua Gate.

Out on West Chang'an Avenue, the broad boulevard bordering Zhongnanhai's southern perimeter, an explosion of strobe lights resembled a street-level lightning storm.

White-gloved traffic policemen standing on the street outside the compound tweeted through silver whistles, hand-signaling vehicles in the motorcade to move forward.

The presidential limousine rolled onto West Chang'an Avenue through another explosion of strobe lights.

Dozens of television cameras lined the exit route. And beyond the cameras, throngs pushed up to roped police lines on both sides of the boulevard, holding signs proclaiming:

VICTORY ...

and LONG LIVE THE PRC ...

and TANG—THE PEOPLE'S PRESIDENT! ...

and THANK YOU TANG QHICHEN! ...

and LONG LIVE TANG THE IMMORTAL!

Standing in front of the crowds and the police lines, stretching as far down the street as the eye could see, were children clothed in white suits and dresses, tossing rose petals in front of the presidential limousine as it passed.

With goose bumps on his arms, Tang settled back and let the aura of the historic moment sweep away all concerns about the *Shemnong.*

CHAPTER 19

President Douglas Surber sat alone in the Oval Office on one of the two black leather sofas positioned in front of his large mahogany desk. He was munching on a small bag of trail mix, a concoction of almonds, cashews, peanuts, and raisins that he had developed an addiction to after his daughter Stephanie had given him five bags of the stuff from the Barnes & Noble café last Christmas.

On two flat-screen televisions mounted on the wall were live images streaming from a sun-baked morning in Tiananmen Square in Beijing, halfway around the world. In fifteen minutes, the president of China was to address his country concerning China's actions in the South China Sea.

The broadcast was being narrated by the venerable Fox News anchor Tom Miller, whose image, complete with wire-rim glasses, was superimposed in the lower left corner of the screen. Across the bottom of the screen were the words: "FOX NEWS SPECIAL REPORT—WAR IN THE SOUTH CHINA SEA."

The scene reminded Surber of a Russian Mayday parade. Red flags waving. Streaming red banners. Kids tossing flowers at a dictator's limousine. Old men and women with tears streaming down their faces.

Alternating cutaway shots flashed from the motorcade to Tiananmen

Square, where thousands were jammed in a sea of humanity before a vacant stage and podium. Positioned prominently on the stage was the red Chinese flag. The Beijing Orchestra was playing the "Overture to a New China," which Fox News anchor Miller explained had been composed for Tang's installation as president.

The scene switched back to the motorcade just as the speakerphone on the desk buzzed. "Mister President," Gayle Staff, the longtime presidential secretary, said.

"Yes, Gayle."

"Sir, Secretary Lopez and Secretary Mauney are here, along with Admiral Jones and Miss Hewitt."

"Is the vice president here?"

"Not yet, sir."

"What about the chief of staff?"

"No, sir."

"Okay, send the others in."

"Yes, sir."

Surber stood as his four national security advisers walked into the Oval Office. "Have a seat. Still a big hullabaloo going on over there, but he's not started his speech yet." He motioned at the flat-screens. "They've gone all out with the propaganda."

Cynthia Hewitt sat on the sofa beside him. Secretary of State Robert Mauney and Secretary of Defense Lopez took the sofa across from them. Admiral Jones sat in one of the four wingback chairs.

"Mister President," Secretary Mauney said, a troubled look on his face. He was holding a single sheet of paper.

"What is it, Bobby?"

"Sir, the Chinese know we have the *Shemnong*. We just received this communiqué from the PRC embassy." He laid a sheet of paper on the coffee table between the two sofas.

Surber picked up the communiqué.

**EMBASSY OF THE PEOPLE'S REPUBLIC OF CHINA
IN THE UNITED STATES OF AMERICA**
2201 Wisconsin Avenue NW
Suite 110
Washington, DC 20007
Communiqué

FROM: Liu Tanchong, Foreign Minister of the People's Republic of China
Huang Yi, Ambassador of the People's Republic of China to the
United States of America
TO: Hon. Douglas Surber, President of the United States of America
Hon. Robert Mauney, Secretary of State of the United States of
America
RE: Status of M/V *Shemnong*

Dear Mister President and Mister Secretary,
Fifteen hours prior to the issuance of this communiqué, the M/V
Shemnong, a freighter navigating the high seas and last located in the
South China Sea, 100 miles off the coast of North Vietnam, vanished
from all radio contact with PRC authorities.
At 0530 hours local time, the M/V *Shemnong* was spotted by PRC
military aircraft 150 nautical miles off course and under escort by
American warship USS *Vicksburg*.
Efforts to establish radio communication with the M/V *Shemnong*
by PRC aircraft failed. Such efforts were hampered by powerful elec-
tronic jamming from USS *Vicksburg*.
As a PRC military plane approached the M/V *Shemnong* and USS
Vicksburg, USS *Vicksburg* locked onto PRC aircraft with fire-control
radar and warned PRC aircraft against overflight, although USS *Vicksburg* was operating in international waters and PRC aircraft was flying
in international airspace.
Be advised that the People's Republic of China considers the USS
Vicksburg action in locking fire-control radar on PRC aircraft, thereby
threatening PRC military aircraft against their legal right to fly in international airspace, to be belligerent, and the People's Republic of China
does hereby launch this PROTEST in response to the belligerent actions
of USS *Vicksburg*.
Furthermore, the People's Republic of China does demand a full
explanation from the United States as to why one of its warships, the
USS *Vicksburg*, is engaged in armed escort of the M/V *Shemnong*.
The United States is warned against any attempt to prevent military forces of the People's Republic of China from boarding or taking
control of the M/V *Shemnong*, a vessel flying under the protective flag of
the People's Republic of China with full international navigation rights
on the high seas.

Failure to comply could result in military and economic retaliation, including a full reevaluation of China's policy of holding United States Treasury debt, both short-term and long-term.
We await your expedited reply.

> Respectfully,
> Liu Tanchong, Foreign Minister
> of the People's Republic of China
> Huang Yi, Ambassador of the
> People's Republic of China to
> the United States of America

Surber laid the communiqué down. "Okay. This changes things. You all had recommended that we get the freighter out of the South China Sea before we confronted them on the cargo. But this forces our hand sooner than I'd hoped, which, in my opinion, makes the situation much more dangerous for our ships in the South China Sea." He looked at each one, then looked down at the message again. "You're all getting paid the big bucks to advise the president. Your thoughts on this?"

Admiral Jones said, "Sir, my first reaction in reading between the lines is that they are going to try some sort of military operation to retake the *Shemnong*."

"Agreed," Secretary Lopez said.

Cynthia Hewitt nodded in agreement. "Sounds like economic blackmail with that last quip about dumping debt."

"I anticipated that," the secretary of defense said. "But the more pressing question, Mister President, is whether you're going to order the *Vicksburg* to intervene if the Chinese try to remove the *Shemnong* from our custody."

Surber looked surprised. "Those are the orders I've already given, aren't they?"

"Yes, Mister President," Secretary Lopez said. "I just wanted to make sure that your orders still stand."

"Why would they not?" Surber asked. "We're talking about several thousand babies murdered in China, likely with the knowledge of the Chinese government. If we, as a nation, no longer stand for the rights of the most defenseless among us, then we have lost our soul as a nation. That will *not* happen on my watch."

Surber glanced at the two flat-screen televisions, showing images of the Chinese president's police-escorted limousine making a left turn into Tiananmen Square, easing through the throngs of cheering citizens.

"Mister President?"

"Yes, Secretary Mauney."

"I don't think we can sit on this thing any longer, sir."

"Agreed, Mister Secretary. What are your thoughts?"

"A great man once said, 'The truth shall set you free.'"

"Yes, I know," Surber said. "I talk to the man you're quoting every day."

"I thought you did, sir." Mauney smiled. "I recommend that first, we inform them that we took Chinese sailors off that ship who had been shot in the Taiwanese Navy's attack. We tell them where the sailors are being treated. We also let them know that we have the bodies of sailors killed by the Taiwanese, including the captain, and that the wounded sailors and the bodies are available for repatriation. We tell them we did not attack the *Shemnong*. Then we urge them to stand down their military confrontation with Taiwan and let us mediate this dispute."

"Agreed." Surber nodded.

"We need to be frank and tell them that we're aware that the ship contains the bodies of thousands of murdered babies. Tell them that we've taken custody of the ship, that we intend to make an issue of this with the UN and, therefore, we aren't going to relinquish custody at this time. We will repel any attempt to wrest control of the ship from us. We consider this issue separate from their dispute with Taiwan over the Spratlys."

"I agree with that," the president said.

"With respect," Admiral Jones said, "that last part is going to be hard to pull off."

"What do you mean?" Surber asked.

"I'm no diplomat, sir, but I doubt the Chinese will separate their disagreement on the Spratlys with Taiwan from our dispute over the *Shemnong* because that freighter is carrying not only those dead babies but also weapons for the Communist forces holding Itu Aba in the Spratlys."

"The national anthem of the People's Republic of China," Tom

Miller said on the television, prompting Lopez and Mauney to turn so they could look at the flat-screens.

Tang stood on the elevated platform that had been erected in front of the Great Hall of the People, distinctive with great columns reaching up to a high portico. He was wearing a navy blue pinstripe suit and was holding his hand over his heart. Alongside him were uniformed members of the Chinese military, who were flashing stern salutes in front of flapping red Chinese flags. The Beijing Orchestra was playing the Chinese national anthem.

"You're watching a breaking Fox News Special Report, 'War in the South China Sea,'" Miller said. "These are scenes from Tiananmen Square in Beijing. Chinese President Tang Qhichen is standing on the eastern façade of the Great Hall of the People with his senior military advisers. The Great Hall, with over one point eight million square feet, was completed in 1959 and was one of the Ten Great Buildings erected to commemorate the tenth anniversary of the People's Republic of China. The National People's Congress meets here, but it is a powerless rubber-stamp legislature appointed by the Communist Party. It was also here, in the State Banquet Hall, that in 1972 President Richard Nixon held historic meetings with Communist Party leader Mao Zedong and Premiere Zhou Enlai that led to signing of the Shanghai Communiqué and the subsequent normalization of relations between the US and China. President Nixon was the first president in US history to visit China."

Another buzz from the speakerphone. "Mister President?"

"Yes, Gayle."

"The vice president and Mister Brubaker are here, sir."

"Send them in."

Chief of Staff Arnie Brubaker and Vice President Rock Morgan walked into the Oval Office.

"Welcome, gentlemen," Surber said. "Please, have a seat."

Surber turned to Admiral Jones. "I don't disagree with you, Admiral, but I still agree with Secretary Mauney that we need to tell the Chinese that we view these positions as separate, whether they do or not."

"For the record, I agree with that also, Mister President," Admiral Jones said. "I was just pointing out the difficulties in selling that position to the Chinese."

"So noted," Surber said. He looked at the secretary of state. "Any other recommendations?"

"Yes, sir. I don't think we can delay much longer in alerting the media. I know we had hoped to try to quell the Spratly dispute before making this public, but in light of this communiqué, our hand has been played."

Surber nodded. "Agreed, Bobby." He looked at Brubaker. "Arnie, arrange for me to address the nation at eight in the morning. Have my speechwriters prepare a statement for me to read from the Oval Office."

"Yes, Mister President."

A swell of sustained applause, growing louder by the second, poured out from the flat-screens.

Surber looked up. His Chinese counterpart, Tang Qhichen, looking modern, dapper, and fit in his trademark navy blue pinstripe suit and red tie, was behind the podium making hand motions to quell the long, sustained applause.

"Why can't I get that kind of reaction when I make a speech?" Surber quipped.

"Because we don't have a propaganda ministry to import cheering crowds at gunpoint, sir," Cynthia Hewitt said.

"I guarantee I can get you that kind of reaction, Mister President," Arnie Brubaker said.

"Oh, yeah? When and where?"

"Three years from now," Brubaker said. He grinned. "Republican National Convention."

"You're assuming a lot, aren't you, Arnie?" Surber said.

Tang began speaking, and the translation quickly followed in English. "My fellow citizens. Today marks the dawn of a new era for the People's Republic of China. For less than forty-eight hours ago, military forces from the People's Liberation Army-Navy attacked enemy forces from the renegade territory of Taiwan that had been occupying the island of Itu Aba, which is sovereign PRC territory in the South China Sea.

"Today, thanks to the heroic and valiant efforts of our naval forces, we have destroyed the enemy in the South China Sea, and we have restored sovereign Chinese territory to Chinese control!"

Frenzied cheering erupted. Cameras cut away to show celebrating

Chinese pumping their fists and waving placards with images of the Chinese president.

"Please! Please!" Tang attempted to silence the crowd. "There will be time for celebration. But first"—he waited for the crowd to quiet down—"first there is more I must tell you." The crowd was hanging on Tang's every word.

"While we have destroyed the enemy at Itu Aba in the South China Sea, our mission is not complete! For from this day forward, we shall *continue* to restore sovereign Chinese territory to Chinese control. And no person, and no president, and no nation shall stand in our way!"

More cheering. Pandemonium. The crowd was chanting something.

"What are they saying?" Cynthia Hewitt asked.

"Listen," Surber said.

"Tang Qhichen! Tang Qhichen!"

Over and over again, they were shouting the name of the Chinese president.

"This is scary," Secretary Mauney mumbled, as all eyes in the Oval Office focused on the two flat-screens.

"Please! Please!" Tang again motioned the crowd into silence. "Today we have come to pay honor to our comrades and heroes of our victory. Today we present comrade Senior Lieutenant Wang Ju with the coveted Hero's Medal for his valiant and daring efforts as the lead helicopter pilot in the mission known as Operation Lightning Bolt, the mission that destroyed the enemy at Itu Aba Island!" More cheering. More applause. The camera cut to a young Chinese naval aviator in full uniform, standing at attention on the platform behind Tang. In Chinese, running across the bottom of the screen, were presumably his name and rank. The officer's face sported a jutting chin and a steel-locked jaw. He did not respond to the thunderous applause.

"And for his second in command"—cheering, applause—"to Lieutenant Zhang Li, the coleader of this mission, the Meritorious Service Medal!" More cheering. More applause. A cutaway shot to another young Chinese naval officer who, unlike the first one, was having difficulty suppressing a smile.

"These are the heroes of a new age of world dominance! For this shall mark the first of many victories. For the twenty-first century shall be the Chinese century! The century of the Raging Dragon! For I declare to you this day, the Raging Dragon has begun to roar!"

Pandemonium erupted. "Tang Qhichen! Tang Qhichen!"

Tang shook his fist over the repeated chants of his name. "The Raging Dragon has begun to breathe fire!"

"This guy is crazy and power hungry," Admiral Jones said.

"I agree, Admiral," the secretary of defense said.

"He's looking for a fight," the national security adviser said.

"Arnie, cut this crap off," Surber said. "I can't take any more of it."

"Yes, sir, Mister President." Brubaker reached down and picked up a remote control. The screens went blank.

"Lady and gentlemen," Surber said, "we have a powder keg on our hands. We can't afford any missteps." He nodded at Secretary Mauney. "Bobby, prepare a response to that communiqué, laying out the positions we just discussed."

"Yes, sir."

"Arnie, get the speechwriters ready for my address to the nation in the morning. You know my criteria. Brief. Factual. To the point."

"Done, Mister President."

"Admiral Jones, Secretary Lopez, reinforce the message to US naval forces in the area. We defend ourselves against attacks from anyone. And remind the skipper of the *Vicksburg* that he is to defend against the Chinese or anyone else who tries to wrest control of that freighter from us."

"Yes, sir, Mister President."

"All right, we've got a ton of work to do. Let's get to it."

CHAPTER 20

Z-10 attack helicopter (codename Tiger Three)
People's Liberation Naval Air Force
altitude 2,000 feet
South China Sea
course 094 degrees

10:00 a.m. local time

L ieutenant Pang Wenjun, his right hand gripping the controls of his
Z-10 attack helicopter, looked out to his left and then to his right.

Two MI-17-V7 troop transport choppers carrying armed Marines
from the People's Liberation Army-Navy flew alongside, thundering
east through the bright morning sky over the South China Sea.

The three helicopters and the platoon of Marines were attached to
the Chinese aircraft carrier *Shi Lang*, which was operating at an undis-
closed location in the area. All had taken part in the attack against Itu
Aba Island, where Pang Wenjun had been third in command, behind
Senior Lieutenant Wang Ju and Lieutenant Zhang Li.

Neither Wang Ju nor Zhang Li had been available to fly this morning's mission because they were, at this very moment, about to receive
the Hero's Medal and the Meritorious Service Medal, the highest and
second-highest awards given by the Chinese military, for their work in
leading Operation Lightning Bolt.

President Tang himself would present the medals, and Pang Wenjun knew the entire crew and air wing of the *Shi Lang* was abuzz with
excitement. Rumors were flying all over the ship that the entire squad-

ron would receive a unit decoration when the ship returned to port, and that Tang would make that presentation too.

But the prospect of a unit citation did not excite Pang Wenjun. For when the entire unit received a citation, no one individual stood out. He needed an individual citation to stay abreast of his rival from the Dalian Naval Academy, Zhang Li.

Wang Ju was of no concern, for Wang Ju was four years his superior. But Zhang Li was a different story. The two had been pitted against each other since they stepped on the campus at Dalian, where they were ranked one and two in their class. At Dalian, Pang had bested Zhang Li by a half point.

After graduation, it seemed as if the People's Liberation Navy wanted to let them fight it out to see which one would ascend to the rank of admiral. And now, Pang thought, they had even been placed in the same helicopter squadron for the prestigious assignment aboard the *Shi Lang*, the new and glorious flagship of the PRC fleet.

Although at the academy, it was *he*, Pang Wenjun, who held the slight advantage, since graduation, the slight edge had gone to Zhang Li, as evidenced by his luck in being chosen to receive China's second-highest military honor, the Meritorious Service Medal.

Such was Zhang Li's luck. For if he, Pang Wenjun, had been selected for second in command of Operation Lightning Bolt, it would be he, Pang Wenjun, who would be having the president hang the MSM around his neck. And truth is that Pang Wenjun had come within a cat's whisker of being selected as the number two, as each had flown as Wang Ju's number two on previous missions.

Pang had hoped for one more training mission prior to Lightning Bolt, which would have put him in the rotation for second in command and would have put him in Beijing today.

But now, an opportunity perhaps even more glorious than Lightning Bolt! He smiled.

This time, it was *he*, Pang Wenjun, who was at the right place at the right time. As the senior helicopter pilot on board the *Shi Lang* at the very moment that Wang Ju and Zhang Li were off in Beijing, he had been tapped by the admiral as the flight leader for Operation Extract, the codename for the military operation to rescue the M/V *Shemnong*.

As he cut through clear skies with little headwind at five hundred feet above the water, Pang considered the impact of this mission. He replayed in his mind the admiral's briefing to the pilots and Marines just thirty minutes before takeoff.

"Gentlemen, I cannot stress enough the importance of Operation Extract to the war effort. As you prepare to launch, you will be facing known and unknown dangers. We do not know why the *Shemnong* is under escort by an American warship. We do not know why she is off course. We do not know why she doesn't respond to our attempts to raise her by radio. And we do not know how the Americans will react when our Marines attempt to board.

"But here is what we do know. First, we know that *Shemnong* is carrying weapons and ammunition that our forces on Itu Aba need to repel an invasion by the enemy. This we know . . . and this is important." The admiral had paused and nearly choked up. "Our great president, Tang Qhichen, as you know, was abandoned by his mother as a boy. His mother left him, along with his sister and his half brother, in their flat to die. But they were found by government workers and were taken to a state orphanage in Harbin." The admiral choked up again. "What I have to tell you, gentlemen, is that the captain of the *Shemnong*, Captain Fu Cheuk-Yan, is the half brother of our president!"

Those last words had been ringing in his mind since takeoff. "The captain of the *Shemnong*, Captain Fu Cheuk-Yan, is the half brother of our president!"

Lieutenant Pang Wenjun looked out at the great blue vista of water and sky. Nothing on the horizon. Nothing in the water. And other than the two choppers on his flanks, nothing in the sky.

"Ensign Xu," he said, "what is our current position?"

"Range to target . . . one hundred miles," the copilot replied.

Bridge
USS **Vicksburg**
South China Sea

10:05 a.m. local time

Navigator, what's our time to course correction?" Captain Leonard Kruger asked.

"Course correction to one-three-five-zero degrees is scheduled in three minutes, Skipper."

"Very well," Kruger said. "Steady as she goes, gentlemen."

"Steady as she goes. Aye, Captain."

Kruger checked his watch. Thirty minutes ago, he had ordered a course correction, hoping that changing course to the southeast might throw off any more PRC search planes. The new course would take the ships straight through the middle of the Philippine Islands and provide additional cover from Chinese search efforts. Once they cleared the Philippines, they would set a course due east for Guam.

At this point, Kruger was second-guessing himself in one respect. He almost wished he'd ordered the course change a couple of hours earlier. He did not do that because of his hunch that the Chinese aircraft carrier might be somewhere to the south, and he wanted to steam as far to the east as possible before changing course to avoid cutting into a sector where her planes might be making routine patrols.

Of course, that gamble cut both ways. Part of the problem with having maintained his current course is that it would become very simple for the Chinese to plot his speed, plot his course based on his last bearing, and, after extrapolating his current position, send their aircraft right straight toward the *Vicksburg*.

The decision on when to execute the course change had been one of those "catch-22" situations where the right answer would not be known until after the outcome. But one of his professors at the Naval War College, a retired surface warfare admiral, to be exact, had taught him, "If you're damned if you do and damned if you don't, then pick a dam."

Kruger had picked his dam. Now he wished in his gut that he had picked the other one.

"Two minutes to navigational correction, sir."

"Very well," Kruger said. "Keep me apprised at thirty-second intervals."

"Aye, sir."

Kruger stepped over to the left side of the bridge, picked up his binoculars, and gazed out at the *Shemnong*. The freighter was steaming parallel to the *Vicksburg*, a couple of hundred yards off to port. *Shemnong* was being run by a handful of young officers from his own ship, including the assistant navigator and assistant helmsman and several experienced chief petty officers.

Kruger was grateful for calm seas and good weather, especially since the windshield on the bridge had been shot out during the Taiwanese attack and the bridge had suffered damage. Still, the "second team," as they started calling themselves since this mission began, had displayed excellent seamanship in keeping the freighter on track. Even more remarkable, the "second team" had gotten some unexpected cooperation from the *Shemnong*'s first mate, an English-speaking Chinese mariner who had survived the attack.

On deck, armed Taiwanese Marines could be seen standing guard, their uniforms whipping in the wind.

"Ninety seconds to navigational correction, sir."

"Very well," Kruger said. "Steady as she goes."

"Captain! Three bogies! Inbound from the southwest!" the radar officer yelled.

Kruger dropped his binoculars and wheeled around.

"How far out?"

"Eighty-five miles and closing, sir."

"Airspeed?"

"One-five-zero knots."

"Analysis, Lieutenant!"

"Probably choppers, sir!"

"Okay, let's get both our Seahawks in the air to go have a look! XO, sound General Quarters! All hands to Battle Stations!"

"Aye, Skipper! Sounding General Quarters! All hands to Battle Stations!"

Control Room
USS **Boise**
South China Sea
100 nautical miles north of Itu Aba Island
depth 200 feet

10:07 a.m. local time

The tight-knit submarine service of the United States Navy had an informal motto: There are two types of vessels—submarines and targets. Submariners believed this creed with every fiber of their being. Indeed, a surface ship's greatest nightmare was to have an enemy submarine appear out of nowhere, fire a torpedo, and then disappear into the depths, vanishing from sight and sound.

This creed was embraced by Sonarman Chief Petty Officer John C. King, who earned the nickname Bloodhound in his days as a young sailor because they said he had the best ears in the Navy. As Bach and Beethoven were masters of the classics, the Bloodhound was a maestro at something the Navy called "acoustic intelligence," otherwise known as "ACINT."

To a layperson sitting in the cramped quarters of a submarine, two hundred feet under the surface, listening to a SONAR headset, the sound of a distant fading, bubbling hum might sound like a strange gurgling aquarium.

But to the Bloodhound, such whines and gurgles were a powerful, yet melodic, symphony orchestra.

Only God could grant a hearing ability like that of the Bloodhound, which is why the Navy authorized two special reenlistment bonuses large enough to pay off the remaining $40,000 that he and Ivy owed on their stucco ranch home in Lemon Grove, California, leaving Ivy with enough cash to go shopping at Mission Valley and Seaport Village.

At the moment, Bloodhound was sitting at the SONAR console in the control room of the fast-attack submarine USS *Boise*, submerged two hundred feet in the South China Sea.

His ears covered by his SONAR headset, which resembled the headset of an expensive SONY stereo system, Bloodhound studied the greenish electronic monitor connected to the acoustics computer.

There. He heard something.

Or did he?

No. There. Again!

It was gone, whatever it was.

Now, only the washing sound of the deep. Then the long, melodic moan of a humpback whale in the area. Then staccato-like clicking. Make that two humpbacks frolicking.

The Bloodhound leaned back and closed his eyes. Even in the swirl of the sub's control room, the effectiveness of his job performance depended on his ability to relax and get lost in the sounds of the sea—faint blended sounds, possibly mechanical sounds, somewhere in the distance.

The whale song diminished into oblivion, yielding to the sounds of the watery underworld.

More bubbling and sloshing.

There! Again! A faint hum, but still ... gone again. More wash sound.

There! Again! Another hum. Now ... a whine!

Not another whale! Definitely mechanical!

"Skipper!"

"Whatcha got, Chief?" Captain Graham Hardison, commanding officer of the *Boise*, walked toward the SONAR station.

"I got something, sir! Somewhere to the northeast. Faint, but definitely there."

"You got a make on it?"

"Not yet, sir. Preparing to run a narrowband analysis."

"Let's get on with it," the CO said.

"Aye, Skipper."

"Helmsman, set course for zero-four-five degrees. Let's get a little closer to whatever it is the Bloodhound's sniffing."

"Aye, sir."

Z-10 attack helicopter (codename Tiger Three)
People's Liberation Naval Air Force
altitude 1,000 feet
South China Sea
course 045 degrees

10:10 a.m. local time

Lieutenant Pang," the copilot said. "Two bogies approaching from projected target area! Range fifty miles. Speed one-five-zero, sir."

Pang Wenjun glanced at the radar screen.

"Probably choppers. Seahawks from the *Vicksburg*."

"Agreed, sir."

"Arm 30-millimeter cannon and air-to-air missiles."

"Yes, sir."

Pang picked up the radio and punched in the frequency for the mother ship.

"*Shi Lang*! Tiger Three!"

No response.

Perhaps the Americans were jamming again. Pang felt a bit of panic.

"Weapons armed, sir," the copilot said. "Should I lock on?"

"Not yet, Ensign." A lock-on might be unnecessarily provocative. He depressed the transmit button again.

"*Shi Lang* Control! Tiger Three!"

No response from the carrier.

Maybe he should lock on now. Yes, he had the confidence to lock on. He had been given the authority if in his discretion he decided this was the best thing to do to defend the interests of the People's Republic.

Should he fire the TY-90 air-to-air missiles at the targets before they could fire at him? Should he act now?

Operation Lightning Bolt was a conflict with Taiwanese forces, not the Americans. But Operation Extract, the mission he was now flying, presented a whole different set of military calculations. This he had to keep in mind in his on-the-spot decision-making. Attacking the Taiwanese military was one thing. Attacking the American military was quite another.

But the Americans were jamming his communications with the carrier. That was hostile. And now they had launched their Seahawks to challenge him before the PRC choppers could even make it to the *Shemnong*.

The Americans, he knew, wouldn't roll over like a dead dog and let PRC Marines rope down to the *Shemnong* from the transport choppers. So getting the Marines aboard was up to him.

"Tiger Three, *Shi Lang* Control. Go ahead. Over."

"Finally!" Pang Wenjun said. He pressed the transmit button.

"*Shi Lang* Control. Tiger Three. We have two bogies on radar. Based on speed and direction, bogies are believed to be attack helicopters from USS *Vicksburg*, but no visual confirmation. Over."

"Tiger Three, *Shi Lang* Control. Stand by."

Static over the headset.

"Lieutenant!" the copilot said. "We're receiving an IFF transmission from unidentified aircraft!"

Pang hit the transmit button to the carrier again.

"*Shi Lang* Control. Tiger Three. Receiving IFF transmissions from unidentified aircraft! IFF frequency is American! Repeat. IFF frequency is American! Tiger Three requesting fighter backup. Over!"

Static. "*Shi Lang* Control. Tiger Three. Acknowledge. Scrambling fighter support now! Stand by!"

US Navy SH-60R Seahawk helicopter (codename Seahawk One)
en route between USS* Vicksburg *and unidentified aircraft
over the South China Sea

Vicksburg Control. Seahawk One." Lieutenant Phil Getman, a native of Sitka, Alaska, and pilot of the lead American chopper, kept his eyes forward as he called in. "Inbound bogies are not responding to IFF transmissions. Bogeys are fifty miles downrange. Anticipate visual identification in eight minutes. We're descending to seventeen hundred feet for identification attempt."

"Seahawk One. *Vicksburg* Control. Roger that. Descend to seventeen hundred feet for identification attempt."

"*Vicksburg* Control. Seahawk One. Roger that. Beginning descent."

Z-10 attack helicopter (codename Tiger Three)
People's Liberation Naval Air Force
altitude 1,000 feet
South China Sea

Lieutenant Pang," the copilot said. "Look! Up there!"

Pang Wenjun tipped his head back and looked up through the cockpit windshield.

Two Seahawks were overhead. US Navy SH-60R Seahawks. They executed a hard splitting maneuver, one going off to the left, the other to the right, and he lost sight of them as they moved behind his Z-10.

What should he do? Instinct told him to engage the Americans now. But the choppers had split off in two directions. If he engaged one, he would be at the mercy of the other. Should he wait for more air cover?

"*Shi Lang* Control. Tiger Three. Be advised. We have visual confirmation of two US Navy SH-60R Seahawks. Repeat. Aircraft are US Navy attack helicopters. Distance to targets, approximately five hundred yards. Awaiting instructions. Over."

"Tiger Three. *Shi Lang* Control. Have the Americans locked on or engaged in any hostile action?"

"*Shi Lang* Control. Tiger Three. That's a negative. Anticipate hostilities could be imminent."

Pang looked up to his left. One of the Seahawks had made a wide loop and was now flying alongside one of the troop helicopters. To the right, the other Seahawk had performed an identical maneuver, and the two American attack choppers were now flanking the three Chinese choppers, an air armada of five all flying toward the freighter and the American warship.

Pang now questioned the wisdom of his superiors. Did they think the Americans were simply going to let them fly in, lower the Marines, and take the *Shemnong* back? Perhaps the mission plan had been miscalculated.

"Tiger Three. *Shi Lang* Control."

"Tiger Three. Go ahead, *Shi Lang*," Pang said.

"Tiger Three. Scrambling two J-11 fighters. ETA less than fifteen minutes. Proceed with mission as ordered. Take no provocative actions unless the Americans show signs of belligerency."

"*Shi Lang* Control. Tiger Three. Roger that. Proceeding with mission as ordered. Awaiting J-11 fighter jet air cover."

US Navy SH-60R Seahawk helicopter (codename Seahawk One)
en route between USS Vicksburg *and unidentified aircraft*
over the South China Sea

V*icksburg* Control. Seahawk One," Lieutenant Getman said.

"Seahawk One. *Vicksburg*. Go ahead."

"Sir, we have visual on three PRC helos. We count one Z-10 attack helicopter and two MI-17 troop transport choppers. We're flanking all three choppers now, and they're flying a course straight for you."

Three seconds passed. "Roger that, Lieutenant. Which one's the attack bird?"

"*Vicksburg* Control. Seahawk One. The Z-10 is flying in the middle, with the troop transports flanking it. We're flanking the outside troop transport choppers."

"Seahawk One. Roger that," Captain Kruger said. "We note primary target is in the middle of the formation. I'd advise you and Seahawk Two to spread your distance a bit. If we have to take a shot at the Z-10, I'd hate to have you flying through that fallout."

"Seahawk One. Roger that."

"Seahawk Two. Roger that, Skipper. Moving out another thousand yards."

Z-10 attack helicopter (codename Tiger Three)
People's Liberation Naval Air Force
altitude 1,000 feet
South China Sea

Ensign Xu," Pang Wenjun said to his copilot, "what is our ETA to target?"

"ETA to target is five minutes, sir."

"Fabulous," Pang mumbled. "We will arrive a full ten minutes before fighter cover arrives."

"Sir! The American helicopters are moving away. Perhaps they have become disinterested."

Pang looked out to both the left and the right. Both American choppers were executing "peel away" maneuvers, opening up the distance between them and the MI-17s. "I doubt they are disinterested, Ensign." He checked his heads-up display. Four minutes to target. "I do not have a good feeling about this."

CHAPTER 21

Bridge
USS **Vicksburg**
South China Sea

Preparing to execute course change, sir," the navigator for the USS *Vicksburg* announced.

"Belay that order," Captain Kruger said. "Hold off course change pending further instructions. Maintain current course, Lieutenant."

"Aye, sir," the navigator said.

"No point in having those choppers radio our course change back to the carrier."

"Good point, sir," the XO said.

"Lieutenant Morrison."

"Aye, Captain."

"Open a frequency to those Chinese helicopters."

"Yes, sir." The communications officer punched several buttons at his work station. "Opening frequency now, Captain. Transmit at your pleasure, sir."

Kruger depressed the transmit button. "To the helicopters from the People's Republic of China approaching from the west. This is the captain of the USS *Vicksburg*. You are instructed to turn away from any flight path that brings you in the vicinity of the USS *Vicksburg*. Your failure to do so will be considered a hostile act. You have one minute to comply. Over." He lowered the microphone. "Mark the time for ninety seconds, Mr. Morrison."

"Aye, Captain."

Kruger glanced at the sweeping second hand on the clock mounted on the bulkhead. Then it hit him: He might be the man who would fire the first shot in World War III. All those years of twentieth-century naval doctrine that focused on the former Soviet Union as the military opponent, and now there was a new Raging Dragon on the block.

"WEPS. Prepare to lock on and take out those choppers on my order. Target the Z-10 in the middle first."

"Aye, Captain," the weapons officer said.

With that order, a war fever swept the bridge.

"But Captain." The XO's voice displayed a tinge of fear.

"Yes, XO."

"Sir, are we at least going to issue a warning before we fire on them?" Commander Bennett asked.

"I just issued them a warning, XO."

"But, sir, you told them to turn back. You did not tell them that we were going to fire on them."

"XO …" Kruger paused. He was fuming that his own XO would question him in front of his men. He had to maintain his cool. "XO, I just warned them that if they continue to proceed in this direction for more than one more minute, that would be considered a hostile act. Now the good news for them is that I'm giving them a little bit more than a minute. But if I tell them specifically that I'm getting ready to fire on them, then they just might decide to fire on us first. And that Z-10 helicopter is carrying some rockets under its belly that could make life unpleasant if one of 'em exploded in the middle of this bridge. I have lives that I'm responsible for, and I'm not going to make the same mistake that Captain Brindle did on the *Stark* by waiting too long. My decision is not up for a vote." He paused. "Any other questions, XO?"

"No, sir. My apologies, sir."

"Time, Mister Morrison."

"Forty-five seconds, sir."

"WEPS, prepare to lock and fire."

"Aye, Captain."

Z-10 attack helicopter (codename Tiger Three)
People's Liberation Naval Air Force
altitude 1,000 feet
South China Sea

L ieutenant Pang Wenjun flipped the switch arming the three TL-10 "Sky Dragon" anti-ship missiles hanging under his chopper. The Sky Dragons were equipped with airborne radar based on the "launch and forget" guidance system.

If the missiles did not sink the *Vicksburg*, they would inflict tons of damage and kill a lot of American sailors.

Pang rested his thumb on the "fire" button. He was now in a dangerous game of chicken with the American captain as to who would launch missiles first — or if either would launch any.

"Lieutenant! Freighter and American vessel are in sight!"

Pang looked up. Two ships, steaming side by side, were way out in front of the choppers, cutting a path to the east through the glistening sun-sparkled water. The freighter was off to the left, and American cruiser was to her right, cutting a wake about half as wide as the wake of the freighter. At that moment, Pang again remembered that the brother of the president of the People's Republic was aboard the freighter.

CHAPTER 22

Weapons officer! Fire missiles!"
"Firing missiles! Aye, sir!"

Captain Kruger watched his weapons officer depress the fire-control button. *Vicksburg*'s SPG-62 fire-control radar locked onto the targets, and he heard a clear *whoosh* sound. Two RIM-66 medium-range surface-to-air missiles, each fifteen feet in length, carrying blast fragmentation warheads, streaked into the sky.

This would be a point-blank shot.

Z-10 attack helicopter (codename Tiger Three)
People's Liberation Naval Air Force
altitude 1,000 feet
South China Sea

Beep ... *beep* ... *beep* ... *beep* ...
"Missiles in the air!" the copilot screamed.

Pang looked down in time to see the flashing red missile-warning light.

"Evasive maneuvers!" he screamed and yanked the control stick to the left.

The white-hot blast and explosion would be the last things he ever heard, saw, and felt.

CHAPTER 23

Bridge
USS **Vicksburg**
South China Sea

Bull's-eye, Captain!" the weapons officer said. "Both missiles on target! We got the Z-10 and one of the troop transport choppers, sir!"

Aft television monitors recording the attack showed the remnants of two white fireballs streaking down into the sea.

"Third chopper is turning around, Captain," the radar officer said.

"Can't say as I blame 'em," Kruger said. "WEPS! Initiate electronic jamming! I don't want this reported yet."

"Initiating jamming. Aye, Captain," the weapons officer said.

"Skipper! Two more bogies inbound! Based on speed and range, looks like fighters, sir!"

"Initiate IFF! Get more missiles on the rack! Prepare to fire on my order!"

"Aye, aye, Captain!"

MI-17 troop transport helicopter (codename Hedgehog Two)
People's Liberation Naval Air Force
altitude 1,000 feet
South China Sea

Senior Lieutenant Liao Guo, at the controls of the MI-17 troop transport chopper carrying fifteen armed PRC Marines, pulled hard left on the control stick, turning the helicopter back toward the southwest, away from the American warship.

He punched the emergency transmit button that would activate a frequency wired to the home ship.

"*Shi Lang*! Hedgehog Two! We're under attack! Two choppers down! Repeat. We're under attack!"

Static. Nothing.

Liao switched to air-to-air frequencies for the approaching J-11 fighter jets.

"Leopard Cat! Hedgehog Two! We're under attack! Two choppers down! Tiger Three and Hedgehog One have been shot down! PRC helicopters are under attack! Repeat! We are under attack!"

No response. Only high-frequency interference. The Americans, he realized, were about to put a surface-to-air missile up his rear end! His only prayer was to fly low, just over the surface of the water, get as far away as he could, and hope that the built-in radar on the American missile could not find him.

"Hang on!" he called out to the Marines in the cargo bay, and then it hit him that he had lost his best friend in the world, Lieutenant Pang Wenjun. But he could not think of that now. He was running on instinct—survival instinct—for himself, for his copilot, and for the fifteen Marines in the back of his chopper.

Liao pushed hard on the control stick. The chopper responded, racing down toward the water.

J-11 fighter jet (codename Leopard Cat Leader)
People's Liberation Naval Air Force
altitude 2,000 feet
course 091 degrees
South China Sea

Senior Lieutenant Qui Jian, strapped into the cockpit of the J-11 fighter streaking across the skies above the South China Sea to the east at supersonic speed, glanced at the jet's radar screen. Something seemed amiss. Could it be a computer malfunction? A software problem? A blown circuit?

He flipped on the radio circuit, opening a broadcast channel to the other J-11 jet on this mission, flying one hundred yards off his right wing.

"Leopard Cat Two. Leopard Cat Leader. I've lost our three choppers off my radar screen. Do you still have them on yours?"

"Leopard Cat Leader. Leopard Cat Two. That's a negative, sir. Two of them disappeared off my screen thirty seconds ago. The third appeared to be executing a turn away from the target destination, and then it disappeared off the screen."

"Leopard Cat Two," Qui said, "have you received any radio transmissions from any of the choppers?"

Static. "That is a negative, sir."

"Very well," Qui said. Something was wrong. This wasn't a radar problem.

"Leopard Cat Leader! I'm receiving an IFF from the American warship."

Qui looked at his heads-up display. "I'm getting one too. Stand by while I alert the *Shi Lang*!"

He switched the frequency to contact the aircraft carrier.

"*Shi Lang* Control. Leopard Cat Leader."

"Leopard Cat Leader! *Shi Lang*. Go ahead."

"*Shi Lang*. Be advised that all three helicopters have disappeared from our radar. Choppers were on final approach to target. Also, we've just received an IFF ping from the American warship. I believe this is a hostile situation. Please advise."

Bridge
USS Vicksburg
South China Sea

Skipper!" the weapons officer said. "Third chopper is descending. Looks like they're trying to drop off our radar. Do you want me to take 'em out or let 'em go?"

The bridge was now a swirl of activity. In the midst of it was Captain Leonard Kruger, who knew how imperative it is for the captain of a warship to make the correct decisions, without error, and to do so in a manner that advances his mission, protects the lives of his crew, and protects the interests of the United States of America.

The decision regarding the third PRC helicopter was one such predicament.

"Any change in course for that third helicopter?"

"No, sir, Captain. Still headed two-seven-zero degrees. Due west. Away from our position, sir."

Kruger's mind raced for the correct decision. On the one hand, the chopper had turned away, as it was ordered to do. And, as a troop transport chopper, it posed no direct military threat to the *Vicksburg*.

On the other hand, that chopper would soon be out of the range of the *Vicksburg*'s ability to jam it. Once that happened, it would alert the carrier that the *Vicksburg* has just splashed two of the three choppers and would provide the exact location of the attack.

Kruger was confident in his ability to defend his ship against a plane or two—although even that was a very dangerous proposition. But if the captain of the *Shi Lang* launched his whole air wing against the *Vicksburg*, it would be ball game over.

If he took the third chopper out, that would raise the level of international tensions already certain to be red hot between the US and China. Plus, he might need every surface-to-air missile in his arsenal if *Shi Lang* sent more planes his way, and he knew in his gut that the two jets headed his way right now were Chinese.

"Let the chopper go, Lieutenant. I've got a feeling we're gonna need every spare missile before this is over."

"Aye, aye, Captain," the weapons officer said.

"Captain!" the radar officer said. "IFF verifies those jets are not ours and don't belong to any of our allies."

"Same bearing and speed, Lieutenant?"

"Aye, sir. Still bearing straight down on our position."

"Sir," the XO said, "should we open a channel to warn them to turn back like we did with the helicopters?"

"Let me think about that, XO."

Kruger had maybe ten seconds to make a decision. The notion of warning an opponent before firing had always been a part of a chivalrous American military tradition. Truman had warning leaflets dropped over Japan before the *Enola Gay* bombed Hiroshima. And before that, the Potsdam Declaration had promised Japan prompt and utter destruction if it did not surrender.

But since 1945, in an age of smart bombs and guided missiles, war strategy had been modified by technological necessity. The disastrous lessons of the USS *Stark*, alongside the lessons of HMS *Ardent*, HMS *Antelope*, and HMS *Sheffield*, had been beaten into the heads of every American captain. In an age of missile warfare on the high seas, sometimes, to survive, one had to fire first and ask questions later. But firing first, especially against the world's fastest-rising military power, could mean war.

"No time for warnings," Kruger announced. "Lock onto those jets and fire two missiles now! One for each plane. Then fire two more. Let me know when we've locked onto targets."

"Aye, Captain. Locking on now," the weapons officer said.

"But Captain," the XO said.

"We can't afford to miss, XO. We've got to take out those jets before they take us out."

"I've got a lock, Captain! Missiles ready. Fire at your command, sir!"

"Fire missiles!"

"Firing missiles! Aye, Captain!"

Vicksburg rocked, and they all heard a clear *whoosh*.

Two more RIM-66 medium-range surface-to-air missiles streaked out into the sky, racing at supersonic speeds to the west.

"Fire missiles three and four!"

"Firing missiles! Aye, sir!"

Another *whoosh*.

Kruger folded his arms and watched the closed-circuit television images of four surface-to-air missiles streaking off to the west in the morning sky. He could only wait and pray that those missiles hit their targets before the targets could launch any missiles of their own.

J-11 fighter jet (codename Leopard Cat Leader)
People's Liberation Naval Air Force
altitude 1,600 feet
course 091 degrees
South China Sea

Beep … beep … beep … beep …
"Missile in the air! Make that two missiles!"

Senior Lieutenant Qui Jian looked down at the flashing red missile-alarm light, just as Lieutenant Long Xiang, the pilot of the other J-11, screamed over the air-to-air frequency: "Make that three missiles inbound! Now four!"

"Long Xiang!" Qui said. "Fire and break!"

"Roger that! Fire and break!"

Qui Jian depressed the fire button on his control stick. The J-11 jumped in the air as it fired a PJ-9 air-to-surface missile. Qui Jian pulled the plane hard to the left to pull it out of the direct path of the American missiles.

"Break to the sun!" he barked at Long Xiang, then pulled his yoke back hard, causing the plane to climb. G-forces pushed him down hard into the seat.

The idea here was to pull the plane into a high bank toward the sun's rays, then fire chaff and electronic countermeasures to try to throw the inbound missile off target.

The J-11 climbed, pushing Qui Jian farther down into the cockpit seat.

"Leopard Cat Two. Leopard Cat Leader. Report."

"I got one missile off, sir. Now climbing in evasive maneuver."

The plane shook in its furious climb. Qui Jian found the missile alarm system and flipped on the audible warning system.

"Thirty seconds to missile impact …" the computerized voice said.

"Twenty-seven seconds to missile impact. Twenty-five seconds to missile impact."

Bridge
USS Vicksburg
South China Sea

S kipper, we got two inbound missiles! Looks like they got a couple of shots off before starting evasive maneuvers, sir."

"Time to impact, Lieutenant," Kruger said.

"Forty seconds on the first missile, Captain. Forty-five seconds on the second."

"Launch interceptors."

"Launch interceptors. Aye, Captain."

With two sudden bursts of fire, the aft section of the *Vicksburg* lit up.

Billowing white smoke rose above the fire bursts, and then two SM-3 antiballistic missiles shot straight up and away from the aft deck.

The interceptor missiles climbed into the sky and then curved out from a vertical trajectory into a horizontal one, now flying parallel to the contour of the sea. Behind them streaks of white smoke marked their race to the west.

Internal guidance systems within the nose cones of the interceptors interfaced with computerized data being fed by radar from the ship. This data then steered the interceptors in their flight on a collision course with the inbound enemy missiles.

In theory, this was the way things were supposed to work.

Vicksburg had drilled for this moment a hundred times or more. And now, the real moment had come.

The life-or-death fate of his crew depended on the accuracy of those interceptors. The intercept had worked about 50 percent of the time in drills, which of course meant that the other 50 percent of the time ...

"Projected time to first missile intercept."

"Twenty-five seconds to projected intercept, Captain."

With the sky above the South China Sea streaked with missiles crisscrossing in east-west and west-east trajectories, all Lennie Kruger could do was hold his breath — and pray.

J-11 fighter jet (codename Leopard Cat Leader)
People's Liberation Naval Air Force
South China Sea
altitude 1,600 feet
course 091 degrees

Beep ... beep ... beep ...
"Fifteen seconds to missile impact," the computerized voice continued its countdown.

"Thirteen seconds to missile impact."

Still climbing toward the sun, Lieutenant Qui Jian calculated, in what could be the last few seconds of his life, that he did not know if the missile was heat-seeking or radar controlled. To have any chance of survival, he had to fire decoys designed to fool both. He would have to fire decoys in sequential one-second intervals, then break hard, and if he survived that, execute the same maneuver with the second missile.

"Nine seconds to missile impact ... Eight seconds ..."

Qui put his thumb on the decoy flare. Fire ... *Poof*. Burning flares flew into the air behind the jet.

Half a second later, he depressed the foil chaff release ... Fire ... *Poof*. Electronic chaff shot out to fool the missile's radar.

"Four seconds to missile impact ...

"Three seconds to missile impact."

"Break! Break!" he yelled as he jerked the control stick hard to the left, peeling off like the top of a banana peel being yanked away from the banana.

The centrifugal forces pushed him hard into the seat in the abrupt turn, and the plane shook hard from great g-forces in the sudden turn.

"One seconds to missile impact," the countdown voice said.

Qui Jian closed his eyes ... and then ... the missile alarm went silent.

Out to his right, a fireball lit the blue sky. The first missile had missed!

He exhaled a sigh of relief ...

"Leopard Cat Leader! I cannot shake this missile!"

"Leopard Cat Two! Release chaff! Release flares!"

"Leopard Cat Leader! Flares and chaff malfunction. I can't shake it! Leopard Cat Leader! Help me!"

"Leopard Cat Two! Bail out! Bail out!"

"AAAAAaahhhhhh." Static.

Then, out to the left of his cockpit, Qui Jian saw a huge fireball in the sky. He looked down and saw parts of the obliterated J-11 dropping toward the sea. A wing. The burning tail section.

Beep … beep … beep … beep …

The missile warning alarm. The first American missile had missed, but the second had locked onto him with a vengeance.

"Thirty seconds to missile impact …

"Twenty-nine seconds …"

Bridge
USS Vicksburg
South China Sea

Fifteen seconds to intercept, sir."

Capain Kruger stood, arms folded, his eyes locked on the closed-circuit monitor in the upper-left corner of the bridge. The images on the screen, enhanced by a powerful telephoto lens installed in the closed-circuit cameras on the ship's aft superstructure, showed the SM-3 antiballistic interceptors that had been launched only seconds earlier from *Vicksburg*. The two missiles that looked about the size of a pencil tip streaking through the sky were leaving long white contrails in their wake.

"Eight seconds to intercept, Captain."

Kruger wiped sweat from his forehead.

"Come on, baby!" the XO mumbled.

"Five seconds to intercept, Skipper …

"Four …

"Three …

"Two …

"One …"

The explosion on the right side of the screen set off cheering pandemonium on the bridge.

"Pipe down!" Kruger ordered. "Pipe down!"

The cheering morphed to silence.

"Where's the second missile?" Kruger demanded.

"Sir, second missile is still inbound," the radar officer said. "The interceptor missed it."

"God help us," Kruger said. "Time to impact."

"T minus thirty seconds, sir."

"Weapons officer!"

"Aye, Captain."

"Prepare to fire the Phalanx."

"Aye, Captain. Preparing Phalanx."

"XO. On the 1MC. Alert the crew. Brace for missile impact."

"Aye, sir!" The XO picked up the microphone. "Now hear this! This is the XO! Brace for missile impact!"

J-11 fighter jet (codename Leopard Cat Leader)
People's Liberation Naval Air Force
South China Sea
altitude 3,000 feet

Twelve seconds to missile impact." The computerized voice continued its ominous countdown.

Senior Lieutenant Qui Jian felt a sense of *déjà vu.*

Once again, as he had done earlier when he had evaded the first American missile, he put his J-11 fighter jet into a steep climb and hit the afterburners. He could do this. Just evade one more missile.

"Ten seconds to missile impact."

As he placed his thumb on the electronic chaff-release button, his mind raced to thoughts of his seven-year-old twin sons, Quing and Xu. Before he deployed, they had spent their last day together in the small skiff he had bought them, fishing for mullet in the Yangtze River. The boys, with twinkling excitement in their dark eyes, had caught two mullet apiece. And as the last fish was flopping in the bottom of the boat, Xu made him promise to take them fishing again the day he returned.

"Dear God, if you're there, let me take my boys fishing again!"

"Nine seconds to missile impact.

"Eight seconds."

Qui pressed the electronic jamming button.

Then he hit the decoy flare button.

A buzzing, then a warning light appeared on the control panel.

"Flare Malfunction."

"Five seconds to missile impact."

Beep ... beep ... beep ... beep ...

"Dear God! No! Not this plane too!"

"Three seconds ..."

Qui Jian pulled hard on the stick, jerking the jet into a hard left peeling maneuver.

"Two seconds to missile impact."

"One second ..."

"Please! No!"

The blinding flash blocked his vision, then searing, iron-like heat covered his chest, his back, neck, throat, stomach, arms, face, feet ...

His vision returned, but only long enough to provide a glimpse of the flames burning the flesh of his lap, knees, arms, and hands.

Bridge
USS Vicksburg
South China Sea

Some compared it to a fat white trash can with a short gun barrel protruding from the middle of it. Others compared it to the famous *Star Wars* droid R2-D2.

For the crew of the *Vicksburg*, their lives now depended not just on the human skills of the ship's weapons officer, Lieutenant Drue Jordan of San Diego, but also on the accuracy of the weapon called the Phalanx.

It was a "close-in" weapon of last resort, designed to be used at the last second against inbound missiles—like the one threatening *Vicksburg*—when defensive interceptor missiles failed to block a missile fired by an enemy. Consisting of a radar-guided 20mm Gatling gun mounted on a swiveling base, the Phalanx was designed to fire a virtual wall of bullets, at the rate of 4,500 rounds per minute, at an inbound enemy missile in hopes of destroying the missile before the missile struck and destroyed the ship.

Sometimes the Phalanx worked.

Sometimes it did not.

If it failed, deaths were certain. Perhaps even total destruction of the ship.

Part of the problem, indeed part of the challenge to the weapons system was the great speed at which an opposing missile came flying at a ship.

A slower-moving cruise missile provided an easier target for the Phalanx.

But faster anti-ship rockets fired from screeching jet aircraft came flying in faster than the speed of sound, providing a difficult target even for the sophisticated Phalanx.

The monitor showed a split screen, with the fat R2-D2–like Phalanx on the left and the inbound missile, its image now picked up on a powerful telephoto lens, on the right.

For Captain Kruger, a feeling of helplessness saturated his body. The defense of his ship was now out of his hands. It was all up to a computerized machine gun, the Phalanx, and divine intervention.

"Ten seconds to impact, Captain."

The moving streak on the right side of the screen grew larger. At the tip of the streaking contrail, the image of the missile was now visible.

On the left of the split screen, the Phalanx sat like a silent watchman, its short single Gatling-gun barrel pointing skyward, awaiting its challenge from a deadly opponent. This was an OK Corral–style showdown on the high seas between two machines that would decide the lives of everyone on board the ship. And they could do nothing but watch.

"Prepare to fire, WEPS."

"Aye, sir."

"Missile approaching from starboard, Captain!"

The XO and three other officers rushed to the starboard windows, as if responding to a sick impulse to witness their own death.

Captain Kruger stood at the center of the bridge, continuing his stare at the flat-screen, watching the missile rocketing closer by the second.

"Seven seconds to impact, sir!"

Kruger gripped hard against the captain's chair and gritted his teeth. "Six seconds to missile impact!

"Five seconds, sir!"

"Fire Phalanx!"

"Firing Phalanx! Aye!" The weapons officer depressed the fire-control button.

The Phalanx responded, shaking like an angry jackhammer on the left side of the screen. Like a fire hose streaming pressurized water from the ground up to a burning window on the third floor, it spewed a black stream of incendiary bullets into the sky.

On the right of the screen, the missile continued to rocket toward the ship.

"I see it!" someone yelled.

"Here it comes!"

"Two seconds!"

"One second!"

The explosion lit the bridge and shook the ship. Clanging alarms rang out.

The screen went blank.

Chaos on the bridge.

Kruger picked up the 1MC. "All departments! This is the captain. I want damage reports ASAP!" He looked at Commander Bennett. "XO. Take a crew starboard and aft, assess the situation, and report back."

"Aye, Captain," the XO said. "Chief. Petty Officer Johnson. Come with me."

Just as the XO was stepping off the bridge, "Bridge Engineering."

"Go ahead, CHENG," he replied to the ship's engineering officer.

"Sir, all power systems appear to be up. Not sure about electrical, sir. We lost closed-circuit TV from the explosion. I'm sending a damage-control team out on deck to better assess the situation."

"Very well. Keep me posted, CHENG."

"Aye, sir."

"Bridge. Combat Systems."

"Go ahead, Commander."

"Sir, the Aegis system appears operational. I'm concerned we may have sustained damage to the Phalanx."

"Bridge. Navigation."

"Go ahead, Lieutenant."

"Sir, no damage reported to the ship's navigation systems. That report is preliminary, sir. We're still checking."

"Very well. Update me if that changes."

"Bridge. Operations."

"Go ahead, OPS."

"Sir, our main concern right now is the OC division. Still testing all radio equipment. No evidence of damage, but it's too soon to tell."

"Bridge. Weapons."

"Go ahead, WEPS."

"Sir, we echo the concern combat systems raised about the Phalanx. We think the Aegis is fine. All missiles appear to be operational. But the Phalanx appears to be out. We're working on it, sir."

"Make it fast, Lieutenant. Looks like we nailed both of those Chinese J-11s. But that carrier is still out there. And I'd hate to face another missile attack without the Phalanx."

"Aye, sir."

"Bridge. Supply."

"Go ahead, Pork."

"Sir, no damage to the supply department."

"Very well."

"Bridge. Engineering."

"Go ahead, CHENG."

"Sir, we've got a fire on the aft deck."

"Let's hear it."

"We should have the fire extinguished in thirty minutes, Skipper. The good news is that the missile did not strike the ship. It appears the Phalanx intercepted it over the water about a hundred feet before impact. But the explosion over the water on final approach sent rocket fuel and burning missile parts everywhere. A bunch of it landed in the water. But burning missile debris slammed into the ship, sir."

"How bad, CHENG?"

"Could be worse, Captain, but bad enough. We lost a sailor. And the Phalanx took a direct hit and is banged up."

Kruger paused. "Who?"

"Seaman Recruit Taylor Jones. He was struck in the head by some shrapnel from the missile when it exploded."

Kruger thought for a moment. "Isn't he the kid from Georgia?"

"Yes, sir. From Marietta. He was in my department."

"Dang it!" Captain Kruger shook his head. "Thanks, CHENG."

Just then, the XO returned to the bridge. The bridge had gone silent at the news of the young seaman's death. "I take it you heard about Seaman Recruit Jones, sir."

Kruger nodded. He took a moment, swallowed hard, and bit his upper lip. Tears in front of subordinates in a military command could undermine good order and discipline and confidence.

"I remember his mother, XO. Tall. Blonde. Attractive woman. She'd flown to San Diego for our sendoff at Thirty-Second Street when we deployed for WESTPAC. She made me promise to take care of her boy. Said he was her only kid. Said he had just celebrated his eighteenth birthday when she shipped him off to the Navy, against her better instincts." He shook his head. "Now I've got to tell her that her boy was killed on my watch."

"It wasn't your fault, sir," the XO said.

"Maybe, XO," Kruger said. "But the kid was my responsibility. And his mother won't be thinking about whose fault it is. She'll be too heartbroken mourning the loss of her boy." He looked at the XO. "Have Dr. Jeter brought back over here from the *Shemnong* to prepare the body."

"Aye, aye, Captain."

"All right, people," he snapped, the authority of command returning to his voice, "let's get back to work."

J-11 fighter jet (codename Tiger Cat Leader)
People's Liberation Naval Air Force
South China Sea
altitude 3,000 feet
150 nautical miles north of aircraft carrier Shi Lang

10:30 a.m.

Tiger Cat Leader! Tiger Cat Two! I've got a small armada two thousand yards off my left wing, sir! Steaming due south. Looks like five warships. Check that! Make it six warships. I see three *Kee Lung*–class destroyers and three troop transport ships."

"Tiger Cat Two. Tiger Cat Leader. Roger that." Lieutenant Tan Zongliang put his jet into a large swooping bank to get a better look at the naval armada. Off to the right, about one thousand yards, Tan saw the six warships steaming in a diamond formation, cutting long streaks in the water.

Three bore the distinctive silhouettes of *Kidd*-class guided-missile destroyers — the type that Taiwan had purchased from the United States Navy. These had been dubbed *Kee Lung*–class destroyers, named for the first of the four ships bought from the Americans.

Three others bore the shape of troop transport ships that Taiwan called its *Chung Hai*–class LSTs, which were in reality World War II–vintage LSTs that also had been purchased from the United States Navy.

Tan picked up his microphone and set his radio frequency for the *Shi Lang*.

"*Shi Lang*. Tiger Cat Leader."

"Tiger Cat Leader. *Shi Lang* Control. Go ahead."

"*Shi Lang*. We have a visual on six Taiwanese warships, one-five-zero nautical miles north of your current position. Flotilla consists of three *Kee Lung*–class destroyers and three *Chung Hai*–class LSTs, steaming at twenty-five knots on a course of one-eight-zero degrees. Directly toward Itu Aba!"

"Tiger Cat Leader. Copy that. Six enemy warships headed on course one-eight-zero degrees. Excellent work. Tiger Cat Leader, return to the ship. Tiger Cat Two is to remain on patrol to monitor the position of the enemy flotilla until further orders."

CHAPTER 24

Office of the Minister of National Defense, Chief of Staff
People's Liberation Army-Navy
Zhongnanhai Compound
Beijing, People's Republic of China

11:00 a.m. local time

The office of the minister of national defense for the People's Republic of China was housed in a three-story gray stone building with a red sloping tile roof that was located in the highly secretive Zhongnanhai Compound. The building was across the narrow two-lane street from the Presidential Palace.

Because of fast-breaking events in the South China Sea, General Shang Xiang—the minister of national defense and the highest-ranking military officer in the Chinese armed forces, had stayed away from this morning's nationally televised ceremonies at Tiananmen Square to monitor the military situation.

Shang had dispatched his second in command, Admiral Zou Kai—commander of the People's Liberation Army-Navy—to the ceremonies decorating the two helicopter pilots from Operation Lightning Bolt for their heroism, which seemed appropriate because the pilots were naval officers.

And in the last two hours, the situation in the South China Sea had exploded.

Neither President Tang nor Admiral Zou had returned from

Tiananmen, but Zou was due back any minute. Shang had sent word that he was to report to his office as soon as he returned.

Shang was again reading the second TOP SECRET communiqué that had arrived from Vice Admiral Gu Hongmen, commander of the People's Liberation Army-Navy South Sea Fleet.

The subject was titled: "US NAVAL FORCES ATTACKS ON PLA NAVY AIRCRAFT."

The subject line of the first communiqué, which had arrived about the time that President Tang had been addressing the nation, was titled: "DEATH OF FU CHEUK-YAN CAPTAIN OF M/V SHEMNONG."

Now, only minutes ago, a third TOP SECRET message had arrived. The subject on this third message read: "URGENT – VISUAL CONFIRMATION OF TAIWANESE WARSHIPS STEAMING TOWARD ITU ABA."

A knock on his office door.

"Enter."

Colonel Ding Yiping, the general's chief of staff, stepped in. "Admiral Zou has arrived, sir."

"Send him in."

"Yes, sir."

The commander in chief of the Navy walked in, a broad smile on his face, still basking in the glow of the nationalistic glory that had flooded every corner of Tiananmen Square.

"How did things go at Tiananmen, Zou Kai?"

"You did not watch on television?" The admiral's smile vanished. "Is something wrong, General?"

"Yes. While you were at Tiananmen, we have had a crisis erupt in the South China Sea."

"What's going on, General?"

"We have had three communiqués from South Sea Fleet within the last hour."

"From Vice Admiral Gu Hongmen?"

"Yes. This is the most recent one." He handed the communiqué to Zou.

"Two helicopters and two jets!" Zou snapped.

"Correct, Admiral. All attacked by the USS *Vicksburg*. And we still did not get our Marines on board the *Shemnong*."

Admiral Zou handed the paper back. "Tang is not going to like this."

"No, he is not," General Shang said. "And I fear he will like this even less." He slid the first communiqué across the desk. "This we received about thirty minutes before the one you just read."

Zou grimaced as he read the message. "I've heard that he is close to his half brother and his sister."

"Think about it," General Shang said. "You're sent off to a cold orphanage at nine years old with your sister and your half brother. And it's the three of you against the rest of the world. Could you not see how they would become close to one another?"

Admiral Zou nodded. "I see your point, General."

"Put it this way," General Shang added. "The *Shemnong* did not receive that rich shipping contract to Itu Aba and Bangkok for no reason."

"True, General. And I fear that because of *who* Fu Cheuk-Yan was that this changes the situation."

"My concerns exactly, Admiral. Our military response, including the appropriate levels of force and the appropriate strategy, should be based on the military situation at hand—not on the fact that the individual who was killed just happened to be the half brother of the president."

Admiral Zou, who had been standing, sat down as Shang made that comment. He crossed his legs and toyed with his chin. "It appears, General, that we share some of the very same concerns."

"Admiral, they do not call him the Raging Dragon for no reason."

"True, Shang Xiang. It is not in the best interests to overreact based on this or to misallocate military resources in our fight against Taiwan for the sole purpose of exacting revenge against the Americans for the death of Captain Fu."

"The Americans blame the Taiwanese," General Shang said. "Which may be accurate. But given the fact that the Americans attacked our aircraft, I'm not certain that Tang will buy it."

"Agreed, General. He will blame the Americans for his brother's death."

"Perhaps," Shang said. "But as much as Tang wishes to eclipse the Americans, the fact remains that Taiwan remains our principal opponent in this conflict. Here is the third communiqué we received, which underscores my point." Shang slid the third communiqué across the desk.

Admiral Zou picked up the document. "Three destroyers and three troop transports? They are probably planning to hit Itu Aba with cruise missiles launched from the destroyers, then let their Marines on the LSTs pick up the pieces. And that kind of firepower from those three ships would be more than enough to destroy our forces entrenched on the island." He slid the memo back toward the general.

"I agree with you, Admiral," Shang said. "If they make it that far, our forces would be vulnerable, since they haven't been reinforced with the anti-missile batteries on board the *Shemnong*."

The admiral walked over to the window and looked out. "His motorcade is arriving right now." Zou turned around and looked at Shang. "The question now is, how do we break the news to ensure that his reaction is restrained?"

General Shang stood and walked over to his coat hanger. He grabbed his uniform jacket and put it on. "We should tell him now. Let us hope he contains himself."

Forward Watch
USS **Emory S. Land**
South China Sea

11:05 a.m. local time

The north breeze across the bow offered a fresh antidote to the tropical sun beating down. Standing at the forward watch station, Stephanie brought the binoculars down from her eyes, closed her eyes, and turned her face into the wind.

After crying herself to sleep—something that would have been humiliating had any member of the crew known about it—the XO had approached her this morning at breakfast and lifted her spirits, as only he could seem to do.

"We would never have saved Commander McCormick's life without you, Stephanie," Commander Bobby Roddick had said in that rich Charleston accent. "The captain and I have been talking," he had said. "We can't pick up everything on radar and sonar. And even when we can, we can't always identify what we're picking up. We still rely on human eyes on watch on the high seas. We're promoting you to officer in charge of our external deck watches. It's an important job, especially in times like this. You showed yesterday that you have a knack for it."

While the "promotion" was not an elevation in rank or in pay, it had boosted her with a renewed sense of mission and importance. She had gotten the promotion based on her performance alone. Her father's name had nothing to do with it. His name had not saved Gunner McCormick's life, a point the XO had brought up during morning mess.

The distant thunder of jet engines from behind her made her do a one-eighty to look off the port bow.

Dark silhouettes of two jets, off in the distance, streaking perhaps a thousand feet over the water, bore down in the direction of the *Emory S. Land.* The jets left black streams of smoke in their wake. She pulled her binoculars to her eyes and trained them on the jets.

They flew in fast, and their roar burgeoned from distant, to loud, and then deafening.

Swooosh ...

Swooosh ...

The sleek fighter jets, each with a single orange star on its fuselage, shot across the bow of the ship, perhaps a hundred feet above the deck, the sound of their screaming engines booming throughout the ship.

Startled by a hand on her shoulder, Stephanie jumped back.

"XO!"

He looked up at the jets, now starting a banking turn out in front of the ship for another pass. "Chinese," he said. "We picked 'em up on radar a few minutes ago, and I wanted to come out and have a look. Their carrier is somewhere in the area." He looked at her. "You okay?"

"Yes, sir. Such a low overpass."

The jets made their turn and came rushing back toward the ship for another flyover.

After thundering over the top of them, the jets screamed away from the ship and headed back in the direction from which they had come.

"Are they bullying us with those low overpasses, sir?"

"That's exactly what they're doing." His blue eyes shifted from the disappearing jets to her face. "We just got a message in from Seventh Fleet. Things could get real hot real quick."

"What happened, sir?"

"The *Vicksburg* just took out two of their jets and two of their choppers."

She felt like a cinder block had just dropped into the pit of her stomach. "Shot them down?"

"That's correct."

"When?"

"Just happened. Seventh Fleet message traffic is buzzing. I'm sure that flyover was a muscle-flexing exercise to let us know they're out there. Fortunately, they didn't take a shot at us this time. Unfortunately, we don't have an antiaircraft defense system like the *Vicksburg*."

"What can I do, XO?"

"Be ready to man Battle Stations on a moment's notice."

"Aye, sir."

Under the blazing sun, as mid-morning was turning to noon, war fever was descending on the *Emory S. Land*.

She glanced at her battle-station position, the .50-caliber machine gun that had limited rounds of ammunition. Her battle helmet and flak jacket were in a steel foot locker at the base of the gun. If General Quarters were sounded, she had replayed a hundred times her route to that station from any place on the ship. Something was about to happen, and soon. She could feel it.

"I'll be ready, XO. You can count on me."

Control Room
USS Boise submarine
South China Sea
108 nautical miles north of Itu Aba Island
depth 200 feet

11:00 a.m. local time

Sonarman Chief Petty Officer John King, the legendary "Bloodhound" of the US Navy submarine force, sat at his station in the control room of the nuclear submarine USS *Boise* and adjusted the headset over his ears.

He was born to be enraptured by the gurgling sounds of the sea. But at the moment, through the melodic gurgles and harmonic bubbling, the distant but clear humming of powerful engines turning two large propellers on a very large ship had widened his grin to the point that his cheeks nearly hurt.

"Whatcha got, Bloodhound?" Commander Graham Hardison, skipper of the *Boise*, asked from over his left shoulder.

King removed the earphones and turned around. "Definitely a big gun, sir. She's still a ways away, but I'd bet money that we've found our target."

Commander Hardison, wearing a USS *Boise* ball cap and a navy blue submariner's jumpsuit with silver oak leaves on the collars, unleashed a grin almost as wide as the Bloodhound's. "Chief, if I were a betting man, I'd bet you're right."

"Thank you, sir," the Bloodhound said.

"Helmsman."

"Aye, Captain."

"Float the communications buoy. Alert Seventh Fleet that we've identified the target."

"Yes, sir!"

CHAPTER 25

Office of the President
Presidential Palace
Zhongnanhai Compound
Beijing, People's Republic of China

11:15 a.m. local time

et me see if—" The president of the People's Republic of China stopped midstream, stood up, slammed his fist on his desk, turned around, and walked to the window. He appeared to be looking out across the street toward the Ministry of Defense. He folded his arms, then turned around and glared at the two top-ranking officers in the Chinese military. "We have lost two helicopters and two fighter jets, we inflicted no damage on the attackers, and we still did not take control of the *Shemnong?*"

"I'm afraid that is correct, Mister President," Shang said. "Our aircraft were shot down by antiaircraft missile batteries from the USS *Vicksburg,* the ship that has commandeered the *Shemnong.*"

Tang unleashed a profanity-laced tirade and slammed his fist on his desk again.

"Did we not attack the *Vicksburg?*"

"Mr. President, two of our J-11 fighter jets launched anti-ship missiles at the *Vicksburg,* but the ship's anti-ballistic missiles intercepted our missiles."

"Unacceptable!" More fist slams. "This wasn't part of the plan!" Another string of profanity. Tang turned, grabbed some papers off his desk, balled them up, and threw them against the wall. Then he swept an arm across his desk, strewing documents on the floor while screaming profanities at the top of his lungs.

In a corner of the room, Tang's young military attaché, Captain Lo Chen, stood at an erect parade rest, a stunned look on his face. Seated in a wingback chair just a few feet from where Shang was sitting, Admiral Zou raised an eyebrow, and Shang saw that Zou was attempting to suppress a grimace.

Shang sensed that he and Zou were reading each other's minds. The worst news was yet to be delivered to Tang, and both the general and the admiral knew it.

Shang had considered ordering Zou to break the news. After all, the whole affair now unraveling in the South China Sea, including the death of the president's half brother, was primarily a naval matter. And Zou was China's senior naval officer.

But in the Chinese military, the Navy remained under the command of the Army. And he, Shang, was the nation's top-ranked military officer. This would be one of those dreaded duties that he would have to shoulder himself.

Shang's concern was the president's emotional stability. Tang had earned the reputation as China's most brilliant leader since Chairman Mao himself, but also the most volatile. And while that emotional tinge in public speeches had been a useful rhetorical tactic in wooing the support of millions, behind closed doors, the president's penchant for explosions had been the hot topic of hush-hush private concern among senior officers of the Army and the Navy.

Tang sat down and folded his arms, as if momentarily out of words, but, based on the contorted look on his face, was still fuming.

Shang looked at Admiral Zou, who looked back and nodded. It was time.

"Mister President, I regret to have to inform you that there is more bad news," General Shang said.

Tang glared at him with almost a hypnotic stare. "General, you are not about to tell me that the Americans have shot down any more of our aircraft, are you?"

Shang resisted the urge to squirm in his seat, opting instead for the unreadability of a poker face. With enough bad news, especially the news that Shang was about to deliver, Tang might launch into another tantrum and unleash his wrath on the military leaders, firing him, firing Admiral Zou, and firing anybody else with any link to the events. Or worse.

"Mister President, we received a TOP SECRET message from the Americans."

"What kind of message?"

"Sir, the Americans claim that the Taiwanese Navy attacked the *Shemnong*. They claim that they were requested by the Taiwanese to provide medical assistance after the attack. They say the Taiwanese attack inflicted casualties on the civilian crew of the freighter."

Tang folded his hands and raised an eyebrow. "Casualties?" A pause. "How bad?"

"Some of the sailors have been shot up. Some with life-threatening injuries. And I regret to inform you, Mister President, that the captain of the *Shemnong* died."

Tang looked at him with an expressionless blank stare.

The president sat there, motionless. The only movement was the expansion and contraction of his rib cage.

"Nooooooooooo!!!!!!!!!!" Tang screamed as he stood, knocking more papers on the floor. "He is my brother!" Tang grabbed the gold lamp off his desk. "Nooooooo!!!!!!!!" He slung the lamp across the room, smashing it. He picked up a figurine and turned and slammed that against the bulletproof glass behind his desk, smashing the figurine.

Then he turned around and stood there, facing the admiral and the general. In a strange voice barely above a whisper, his tone an eerie contrast to the blood-curdling screams he had just unleashed, he said, "And where is the body of my brother?"

"The Americans have proposed flying the body to Hong Kong, sir."

Tang sat down and placed his hands on his desk, palms down. He looked straight ahead, saying nothing, showing no emotion, almost as if he hadn't heard the answer.

"The Americans," he said. "The Americans seem to have involved themselves to stifle our ascendency to military superpower status. Since the Americans have attacked our aircraft and now have killed sailors on the *Shemnong*—"

"Mister President," Shang said, "may I remind you that the Americans are blaming your brother's death on the Taiwanese."

"Do not interrupt again, General Shang. Since the Americans have attacked our aircraft and now have killed sailors on the *Shemnong*, we must strike back with full force!" Tang looked at Admiral Zou. "Admiral, I am ordering the Navy to sink the *Vicksburg* and to do so immediately."

Zou looked over at Shang, as if deferring to him to respond.

"Mister President," Shang said, "executing that particular order right now might serve to compromise our overall mission."

"Why is that, General?"

"The *Vicksburg* and the *Shemnong* are steaming to the east, toward the Philippines. If we bring more air power against the *Vicksburg* at this time, then we would be forced to move the *Shi Lang* farther to the east to pursue her. Part of the problem with that is that our search planes from the *Shi Lang* have just discovered the Taiwanese naval task force sailing toward Itu Aba. Right now, the *Shi Lang* is in the path of that task force. If we send her off to the east in pursuit of the *Vicksburg*, then the Taiwanese have a straight shot at Itu Aba and can retake the island."

Tang started screaming at the top of his lungs again. Then, as if freezing in the midst of his tantrum, he stood still, went silent, and sat back down again. As he sat at his desk, his face became placid, as if under the influence of some spell. The calm and tranquil Tang returned. "So your position, General, is that sinking the *Vicksburg* would not constitute the wisest allocation of our military resources in the area at this time?"

Shang hesitated. "That is a fair assessment, Mister President."

"And you agree, Admiral."

"Yes, sir."

"Just how many ships are in this Taiwanese naval task force?"

The admiral answered this one. "Six, Mister President. Three *Kee Lung*–class destroyers and three troop transport ships."

"Very well," Tang said. "Order the *Shi Lang* to sink them all."

Admiral Zou nodded. "With respect, sir, we recommend letting the flotilla sail a bit farther south into our trap before we attack."

"Very well"—Tang wagged his finger in the air—"but we cannot let the Americans off the hook. What was that other ship that we spotted in the sector? A submarine tender, I believe?"

"The USS *Emory S. Land*, sir," Admiral Zou said.

"I want that ship captured, just like they captured the *Shemnong*," Tang said. Shang and Zou looked at each other. "Can we capture this ship without compromising our attack on the Taiwanese fleet?"

"I will defer to Admiral Zou on that one," Shang said.

Zou nodded. "The sub tender is lightly defended by small arms. Machine guns. That sort of thing." He waived his hand in the air. "The only real danger would be if they happen to have Stinger missiles on board. We could capture her with a helicopter assault from the *Shi Lang*."

Tang rocked back and forth in his chair, nodding, as if contemplating his options. "Then this is my order. Seize the *Emory Land*."

"Yes, Mister President."

CHAPTER 26

USS Emory S. Land
South China Sea

As the sun climbed into the midday sky, Ensign Stephanie Surber, in her forward watch post on the USS *Emory S. Land*, sipped one of the bottled waters she had stored in the small cooler on the deck.

In a way, the hot sun and the intermittent cool wind gusts proved to be a bit of a surrealistic distraction from the blanket of ... well, to Stephanie ... it felt like a blanket of fear. The lead ships of the *Carl Vinson* Strike Group were still several hours away, and until the USS *Shiloh* arrived on the scene, every officer and crew member on board the *Emory Land* knew that in the event of an attack, the tender would be outgunned.

A knot twisted her stomach. Even as she searched the skies and seas for whatever was out there and saw nothing, she could not dispel the foreboding. All around her, crew members walked the main deck, sporting somber faces as they prepared for another sub replenishment at sundown, this time with the new *Virginia*-class submarine, the USS *North Carolina*.

Alarm bells sounded all over the ship!

Men thundered across the deck as the XO's voice resonated over the 1MC: "General Quarters! General Quarters! General Quarters! All hands to Battle Stations!"

Stephanie dropped the bottled water and scrambled to the .50-cal on the starboard side. Her heart pounded like a string of sixteenth notes on a snare drum. Her assistant, Gunners Mate Third Class Charles

Jonas, sprinted to the gun from the stern. "I'll get the belt, ma'am!" he screamed.

"Okay, okay!" She reached the gun and swung it around. "Let's get this baby loaded!"

"Yes, ma'am!" He popped open the transit box on the deck beside the gun.

"Now hear this! This is the XO! Enemy aircraft detected on radar approaching from the southwest. Blips spotted appear to be helicopters. Man Battle Stations!"

Z-10 attack helicopter (codename Tiger Five)
South China Sea
altitude 1,000 feet
ten miles southwest of USS Emory S. Land

Lieutenant He Chong, who was fifth in command at the historic attack on Itu Aba Island and thus bore the handle of Tiger Five, pushed down on the throttle from the lead position of the seven-helicopter V-formation squadron from the *Shi Lang*.

Now He Chong was in command of his own mission. The Chinese Command called this mission Operation Counterpunch.

The target of the mission, the USS *Emory S. Land*, a Navy submarine tender, would become visible in a few minutes. As the attack force thundered through the sunny sky, He Chong felt an anxious excitement.

This was his first shot at command, the result of the fact that the squadron leader and assistant squadron leader had not yet returned from being decorated for heroism by the president.

The anxious feeling that now gripped him came from the fact that the third and fourth in command at Itu Aba, including his close friend Lieutenant Pang Wenjun, both died just hours ago in a mission to retake the freighter *Shemnong* from the American cruiser USS *Vicksburg*.

The call to command, to lead the assault against the *Emory Land*, to capture her rather than destroy her, had not given him any time to grieve for his friend. That would come later.

But Pang's death had reminded him that the Americans are a formidable foe. And even though the *Emory Land* did not contain the sophisticated air-defense missiles that the *Vicksburg* had employed to shoot down two of China's attack helicopters and two fighter jets, the Americans should not be underestimated.

His mission was to attack and disable the *Emory Land's* primitive air defenses, using enough force to allow Chinese Marines to seize control of the ship. But he was not to sink the ship. He could accomplish this by firing two lightweight missiles at the ship.

The air armada approaching the *Emory Land* consisted of four attack helicopters and three troop helicopters. The armed Marines and sailors would board the ship once her air defenses were disabled.

He Chong checked the chronometer on the control panel. It was time.

"Tiger Five to all units. Launch anti-ship missiles in ten seconds. Prepare to move in on my orders."

Forward section, main deck
USS Emory S. Land
South China Sea

N ow hear this! This is the XO. Radar shows two missiles inbound! Port side! All weapons fire! Brace for impact!"

Crew members all over the ship scrambled for cover. The machine guns and the 20- and 40-millimeter antiaircraft cannons on the port side began a thunderous barrage, firing shells into the air in the general direction of the incoming missiles, hoping to strike pay dirt.

"Petty Officer Jonas!" Stephanie yelled.

"Yes, ma'am!"

"Let's get this .50-cal moved over to the port side. We're gonna need all the firepower over there that we can muster!"

"Yes, ma'am!"

"Time to impact!" Another voice over the 1MC. "Fifteen seconds!"

"Don't know if we've got enough time to get it mounted there, ma'am."

"Just do it!" Stephanie said.

"Aye, ma'am," Jonas said. "Got her dismounted. If you can grab the ammo belt, ma'am!"

"Got it! Let's go!"

"Stay low, ma'am!"

"Just move!"

Heads down, they ran to the port side through the thunderous roar of antiaircraft fire spewing out in the direction of the incoming missiles.

"Time to impact, five seconds!" the XO's voice boomed over the 1MC.

"Get that baby mounted, Petty Officer!" she screamed.

"Working on it, ma'am!"

"Three …

"Two …

"One …"

Powerful blasts shook the ship, knocking Stephanie facedown onto the steel deck. Alarm bells rang out.

"Fire!"

"Fire!"

Stephanie looked up. Crackling flames and billows of black smoke poured from the port superstructure of the ship.

"Grab the fire hoses!" someone yelled.

"I got it! I got it!" someone else screamed.

"Hurry!" a chief petty officer shouted.

The ship's portside antiaircraft batteries had gone silent. Mixed with the crackling sound of flames and screaming voices, the sound of helicopter rotors now could be heard in the distance.

"Here they come!"

"They're coming!"

Sick bay
USS Emory S. Land

Gunner woke up to the sound of alarm bells, then heard the call to General Quarters over the 1MC. He was thrown from his cot when the missiles hit the ship and exploded.

He was all alone in the ship's sick bay. Gunner pushed himself up off the floor. "*AAAAaaahhh.* Oh, man." He snatched both IV needles out of his arms and pulled himself up.

He looked around for his clothes, then remembered his seabag underneath his cot. It was gone. He finally saw his khaki uniform draped over a chair beside one of the examination tables. His shoes were on the floor next to it. Fighting pain and a sudden rush of wooziness, he slipped on the pants, the shirt, then tightened the belt. He stepped into his shoes and tied them.

Gunner scanned the room. There! A small-arms locker in the opposite corner! He opened the safety-latch door and took out a .45-caliber pistol and an ammunition clip and stepped out into the empty passageway.

Forward section, main deck
***USS* Emory S. Land**
South China Sea

Sailors were pointing off the port side of the ship. Visible through the clearing smoke, seven helicopters, stretched in a straight line, were flying in toward the *Emory S. Land.*

"Let's get this .50-cal mounted, Petty Officer!" Stephanie shouted.

"Aye, ma'am!"

"Ensign Surber!"

Stephanie turned around and saw Senior Chief Vasquez, the senior gunner's mate that the XO had assigned to mentor her. "What is it, Senior Chief?"

"Ma'am, there's no point in mounting the .50-cal! They've taken out our 20- and 40-millimeter antiaircraft guns. That .50-cal's like taking a pea shooter to a gunfight at OK Corral. There's nothing we can do! Highly recommend that you get belowdecks, ma'am!"

As Petty Officer Jonas finished mounting the .50-caliber machine gun on the port side, Stephanie shot back at the senior chief, "In other words, I'm supposed to run and hide because I'm the president's daughter? No way! I'm a naval officer, and I'm the weapons officer of this ship, and I'm going to stand and defend my ship no matter the odds!"

"But ma'am!" Vasquez pleaded.

"Sorry, Senior Chief!" Stephanie snapped. "I'm overriding you!"

"Yes, ma'am!" The senior chief hurried away, rushing through a hatch into the ship's superstructure.

"Petty Officer Jonas! Prepare to fire! Be ready with that belt!"

"Aye, ma'am!"

"Just a few more seconds!" She swung the machine gun to her left, aiming at the lead chopper. "Ready?" Her hands shook as the choppers flew closer.

"Yes, ma'am!" Jonas said. "Ready!"

"Okay!... Three ... two ... one ..." She squeezed the trigger. The .50-caliber responded, firing a string of lead into the sky. She held on tight to the shaking gun and didn't let up on the trigger.

And then ... the helicopter on the far right burst into flames. Seconds later, it plunged into the sea!

"Yes!" Stephanie screamed, pumping a fist in the air. "We got one, Jonas! Woohoo!"

"Yes, ma'am!"

"Let's get another one!"

"Yes, ma'am!"

She squeezed the trigger again.

Two of the choppers began returning machine-gun fire! A stream of bullets flashed across the water in a line and up onto the deck of the ship, pinging and ricocheting all around Stephanie. She fired back, overcome by the fervor of the moment and in such an adrenaline-rush that her instincts had taken over.

"Stephanie! Get down! Get down!" The XO's voice startled her. She turned, and he rushed in and tackled her like a free safety blitzing the quarterback.

She hit the deck hard, and his body was on top of hers, just as another round of bullets pinged across the steel deck from the attacking aircraft.

"Stay down!" he ordered, pinning her down with his powerful arms. And then his body jumped, as if a bolt of lightning had struck him.

"Noooo!" she screamed as his blood started flowing down onto her arms. She tried pushing herself up, but his weight was too heavy. "XO! XO! Bobby! Please! XO!"

"Stay down, ma'am!"

She craned her neck over to the left and saw Jonas, crumpled in a heap on the deck, face down in a pool of blood. Senior Chief Vasquez was crouched low in the open passageway leading into the ship's superstructure, just a few feet away. "Stay down!"

More bullets pelted the deck, whizzing the air above her head. A second later, she felt a tug and then a yank on her right ankle. She felt herself sliding, butt down, across the deck. Senior Chief Vasquez dragged her to the open passageway and yanked her inside the superstructure.

"Seal the hatch!" someone yelled.

The steel door slammed shut just as more bullets pelted the outside of the ship.

Z-10 attack helicopter (codename Tiger Five)
South China Sea
altitude 300 feet
two hundred yards west of USS Emory S. Land

From the point formation just off the port side of the American ship, Lieutenant He Chong hovered the Z-10, his thumb on the machine-gun trigger.

The Americans had stopped firing back. The American sailors were using high-powered water hoses to spray water on the flames still flickering on the left side of the ship. Black smoke billowed from the vessel, but the American sailors seemed to have the fire under control.

One of the troop transport choppers hovered over the bow of the ship while People's Republic of China Marines were sliding down ropes from the chopper onto the deck of the *Emory Land*.

He Chong and the one other remaining Z-10 attack helicopter — the one that had not been shot down — hovered off the port side, ready to deliver the coup de grâce with anti-ship missiles fired from point-blank range if the ship resisted.

This battle was not over, not yet anyway.

But as he watched the Chinese Marines fanning out along the main deck, with defenseless American sailors throwing up their hands, Chong sensed the thrill of victory fluttering in his chest.

Chong's mind wandered. This mission, of which he was the air commander, had been personally ordered by the president. In just a matter of minutes, if the Marines could secure the *Emory Land* ...

He dismissed that thought. There would be time for accolades later. Continue to focus. This mission was not over.

CHAPTER 27

Bridge
USS Emory S. Land
South China Sea

From the center of the bridge, with his hand glued to his .45-caliber sidearm, Captain Auclair Wilson, commanding officer of USS *Emory S. Land*, looked out at the six Chinese Navy helicopters hovering around his ship.

In a matter of minutes, the situation for the *Emory Land* had grown beyond urgent.

Either of the two attack choppers could fire a rocket or machine-gun bullets into the bridge at any moment, and there was nothing he could do about it. His ship had become defenseless.

Looking down at the main deck, he saw Chinese Marines carrying AK-47s and sub-machine guns swarming all over the deck. His crew was largely unarmed. It was only a matter of time before the Chinese made their way up to the bridge.

Soon the forty-five-year-old captain would have to make a decision: Fight to the death or surrender his ship.

"Lieutenant Rogers. How's that FLASH message coming to Seventh Fleet?"

"Can't get the message off, sir," the communications officer said. "Frequencies are still jammed."

Wilson cursed. "Can you verify if we got the earlier message off?"

"Still can't say with any certainty. We depressed the send button, but the Chinese were already jamming, and we never got a response."

Three sharp raps on the closed bridge door.

"They're here!" someone said.

"Draw arms!" the captain ordered. He pulled his pistol and pointed it at the steel door.

"Captain!" a voice shouted from the other side of the door. "It's Senior Chief Vasquez. I have Ensign Surber!"

"Master-at-Arms! Open the door!"

"Aye, Captain!"

The master-at-arms opened the bridge door, and the loud roar of helicopters flooded into the bridge.

Captain Wilson reholstered his firearm.

Senior Chief Vasquez, visibly winded, stumbled onto the bridge with the First Daughter of the United States in tow. Stephanie's face looked pale, her sparkling green eyes a mix of fear and anger.

"Reseal the door!" Captain Wilson ordered, yelling to be heard over the helicopter rotors.

"Aye, sir!" The master-at-arms complied, sealing the steel hatch.

"What's going on down there, Senior Chief?"

"Not good, sir." Vasquez's face was grim. His voice and his hands were shaking.

The captain looked over at Stephanie. Her eyes were transfixed on the bulkhead, as if she was in a daze.

"Where's the XO?"

Vasquez dropped his head, his eyes to the deck. His lips trembled. "I'm sorry, sir. The XO was a good man." The senior chief rubbed his eyes.

The senior chief's words were a jarring punch to the captain's midsection. Bobby Roddick had been Wilson's right-hand man. And he wasn't just a good man. He was a great man of promise who was destined to command a naval warship. Roddick was the best naval officer Wilson had ever been around.

Captain Wilson turned and walked over to the windshield. He looked out. A second Chinese troop chopper, black with a single orange star on its tail, was unloading a second group of Communist Marines down below.

As he watched, the weight of a thousand bricks descended upon his shoulders.

He faced a decision that only the captain of a warship could face—to surrender his ship or to fight to the death.

CHAPTER 28

Headquarters
United States Seventh Fleet
US Naval Base
Yokosuka, Japan

Sir, could I see you for a moment?"

Captain Dave Draxler, grateful that he had not been relieved of his duties as chief of staff to Seventh Fleet, looked up from behind his desk at his assistant, Commander Wesley Walls.

Walls was holding a single sheet of white paper. He looked worried.

"Sure, Wes. What's up?"

"We've got a problem with the *Emory Land*."

"What are you talking about, Wes?" Draxler whipped off his glasses. "Is Ensign Surber okay?"

"We don't know. But they tried to send a FLASH message twenty minutes ago. The message was broken up. Our efforts to contact the ship have failed. Take a look at this FLASH message, sir." Walls slid the paper onto Draxler's desk. "I'm afraid they might be under attack."

"What?" Draxler picked up the message and slipped his glasses back on.

FROM: Commanding Officer, USS *Emory S. Land*
TO: Commander Seventh Fleet
PRECEDENCE: FLASH
CLASSIFICATION: TOP SECRET - URGENT

1. Shipboard radar shows seven (7) enemy aircraft approaching from the southwest.
2. Based upon speed and acoustic and electronic signature, approaching aircraft are believed to be PRC military helicopters.
3. Request immediate air support.
4. Current coordinates of USS *Emory S. Land* are

END TRANSMISSON

Draxler looked up at Walls. "So the message breaks up before we could copy coordinates?"

"Correct."

"This doesn't look good."

"Agree, sir."

"Sounds like they're trying a helo assault," Draxler said. "Just like they tried against the *Vicksburg*."

"Agreed, sir," Walls said. "Except messing with the *Vicksburg* is like trying to pick a fight in a back alley with Iron Mike Tyson. Messing with the *Emory Land* is more like arm wrestling the tooth fairy."

"When did we last get a mark on the ship's coordinates?" Draxler asked.

"Last night, sir. She replenished USS *Boise* and then at sunset local time, she rescued Lieutenant Commander McCormick. Nothing since then."

"When will *Carl Vinson* be in range?"

"Another six hours before her jets are in range."

"Dang." Draxler pounded his fist on the table. "What about USS *Shiloh*?"

"Aside from the subs out there, with *Vicksburg* steaming out of the area, *Shiloh* is the only show in town."

Draxler thought for a second. "Okay. Message the *Shiloh*. Tell the skipper to get both choppers up and scour the area for any signs of the *Emory Land*. I'll notify Admiral Wesson. I'm sure he will want to message Washington." He paused. "I can't even imagine how the president will react to this."

Control Room
USS **Boise**
South China Sea
150 nautical miles north of Itu Aba Island

The Bloodhound tried suppressing his grin. For this was a mental game that he had played over and over again against the acoustics computer. For him, this was man against machine. His pure instinct and hearing ability pitted against a sophisticated array of circuits and microchips and electronics.

He glanced again at the computer, which displayed numbers rolling across the screen at a lightning pace, reflecting the sonar computer's fast-and-furious attempt to match the sound pouring in from the sub's passive radar sensors against the thousands of ship engine sounds programmed into its database.

Bloodhound already knew. He was waiting for the computer to catch up.

If it ever got to the point that the machine was beating him more than he beat the machine, he would submit his retirement papers on the spot.

So far, he had not submitted his retirement papers. Not even close.

And at the moment, King sensed the exhilarating thrill of victory over the computer—once again!

On the screen, the numbers turned faster and faster ... then faster ...

And then ...

TARGET MATCHED
Vessel Type: Aircraft Carrier
Varyang/*Shi Lang*–class (PLA Navy)
Probability of Accuracy Based upon Acoustical Data: 85%

"Yes!" The Bloodhound pumped his fist in the air to celebrate having laid another butt-kicking on the computer.

"Whatcha got, Chief?" Commander Graham Hardison asked.

"Sir, I was right. The computer verifies it. We've found ourselves a Chinese aircraft carrier!"

"Estimated range?"

"Six ... maybe seven miles, I'd say."

"Helmsman," the skipper said. "Let's get in behind that carrier. Stay in her wash and hide behind the sound of her engines. Last thing we need is to let them know we're on their tail."

"Aye, Skipper."

"Great work, Bloodhound!" Captain Hardison delivered an affectionate slap on the back. "Keep those super-ears peeled. I want you to tell me about every little squeak that carrier makes. I want to come into periscope depth for a look when we're close enough."

"Aye, aye, Captain." The Bloodhound broke into a grin.

Bridge
USS Emory S. Land
South China Sea

At most, he had a couple of minutes. Perhaps only a few seconds. Chinese Marines were about to kick down the hatch into the bridge.

For Captain Auclair Wilson, this was the moment of truth. Either defend his ship to the death or surrender it.

He looked around at the men on the bridge. And at the one woman. All eyes were on him.

Why did Bobby Roddick have to die? If the XO had lived, at least he would have been another seasoned and experienced officer to discuss the matter with. But now ... the officers left on the bridge were so young ... so green.

He remembered the words of the English poet John Donne: "No man is an island."

But today, at this heavy moment, Captain Auclair Wilson was an island unto himself.

"Skipper," his communications officer said.

"Yes, Lieutenant."

"Permission to speak."

"Better make it fast, Lieutenant."

"I say let's fight 'em, sir! I'll stand with you and fight 'em to the death."

"Yeah!" someone said.

"Me too!" This was from a young petty officer standing on the left side of the bridge.

"Sir. Permission to speak!"

The woman's voice drew Wilson's gaze to his right, where Stephanie Surber stared at him, her green eyes blazing with fire, her jaw steeled with determination. An incredible metamorphosis had erased her vacant shell-shock look.

"Same thing I told Lieutenant Rogers. Make it fast."

Bang-bang-bang! Hard raps on the bridge door. "Open up! We are Marines of the People's Republic of China! Open the door or we will kill you!"

"Captain!" Stephanie said. "Do not surrender the ship. Not on account of me!" Her eyes were pleading. "I want to fight them, Captain! We all know we're outnumbered and outgunned. But I will give my life for my country, and I want to take them out with me! Right here! Right now! I am with you, sir!"

Residence of the Secretary of Defense
Arlington, Virginia

thirty minutes past midnight local time

Secretary Lopez had turned in early, with plans to rise at 4:00 a.m. to head to the White House, where he would help the president put the final touches on his national address at 8:00 a.m.

But when the hotline from the Pentagon buzzed at thirty-three minutes after midnight, Lopez knew there would be no more sleep.

"Secretary Lopez."

"This is General Gordon at the Pentagon, sir. We've lost contact with USS *Emory S. Land* in the South China Sea."

"How did that happen?" Lopez waited as the officer explained that Seventh Fleet had received a broken message indicating a possible air assault by Chinese helicopters. "Okay, thanks. Convene the joint chiefs in the tank. I'll call the president."

Lopez hung up the Pentagon hotline phone and picked up the line to the White House chief of staff. Almost instantly, the tireless Arnie Brubaker was on the other end.

"Has the president gone to bed, Arnie?"

"He's been in bed for an hour."

"Get him up. Something's breaking with the *Emory Land*. We've lost contact. It doesn't sound good. I'm on my way."

Bridge
USS Emory S. Land
South China Sea

12:31 p.m. local time

Ladies and gentlemen." Captain Wilson eyed his officers and senior enlisted men who were with him on the bridge. "I am proud to be your captain and moved by your courage."

His words were interrupted by continued kicks on the door.

"We will blow open this door in fifteen seconds!"

Wilson looked at Stephanie. Her eyes showed strength and grit and willingness to fight.

The young woman was a national treasure. But she was also someone's daughter. Forget the fact that she was the president's daughter. What if she were his own daughter?

"You have ten seconds!"

"I am moved by your bravery. But I cannot in good conscience order you into a battle that will result in suicide. Even if we fight them off here, we can't survive another anti-ship missile fired from a chopper at point-blank range. I have no choice but to surrender the ship. I am ordering you to lay down your weapons. Hands in the air! Now!"

"Five seconds!"

"Senior Chief Vasquez! Open the hatch!"

"Aye, sir!"

Vasquez unlatched the door.

Angry-faced Marines of the People's Liberation Army-Navy streamed onto the bridge. They wore dark green camouflage uniforms, and they aimed their guns at every American on the bridge. "Who is the captain?" The one who had jammed his gun barrel at Wilson's face screamed this in English.

"I am the captain," Wilson said. "What do you want?"

"We want your ship, Captain! Either surrender it, or your crew will die!"

Belowdecks
USS Emory S. Land
South China Sea

12:33 p.m. local time

The spaces on a naval warship known as "belowdecks," meaning the lower decks within the ship's hull that are far below both the ship's superstructure and its main deck, could be a confusing labyrinth to a first-time visitor to the ship.

Because each ship had its own unique belowdecks design, even new sailors coming aboard sometimes needed days or even weeks to figure out what was where. Some new sailors often carried maps showing all the passageways and twists and turns and compartments on their new ship.

As a submarine tender, the *Emory Land* was one of the larger ships in the Navy, and Gunner had never been aboard before. The intricate configurations of the passageways and hallways constituted a maze of gray steel, grated decks, and fluorescent lights. The confusion was compounded when they plucked him from the water, disoriented, and hauled him down to sick bay.

Gunner clasped the .45-caliber pistol and, like a hunting dog sniffing its prey, moved through the empty spaces. He knew if he kept moving, he would eventually find ladders leading to the main deck. The main deck, he suspected, was where the action was.

Moving cautiously down the gray passageway, he passed enlisted living quarters, small quarters with six to eight bunks in each quarter, all vacant. After a few more steps, he came to another passageway leading off to the right. Above the passageway, a blue-and-white sign proclaimed "OFFICERS COUNTRY." This was where the commissioned officers' living compartments are located. On most ships, Officers Country had one or more ladders leading to the upper decks to allow the ship's commissioned officers quick access to Battle Stations in the event the ship was under attack.

Gunner pushed open the doorway and stepped into the passageway. He saw no one.

A whistle over the loudspeakers signaled an announcement over the 1MC.

"Now hear this. This is the captain."

Gunner stopped.

"As you know, the *Emory S. Land* has been attacked by naval air forces of the People's Republic of China. Even though our ship is not a full-fledged man-o'-war, we resisted the attack to our maximum capability, and I am proud of each and every one of you."

There was a pause.

"You fought bravely. However, our ship is a submarine tender. While our mission is vital to the Navy, we are not designed for combat.

"We have been struck by two anti-ship missiles. Our fire crews have extinguished the flames and contained the damage. Our navigational systems are still operational. But we cannot stand another missile attack."

Another pause. "We have been boarded by Marines of the People's Republic. In fact, armed Chinese Marines are here on the bridge with me as I speak. They have demanded that I surrender the *Emory Land* to them. And I have ... with great reluctance ... and for the benefit and safety of all of you ... acceded to that demand. I am surrendering ... the ship. You are to stand down from General Quarters. You are ordered to lay down ... all weapons. All officers on board"—the captain's voice cracked—"All officers are to report to the fantail for muster immediately. All officers will then be escorted by Chinese Marines to their staterooms, where they will remain under guard until further orders.

"All enlisted and civilian personnel are to report to your regular duty stations to await further orders from either me or from Chinese military personnel. You are ordered to give your full cooperation to the Chinese. I regret having to make this decision, but as your captain, I must consider that several members of this crew have already died, including our XO, Commander Roddick. Your safety and well-being are my responsibility. All officers. Report to the fantail for muster immediately. This is the captain."

The Lincoln Bedroom
the White House

12:40 a.m. local time

Under the silk satin sheets and the white presidential bedspread, President Surber twisted, and turned, and then twisted again. The plan to get four hours of sleep before his national address at 8:00 a.m. wasn't working.

Maybe he should just get up and head down to the Oval Office and monitor the situation from there. At least Hope-Caroline might be able to sleep.

A jarring static buzzed from the hotline beside the bed, accompanied by a flashing red light that interrupted the dark.

Surber reached over and picked up the phone. "Whatcha got, Arnie?"

"Mister President, Secretary Lopez called. We've lost contact with the *Emory Land*. Seventh Fleet thinks the Chinese have attacked her."

"What? Are you sure?" The president felt a lead ball drop to the bottom of his stomach.

"I'm sorry, sir. Secretary Lopez is on his way."

"Okay ... okay. I'll be right there."

"Doug what's going on?" This was the smooth, velvety voice of the love of his life, the beautiful First Lady of the United States, Hope-Caroline Surber. It had been that voice, along with her magnetic smile and shapely legs and that intriguing southern double name that drove him batty over her all those years ago, when he first met her at SMU, and in fact still drove him batty.

"Nothing, honey. Go back to sleep. I've got to meet Arnie about something."

He flipped on the lamp beside the king-size bed. The light made him squint. His conscience nagged him. He had just lied to his wife. She would find out anyway. Stephanie was her daughter too.

"Actually," he said, "something's going on with Stephanie's ship."

"What?" She sat up and rubbed her eyes. "What about it? Is Stephanie okay?"

The president slipped on a pair of khaki slacks. "Arnie says we've lost contact with the *Emory Land*. Irwin Lopez is worried about an attack by the Chinese."

Hope-Caroline buried her face in her hands. "I knew it was a mistake for her to go to Annapolis."

Surber walked to the closet to grab a shirt. "I'm going to the Situation Room to meet with Arnie and Irwin."

"Doug, I want to come."

"That's not a good idea."

"But this is our daughter!" She threw the sheets off her legs. "I want to know what's going on!"

"I understand. But there are about thirteen hundred other parents with sons and daughters on that ship, and I'm responsible for their lives too." He kissed her on the cheek. "I gotta go. Pray for Steph."

Fantail
USS Emory S. Land

1:00 p.m. local time

Under the blazing sun, in whipping winds, they lined up in four rows of twenty, from highest to lowest rank, and were surrounded by armed Chinese Marines.

Stephanie stood at attention in the back row as a newly minted ensign with the most junior of the junior officers, six other ensigns, and the ship's warrant officers.

The USS *Emory Land* had eighty-one officers on board, and now, with the death of the XO, there remained eighty.

"I am Captain Wang Ligin of the Marine Corps of the People's Liberation Army-Navy." The short, stocky officer was in front of the first row, pacing back and forth. Stephanie saw his head appear and disappear and then appear again in between the heads of the officers in the three lines in front of her. His English was broken, but understandable. "You are in the custody of the People's Republic of China. Our decision to attack your ship and to take you into custody was made after your president ordered a civilian freighter flying the sovereign flag of the People's Republic seized, and after your Navy shot down aircraft of the People's Liberation Army-Navy—"

A wind gust interrupted the officer's explanation.

"We Chinese are compassionate people. If you cooperate with us, you will live, just as the crew of the P-3 Orion that invaded our airspace in 2001 was allowed to live. But if you disobey us or take any action which interrupts good order and discipline, you will be shot on the spot—" Another wind gust. This one nearly blew Stephanie's cover off her head. "You will be led to your staterooms," the Chinese Marine continued, "row by row, starting with the higher-ranking officers first. Each row will be assigned two armed Marines.

"Your captain will accompany our Marines to ensure that each of you arrives in your stateroom. When you arrive in your staterooms, you will remain there pending further orders from me. Raise your hands over your heads and keep them there until you are in your staterooms. If you fail to do so, you will be shot in the back! Now, first row! Hands up! Let's move!"

Office of the President
Zhongnanhai Compound
Beijing, People's Republic of China

1:05 p.m. local time

"Mister President, two urgent items demand your attention," General Shang announced.

President Tang peered across his desk with the angry eyes of a hissing snake. "You are not going to tell me that the Americans have shot down any more of our aircraft are you, General? Because if you are, I may decide not only to fire both you and Admiral Zou, but perhaps I will have you both shot on the spot and promote someone who can handle command of the armed forces of the People's Republic. Perhaps I will even promote young Captain Lo here as my minister of national defense."

Shang glanced at Admiral Zou, who was sitting a couple of feet away in the other chair in front of the desk of the president. And it seemed, based on the look on Zou's face, that both senior officers were thinking the same thing. The Raging Dragon was about to become uncorked.

"So, General," Tang continued, "please tell me that I am not going to have to first fire you both, and then shoot you both, and then promote young Captain Lo to do your jobs for you because of your continued professional incompetence." The Dragon stood up, crossed his arms, and shifted his gaze from first the general, then to the admiral, and finally to the young officer.

Several weeks ago, even before the execution of Operation Lightning Bolt, Shang had begun to worry about the president's mental fitness to serve as commander in chief in the midst of actual military hostilities. Not that he questioned the president's genius or his charisma. But he had noted an odd response. It made him uneasy. Nothing he could explain. And history showed that sometimes genius and ambition while in command of a great military machine could brew together in a recipe of colossal disaster. Alexander. Napoleon. Hitler.

Shang suspected that Admiral Zou was thinking the same thing, although he had not dared mention his thoughts. At least not yet.

"The good news, Mister President, is that I am pleased to report to you that Operation Counterpunch has been completed, and it is a resounding success."

The scowl on Tang's face dissipated, then morphed neutral, and then his lips curled into a smile. "Are you telling me our forces have captured the *Emory Land*?"

"Yes, Mister President," Shang said. "Our Marines are on board the ship. Their captain has surrendered, and their officers have been placed under arrest and are being sequestered even as we speak. The ship was damaged by our missile attacks, but she remains operational, and we can steer her anywhere we would like. Congratulations on your command of another successful operation, Mister President."

"Excellent! Excellent! Now perhaps we will have some leverage with the Americans. And not only leverage, but also respect!" Tang pumped his fist.

"Unfortunately, we won't have much time to celebrate, Mister President. There is another issue that calls for your immediate attention, sir."

"What is it, General?"

"It is the Taiwanese flotilla, sir. The lead ship is now about one hundred miles from the *Shi Lang*. If we are going to interdict the Taiwanese, it is time to act, Mister President. And we cannot afford to spare any planes chasing the *Vicksburg*. We will need every plane in the *Shi Lang*'s arsenal to deter a flotilla of this size."

"Very well," Tang said. "General. Admiral. Deploy all of *Shi Lang*'s firepower against the Taiwanese flotilla. Send all six of those ships to the bottom of the sea."

"Yes, sir, Mister President."

"And as far as the *Emory Land* is concerned"—he leaned back, interlocked his fingers across his belly, and smiled—"this is our most significant war trophy in a hundred years!" He stood. "Don't you agree with me, gentlemen?"

Admiral Zou raised an eyebrow.

Capturing a lightly armed ship, even an American ship, was hardly an event that would be marked as one of the brilliant tactical maneuvers in the annals of military history. Still, General Shang wasn't about to spoil the boyish enthusiasm of the Raging Dragon. "Mister President, the success of this operation is a testament to the professionalism and precise execution of our naval air forces, under the command of my colleague Admiral Zou, and, ultimately, a testament to your vision and leadership in rebuilding our Navy, sailing under its magnificent flag-ship, the *Shi Lang!*"

"Yeeeeessssss!" The president sat back down, with a look of smug satisfaction. "Gentlemen, this victory marks a historic turning point. While the capture of the American P-3 aircraft in 2001 was a forerun-ner of things to come, in that our military embarrassed the Americans and forced them to apologize, this capture of this great ship will be earmarked by the historians as the pivotal moment on which history turned!" He pounded his fist on his desk. "The moment of emergence of the Great Dragon! The moment of decline for the fading Eagle!"

Tang was not finished. "We must make this a moment of national celebration. I am ordering the *Emory Land* to be taken to Hainan Island, the same place we took the P-3. I will go there and make a speech from the deck of this ship. That will make a statement of tremendous propor-tions, historically, that will rival MacArthur on the battleship *Missouri* at Tokyo Bay!"

Still more glances between Shang and Zou.

"Mister President," Admiral Zou said, "may I make a suggestion?"

"What is it, Admiral?"

"Sir, with all due respect, I do not believe that it is a good idea."

"What do you mean?" the president snarled.

General Shang said, "Mr. President"—there was no point in letting Admiral Zou take the heat alone—"perhaps the admiral is suggesting that Hainan Island may be among the first places the Americans would search for the ship. Their satellites photograph our bases there every two hours. Perhaps he is suggesting that we may be able to maximize our leverage against the Americans if we move the *Emory Land* to a place that makes it difficult for the Americans to find her."

The president's expression changed to a look of curiosity. "What do you suggest, gentlemen? Surely their satellites are watching all our ports."

"Would you like to address this, Admiral?" Shang waved at his Navy colleague.

"Certainly, General." Zou looked back at the president. "Mister President, the easiest place to find a ship is in port. The hardest place to find a ship is at sea. I suggest that we move the *Emory Land* farther out to sea, under armed escort, and keep her away from any port until we decide how we will dispose of her."

Tang scratched his chin. "Mmm. I can see the strategic logic of that. However, I do not want to pass up the historical significance of this. The world must know that we have captured one of America's great ships."

Shang, Zou, and young Captain Lo said nothing. No one was willing to give Tang advice on his attempt to gain propaganda from a sensitive military situation.

"I have made a decision!" the president announced. "General Shang. Order CCTV to set up in my office in two hours. I will announce to the world on live television that we have captured the *Emory Land*. And"— he held up his right index finger—"I will have a special message for President Douglas Surber."

CHAPTER 29

Fantail
USS **Emory S. Land**

Get hands up!" the Chinese Marine barked in broken English. Under the broiling tropical sun and breezy blue skies, the American officers began raising their hands.

Stephanie wanted to puke. The thought of surrender cut against the core of her being. Like her father, she was a born fighter. But now she was surrendering because her commanding officer had ordered her to. Reluctantly, she raised her hands.

They were down to the last row now, the row with the most junior officers on the ship. Only Captain Auclair Wilson remained out on the deck with his junior officers. The skipper was being held by the Chinese at gunpoint, forced to show the armed Chinese Marines where all the officers' quarters were located.

Stephanie was the second most junior of all the ensigns, senior in rank only to the older warrant officers, and thus was in the very center of the last line.

"Turn to your left and prepare to move to your staterooms."

Stephanie shuffled in behind Ensign Bob Mason, a junior ensign who had graduated from the ROTC program at the University of Wisconsin. They had taken three or four steps across the hot steel deck when the Chinese Marine screamed from the front of the line, "I said raise your hands!"

"Go kiss off, Commie!" The thick New Jersey accent revealed the voice of Ensign Steven Lapuro, a recent Rutgers ROTC grad with the reputation of a hothead. Lapuro was four officers ahead of Stephanie in line. She could not see him because Mason was blocking her view. But Lapuro's thick accent was distinctive.

"I said hands up now!"

"I'm an American naval officer!" the New Jerseyite snapped. "I don't raise my hands for no Commie!"

The Marine pulled a pistol from a holster, aimed it straight out, and fired.

"Aaaaaaaaah!"

With a thud, Lapuro's body slumped to the deck, his head bouncing against the steel deck, bleeding.

"Corporal! Sergeant! Throw him overboard."

Two Marines picked up Lapuro's body. With one holding Lapuro under his arms and the other holding his feet, they stepped to the back of the fantail and chucked Lapuro over the stern, into the churning water in the wake of the ship's propellers.

"Who else wishes to challenge my authority?"

The Lincoln Bedroom
the White House

1:20 a.m. local time

Hope-Caroline Surber couldn't sleep. She had known something was wrong even before that call from Irwin Lopez. Doug thought she was sleeping. He was wrong.

This whole harebrained idea of Stephanie going to the Naval Academy had made her sick from the beginning. But who could tell Stephanie anything? She was bullheaded. Just like her father!

Why couldn't Stephanie have been a Tri Delt? Why not a sorority girl in search of a successful husband, like Hope-Caroline had been all those years ago?

She leaned over and flipped on the lamp to the left of the bed.

Inside the gold eight-by-ten-inch frame, in her choker white naval uniform, her hand resting on her hat, and sitting in front of the

American flag, her baby girl smiled with a radiance that filled the room, even from her image in a picture frame.

The Navy was what Stephanie wanted. The Navy was what she had achieved. And now, Hope-Caroline felt it in her stomach, the Navy would take her life at all too young an age.

All of her prayers in her lifetime had been answered, it was just that sometimes the answer was "no." Why could she find no peace about this? Why was her prayer for Stephanie not calming her soul?

Here she was, the most popular woman in America, living in the best-known house in the world, surrounded by servants, guards, and staff members ready to jump at her very command. But in the midst of all of it, she felt supreme loneliness. None of it mattered now. Not the power. Not the popularity. Not the pandering nor the pampering. Nothing could remove the sick feeling that her only child was about to die.

She had already lost one child. She could not bear to lose another.

She rolled over, then rolled back again. She reached over to the ornate nightstand beside her bed, pulled open the drawer, and pulled out the family Bible that had been her grandmother's. She opened it. And it opened to the thirty-second chapter of Psalms.

"You are my hiding place; you will protect me from trouble and surround me with songs of deliverance."

"That's fine, Lord." She closed the Bible. "But it's not me I want you to protect. It's my daughter! Please protect her."

Officers Country
USS Emory S. Land
South China Sea

1:25 p.m. local time

As they stepped into the air-conditioned passageway, which was a stark contrast to the searing heat on the fantail, Stephanie held her hands high in the air, prodded by the gun barrel jammed in the middle of her back.

"Her stateroom is the last on the right," Captain Wilson said as they arrived at her door. Stephanie had wondered if she was going to get shot in the back before she ever got to her stateroom, which was off by itself, far down the passageway from the others. Or perhaps she would be forced into her stateroom and gang-raped by a half-dozen thug Chinese Marines.

Thank God, they hadn't recognized her, she thought.

"In the room!" The Marine rammed the gun barrel harder into her back.

"It's going to be okay, Stephanie," Captain Wilson said. "Just go in and stay put."

"Yes, sir." She put her hand on the steel knob, turned it, stepped inside and closed the door behind her.

With her back pressed against the closed door, her heart pounded like a bass drum as she caught her breath. Thank God, they had not shot her like they had Lapuro.

Stephanie stood there for a few seconds, then, feeling more under control, she stepped away from the door, toward the back of the stateroom.

A hand grabbed her from behind! Gripping her mouth! Another hand and arm was around her waist!

The Chinese bastards were going to rape her!

She tried jamming the man's rib cage with her elbow. But his grip was too tight.

"*Shhhhhhhhh!!*" The command was blown into her ear.

She tried kicking him.

"Quiet!" An angry whisper. "*Shhh!* It's me, McCormick! Keep your voice down!"

She exhaled, and he let go.

She turned around. "How did you get in here?"

"Keep your voice down. I saw your name on the door. You saved my life, so I thought you might like the company."

"You know what's going on?"

"I figured it out," he whispered.

"Be careful," she said. "They wanted all officers on the fantail, and now they've ordered us to quarters. If they find out you're here, they'll shoot you. They just shot one of our ensigns in the head. Threw his body overboard. The XO was killed during the attack."

Gunner winced. "Roddick's dead?"

Stephanie wanted to cry at the very question. But she could not. Adrenaline would not allow it. "Yes. And it looks like you're the only officer on board not accounted for."

"And I'll bet I'm the only officer with one of these unaccounted for." He pulled out the .45-caliber pistol and held it straight up.

"Where'd you get that?"

"Sick bay."

"You can't use it. If they hear that go off, they'll track you down and shoot you in the head."

"Maybe. Maybe not. But at least maybe I'll take a few of them with me."

"You're crazy, sir."

"So I've been told." He stuck the pistol under his belt. "First off, we're going to lay low for a while. Then I've got a plan. But it's risky.... It's dangerous." He put his hand on her shoulder and looked her in the eye. "I'll have to think about it."

"Sir, if you're having to think about protecting me, please. Sir, we're at war." She stared him straight in the eye. "The XO and Ensign Lapuro did not have the benefit of protection." She touched his arm. "It doesn't matter whose daughter I am. We're naval officers. Do not give me special protection. We are one and the same."

He winced. "Okay. We still have to wait an hour or so. Then I'll tell you the plan."

"Aye, sir."

Situation Room
the White House
Washington, DC

2:30 a.m. local time

Sitting at the end of the conference table, President Douglas Surber felt like his abdomen had been invaded by an octopus with a hundred tentacles squeezing his insides. He waited for Admiral Jones to finish a telephone call, hanging on every word the admiral was saying.

"Are you sure?" Admiral Jones asked. He was speaking on a secure line to the Pentagon, and every eye in the room, including the eyes of the vice president, the secretary of defense, and the secretary of state, were fixed on him. "Repeat that? Still no news on the whereabouts of the *Emory Land*? . . . Okay . . . Do we have a chopper up from the *Shiloh* searching the area? . . . Good . . . What? . . ."

Surber took a swallow of black coffee. The caffeine jolt might energize him, but it could do nothing to untangle his nerves or his mental image of Stephanie.

Jones was still on the phone. The expression on his face showed that something else had gone wrong.

"When? . . . Now? . . . Okay, let me hang up. I'll tell the president."

"What's going on, Admiral?" Surber demanded.

"Mister President, we haven't located the *Emory Land* yet. But we've been in touch with the British, and the Royal Navy has agreed to join in the search. Also, the Russians are calling for a total cease-fire. And I just learned that Tang is getting ready to address the nation live about military developments in the South China Sea."

"When?"

Jones checked his watch. "About two minutes, Mister President."

"Arnie, get us a video feed in here. Now!"

"Yes, sir." The chief of staff picked up one of the phones and started barking instructions.

"Any idea what he's gonna say?" Surber asked the admiral.

"No, sir," Jones said. "A sudden thing."

"We've got a connection," Arnie Brubaker said.

A second later, flat-screen televisions lit up on the walls of the Situation Room. The Chinese president, in a blue pinstripe suit and a red tie, appeared on the screens.

"Comrades of the People's Republic and workers of the world. Greetings from Beijing. I bring you important news of developments from the South China Sea, because you deserve to know the truth, and because these developments could affect the security of the world.

"I regret to inform you that, within the past two days, the United States has taken belligerent naval action toward sovereign ships of the People's Republic in the South China Sea.

"First, the US Navy attacked and then captured an unarmed civilian freighter, the M/V *Shemnong*, flying under the flag of the People's

Republic. When we demanded that America release this civilian Chinese freighter, America refused. Then when our naval Air Force attempted to rescue the freighter, American missiles from the USS *Vicksburg* shot down several People's Republic helicopters.

"Let me make it clear"—Tang shook his finger at the camera—"no one attacks the People's Republic of China with impunity. Therefore, today I ordered Chinese naval forces to attack and capture the American warship USS *Emory S. Land*. Today I report to you that this military operation has been a success, and the American captain of the *Emory S. Land* has surrendered his ship to our naval forces. The *Emory Land* is in Chinese custody and will be returned only under the following conditions:

"First, the United States government in general, and President Douglas Surber in particular, must publicly apologize for its capture of the *Shemnong*."

"That's blackmail!" Vice President Rock Morgan exclaimed.

"Yes, sir, it is," Secretary Lopez said.

"Second," Tang continued, "America must release the *Shemnong* to the custody of the Navy of the People's Republic."

"No way I'm doing that!" Surber hit the table with his fist.

"Third," Tang said, "America and other nations must understand that the South China Sea is uniquely within the naval influence of the People's Republic. I am sure that the American people would not appreciate it if I were to order the Chinese Navy into the Gulf of Mexico to interfere in internal American affairs."

"That's rank political pandering," Arnie Brubaker said.

"Therefore, in addition to a public apology and the return of the *Shemnong*, America must withdraw all of her naval vessels from the South China Sea immediately and stop interfering with internal Chinese affairs. Without immediate compliance, I am today instructing my government to begin liquidating our holdings in more than $1.2 trillion in United States Treasury issues.

"This sell-off will continue until our demands are met. We are prepared to liquidate all of our holdings of American Treasuries if necessary. America must comply with all my demands within twenty-four hours or, in retaliation for the American attacks against Chinese aircraft, we will sink the *Emory Land*. President Surber, you have twenty-four hours." The screen went blank.

Surber's stomach seemed to fall through the floor. He was the commander in chief. But all he could think about at the moment was his daughter. Jesus. Please.

"Not good. He beat us to the airways," Secretary Mauney said. "Not good."

"Couldn't be helped," Secretary Lopez said. "We were trying to keep it quiet until we got the *Shemnong* out of the area."

"Mister President."

"What is it, Bobby."

"Sir, with respect," the secretary of state said, "we do need to discuss the issue of your daughter being on board the *Emory Land* and how that may change the diplomatic and military calculus of the situation."

"It doesn't change the calculus, Bobby. I can't capitulate out of a special favor to Stephanie. That wouldn't be right."

"I understand, sir, but even if Stephanie weren't on board, we now have a situation where we could lose an entire warship and its crew. So it's not just about Stephanie."

"Maybe not, Bobby, but if I capitulate, it will look like it was about Stephanie."

"Not if the public doesn't know she's on board, sir," the secretary of defense said. "And that information has not been made public."

"And how long can we keep that bottled up, Irwin?"

"Don't know, sir," Secretary Lopez said. "But at this point, the Chinese don't appear to know."

"Eventually, it will come out," the president said. "And it would be perceived as special favors." Surber wiped his forehead. "Not only that, but we can't just let evidence of mass atrocities disappear."

"But it's crucial right now that the Chinese don't appear to know," Secretary Lopez said. "If we're going to get the ship back, we have a much stronger negotiating hand if they don't know they have your daughter. With respect, sir, she would become a very valuable ace in Tang's hand if he knew he had her, and he might demand more than he's already demanding."

Surber looked at Bobby Mauney.

"With respect, sir," the secretary of state said, "I agree with the secretary of defense. We don't want Stephanie to become a pawn giving greater leverage to the Chinese. But if they discover that she is on board..."

Surber sat there. He had already lost one child. It would be so easy to just release the freighter. But still … the images of the dead baby girls …

"Mister President."

"Mister Vice President."

"Sir, both the secretary of state and the secretary of defense make valid points. But even if no one ever discovers that Stephanie is on board, we must examine the question of what kind of precedent we are setting with Tang if we appear to back down too easily."

Surber felt paralyzed, torn between thoughts of Stephanie … sitting on his knee as a little girl … graduation from high school … from the academy … and visions of those murdered babies.

He was the president. He *had* to make a decision. This was the first crisis of his young presidency. But never did he ever imagine that he would be caught up in a life-or-death decision involving his own daughter.

"Gentlemen, excuse me a second." He stood. Others stood. "Sit down. I'm just going to the restroom." They sat down. He walked across the room and went into the restroom adjacent to the Situation Room.

The lights were already on. He closed the door, locked it, and went to his knees. "Lord, what do you want me to do? I'm torn up!"

He clasped his hands together. "Tell me what to do!"

Nothing.

"Please, I've got to make a decision!"

Still nothing. "You said you would provide wisdom!"

He waited. "You know, my national security team would think I'm nuts if they heard me in here trying to pray like this."

Enough was enough. He wasn't going to get an answer. For whatever reason, God would let him decide this one on his own. He got up off his knees and stood.

"What? Mount Moriah?" These two words popped into his mind. *Mount Moriah.* "You want me to sacrifice my daughter? Is that it?"

Surber felt sudden anger. Anger at the Chinese. Anger at Tang. Yes, even a tinge of anger at God himself. But anger or not, he had to do the right thing.

He stepped back into the Situation Room. "Everybody sit!" he ordered. "Secretary Mauney."

"Yes, sir."

"Draft a communiqué to the Chinese. Mark it urgent for instant delivery. Tell them we are not going to turn over the *Shemnong* until we have disclosed its contents to the world. And if any harm befalls the *Emory Land* or any of her crew members, they will have hell to pay. Tell them I personally guarantee it."

The secretary of defense and the secretary of state stared at each other with quizzical looks.

"Anything ambiguous about my instructions, Mister Secretary?"

"No, sir," Mauney said.

MSNBC newsroom
Washington Bureau

2:50 a.m. local time

Ever since the White House had alerted the networks that the president would be addressing the nation with a major announcement about the breaking situation in the South China Sea, the newsroom at MSNBC's Washington Bureau had been a blur of activity.

Longtime White House correspondent William P. "Wylie" Shepherd, his tie long since tossed aside and his sleeves rolled up, was craving another cigarette. But that would mean stepping outside into the dark again. Not enough time for that.

Wylie popped peanuts in his mouth to help keep himself awake as he studied the hot-off-the-press transcript of the Chinese president's speech.

A war had erupted in the South China Sea, and the enemy made the first announcement. Tang beat Surber to the punch in the public-relations war that accompanies any real war. That, alone, was a major story.

Wylie wasn't a Surber fan, and to see Surber get trumped by the Chinese president—and the surefire embarrassment from that— wasn't something he would lose any sleep over.

As usual, the White House had been mum. Calls to the White House press room had generated no comment on Tang's claims, including the incredible claim that an American warship had been captured.

Wylie leaned back and studied Tang's words. As a journalism student at Berkeley, he had studied Tang's doctoral thesis from Tang's days at Harvard. The thesis was admired and studied in detail at the best American liberal arts schools—Berkeley, Yale, Harvard.

Tang's thesis, he had decided, was a brilliant exposé by a brilliant young political mind condemning the American practice of big-stick hegemony for what it was. The concept of international coexistence in this age of postmodernism, they had taught at Berkeley, meant that no nation should assert its will over other nations. All is relative, he learned at Berkeley. The truth is not absolute. All nations, all cultures, and all religions are equal.

His professors at Berkeley had argued that Tang's thesis philosophically embraced postmodernism. This debate—whether Tang intentionally embraced postmodernism—dominated scholastic debates about the thesis.

He smiled, just thinking about the brilliance of the man Tang.

"Phone call, Wylie," the young, leggy blonde copyeditor announced.

"Can't take it right now, Mary. I've got to finish this story before daybreak."

"Might want to rethink that." The blonde raised an eyebrow and batted her big blue eyes at him. "Some guy claims he knew Stephanie Surber from the Naval Academy. He's got some fascinating info that I think you'll be interested in."

"Knew her from the academy?"

"That's what he says."

"What line?"

"Three."

He picked up the receiver and punched the line. "Wylie Shepherd."

Bridge
People's Liberation Army-Navy aircraft carrier Shi Lang
South China Sea

3:00 p.m. local time

Turn the *Shi Lang* into the wind!"
"Aye, Captain!"

With the tropical afternoon wind whipping across the flight deck, Captain Xue Haifeng stood on the flight bridge, his binoculars trained on the first two J-11 fighter jets positioned on the catapult below.

In a moment, the great ship under his command would launch the most powerful and significant carrier attack since Pearl Harbor! *Shi Lang* had a maximum capacity of fifty jets. She was currently at 80 percent capacity and carried forty J-11BH fighter jets on board.

And of those forty jets, thirty-eight were about to be launched for the mission at hand.

This launch would leave the *Shi Lang* severely depleted from effective defensive air cover. This made Xue a bit nervous. But it was imperative that the mission succeed, and if that meant launching thirty-eight out of their forty attack jets, then so be it.

"Captain. The *Shi Lang* is into the wind, sir. Steaming into a headwind of five knots. Ready for launch."

"Very well. Launch air wing!"

"Launch air wing! Aye, Captain!"

The roar of the two jets below grew to a loud thunder. Then, a few seconds later ... *swooosh* ... the first J-11 climbed into the sky, followed by *swooosh* ... the second J-11 rocketed off the deck.

Down below, flight crews prepared two more jets for launch.

Officers Country
USS Emory S. Land
South China Sea

3:59 p.m. local time

Stephanie checked her watch. One minute to go.

Her heart pounded, knowing that her life, in a matter of minutes, might soon be over. She felt she was about to hyperventilate. Images of her father and her mother and yes, of Commander Roddick and Ensign Lapuro, had been swirling in her head.

Commander McCormick—who had insisted on her calling him Gunner in private—stood beside the door.

Gunner gave her the thumbs-up. It was time.

Hopefully there was only one Chinese Marine in the passageway out in front of her stateroom. Would she get shot the second she stepped out?

She silently prayed, took a deep breath, put her hand on the knob — this was it — and turned it.

She stepped into the passageway. One Marine, carrying his rifle, was walking away from her, but almost ready to do an about-face.

"Help!" She started coughing and bent over. "Help me!"

The Marine turned and pointed his rifle at her.

"Help!" More coughing. She stepped back into the stateroom and walked straight to the back and feigned puking.

A second later, she heard a clang. She turned and saw that the Communist's rifle had dropped on the floor.

As the Marine staggered, still on his feet, Gunner whacked him in the back of the head again with the butt of his pistol.

The man twirled like a ballet dancer, and then hit the deck with a thud.

"Close the door," Gunner ordered. He felt for a pulse, found none, then pulled the body toward the back of the cabin, leaving a trail of blood from the gash in the back of the head. "Okay, get his gun."

"Yes, sir."

"You know how to use that thing?"

"You bet."

"We'll stuff his body under your rack."

They pushed the Marine's body under the lower bunk rack.

"Okay, stuff some blankets down there to cover him up. And wipe that blood off the deck."

Stephanie reached into the footlocker and took out two gray wool blankets. She wiped up the blood trail with the first blanket and pushed it against the man's body, covering it. She stuffed the second blanket under the rack for good measure.

"You remember how to get to sick bay?" he asked.

"Yes, sir."

"Okay, take the rifle. I'll keep the pistol. Hopefully they won't have anybody posted down there. But if we have to take 'em out, we'll take 'em out. Ready?"

"Yes, sir."

"Okay. Stay quiet and stay low. Let's go."

They stepped into the passageway, then through the door leading out of officers country and moved past the galley. The passageways just outside her stateroom were all empty.

Belowdecks resembled an eerie ghost ship. Bright fluorescent lights were flickering in empty passageways. The humming roar of the ship's engines was the only sound. All enlisted members were corralled topside, and all officers were being kept in their quarters.

Soon, someone would notice that the Chinese Marine was missing, and then his body would be found, prompting a manhunt throughout the ship. They had to move quickly.

The Situation Room
the White House

4:08 a.m. local time

The secretary of defense hung up the phone. "We've got a problem, Mister President."

"What now, Irwin?"

"The press room got a call from our favorite liberal, Wylie Shepherd at MSNBC. He heard Tang's speech. Somebody's tipped him off that Stephanie's on board the *Emory Land*. He wanted our comment before he goes public with it."

Surber pounded his fist on the conference table. "I knew we wouldn't be able to keep it corked up. But I had no idea it would come out this fast." He stood up.

"Mister President."

"You got any ideas, Rock?"

"Yes, sir, I do."

"I'm all ears."

"Let's invite Wylie over here right now," Vice President Rock Morgan said. "We can have a friendly little chat and explain to him that if that information gets to the Chinese, it could endanger the lives of the entire crew. We can ask him to consider holding the information until the crew is safe and secure." The vice president paused. "He must have some love of country and some sense of responsibility to use restraint with that information when lives are on the line."

The secretaries of state and defense nodded in agreement with the VEEP's suggestion.

"Okay. Why not?" Surber said. "Arnie, extend the invitation. Tell him we'll send a car over for him."

"Yes, sir."

Belowdecks
USS **Emory S. Land**
South China Sea

4:12 p.m. local time

A bout fifteen more feet up on the left," Stephanie said.
"Ready your weapon, just in case," Gunner said.

"Aye, sir."

It was a good thing Stephanie was with him, Gunner thought. All the drab passageways belowdecks looked the same.

When they got to the entrance to the ship's sick bay, the door was closed. If the Chinese were anywhere belowdecks, it might be in sick bay, especially if any of them had been wounded in the attack.

Gunner drew the pistol with his right hand and reached for the door latch with his left. "Wait here till I call you in," he whispered.

He aimed the gun out in front and pushed the door open.

Bright lights flooded the empty space. Not a soul in sight. Except ... except on the very cot that he had been lying on just a few hours earlier, a body, covered by a sheet from head to toe. Or was it a body? Or perhaps a ruse?

Gunner stepped toward the stretcher. He stood over it with his gun aimed at what appeared to be the head under the white sheet. With his left hand, he snatched the sheet back.

"Oh, my ... Stephanie, get in here."

"Oh, no!" Stephanie said. "One of the Chinese!"

"One of their Marines. Looks like he took a bullet to the neck. Might have been one of your bullets."

"That means they've been down here. They know how to get here," Stephanie said.

"Yes, it does." He pulled the sheet back over the corpse. "They must've brought the body down and headed back up topside. But they know how to get here. Hold this for a second." He gave her his pistol. "Close the door. If one of them shows up, put a bullet through his head."

J-11 fighter jet (codename Cougar Leader)
People's Liberation Naval Air Force
South China Sea
altitude 2,000 feet
course 375 degrees

4:15 p.m. local time

The descending sun was off to the left, casting an orange light in the cockpit of the jet as Senior Lieutenant Jong Jun checked his instruments.

Range to lead target ... seventy-five miles.

Flying lead in the aerial assault against the approaching Taiwanese battle group was of highest strategic importance to President Tang and the People's Republic.

This mission was potentially deadly. The assault against the *Vicksburg* had demonstrated the sophistication of American naval antiaircraft systems.

Of the six ships steaming toward Itu Aba, the three *Kidd*-class destroyers that Taiwan had purchased from the American Navy would be the most problematic, offering sophisticated jamming and antiaircraft missiles. The three troop transports were not heavily armed, but the ground forces that they carried would be more than enough to overwhelm the small Chinese contingent on the island.

While the Taiwanese destroyers did not possess the same level of antiaircraft sophistication as the American cruiser, there were more of them, and they were deadly accurate. The threat was enough to warrant having launched almost the entire air wing.

This attack would become the biggest test yet of the new Chinese naval muscle swirling around the great aircraft carrier *Shi Lang* and her battle group of escort ships.

The battle plan called for the first wave of thirteen jets, of which he was a part, to launch missiles and then peel off. The second and third waves of thirteen and twelve jets would do the same.

He again checked the target-tracking computer.

Range to lead target ... sixty-five miles.

It was time. "Cougar Leader to first wave. Arm missiles. Prepare to fire on my mark."

Jong reached down and flipped the switch arming his two anti-ship missiles, targeted for the lead troop carrier.

"Five.

"Four.

"Three.

"Two.

"One.

"Fire missiles!"

The J-11 jumped as two missiles shot out straight ahead, leaving white contrails in their wake. To his left and right, a battery of other missiles from the first wave streaked through the skies.

The Taiwanese would have their hands full.

Sick bay
USS **Emory S. Land**
South China Sea

4:17 p.m. local time

Where is it?" Gunner opened another drawer along the bulkhead just above the body of the dead Chinese Marine. This one contained surgical supplies, including several scalpels, knives, and sutures.

The long surgical scalpel might be helpful in the short run. He took it and stuck it under his belt. But the scalpel wasn't why he had come.

"What are you looking for?" Stephanie asked.

"My seabag," Gunner said. "The one you put under my cot. Someone's moved it. Probably a corpsman. There's something we need."

"You need me to help you look, sir?"

"No. Just guard the door. Crack it open and keep your ear peeled for any noise out in the passageway. I'll check one other place. Then we've gotta get out of here."

"Aye, sir."

There was one other possibility. The coat locker was bolted to the bulkhead on the other side. Gunner hurried across the room and opened the locker door.

There! On the deck!

Gunner picked up the seabag and ran his hands through it. In the bottom, he felt it. Yes! The lost-at-sea transmitter was still there. He pulled it out and pressed the "transmit" button. Nothing.

"Come on, baby! Work!"

He pressed the button again.

Nothing.

"Come on!"

"Sir! I hear steps!"

Gunner dropped the transmitter back into the bag. He dropped the bag back in the locker and rushed over and pressed his back against the bulkhead, his shoulder next to Stephanie's.

They lined up next to the hinge side of the door so that if anyone opened it, the door would block them from view for a split second.

The *click ... click ... click ...* of boots against the deck grew louder.

Gunner felt for the handle of the scalpel. He whispered to Stephanie, "I'll take him out by hand. But if I get into trouble, shoot him in the head."

Stephanie nodded.

The door opened a crack, then swung open.

A Chinese Marine, his back to Gunner and Stephanie, walked toward the cot and stood over the body of his dead comrade.

Gunner charged forward, and the Marine turned with a startled look on his face. Gunner rammed the scalpel into his Adam's apple.

The man staggered, grabbed at the scalpel in his throat, but as his black eyes crossed, he dropped to the floor, limp.

Gunner stood over the man and looked down. The eyes were frozen open and the mouth hung open. Blood spurted from the wound around the blade of the scalpel.

Gunner grabbed the stainless steel handle and pulled the scalpel from the man's throat. He wiped off the blood against the man's pants leg and stuck the scalpel-turned-dagger back under his belt. He picked up the Marine's rifle and slung it over his neck.

That gave them two rifles, a pistol, and a scalpel. Still not enough against all those Chinese on deck. But better than nothing.

"Are we going to do anything with the body, sir?"

"Not enough time," Gunner said. "They'll be here soon and we need every second."

"What about the transmitter? Shouldn't we take it, try to fix it?"

"I'm an intel guy, not an electronics tech. Wouldn't have a clue and don't have any equipment even if I did. No, let's leave it hidden. It would just be in the way, and we need to collect weapons. We've got to move."

"Where to?"

"Aft engine room. If this is like every other ship I've been on, that's as far away as we can get. And there are plenty of spaces to hide down there. Let's get moving."

J-11 fighter jet (codename Cougar Leader)
People's Liberation Naval Air Force
South China Sea
altitude 2,000 feet
course 375 degrees

4:30 p.m. local time

Senior Lieutenant Jong Jun swung his J-11 attack jet in a wide loop. Off to the right, visible at a distance of two miles, three of the six ships in the Taiwanese battle group sat dead in the water, engulfed in orange flames leaping into the sky. Thick black smoke plumes billowed into the heavens.

Chinese missiles had destroyed two enemy troop carriers and one enemy destroyer.

The remaining three ships, two destroyers and one troop carrier, had broken course and turned away from Itu Aba.

With the three ships retreating, the mission had been a success. The assault, however, had not been without costs. Ten of the thirty-eight jets flying the mission had been shot down by antiaircraft missiles. When the remaining three ships changed course, the *Shi Lang* wing commander had ordered the jets to break off pursuit to avoid more losses.

It was a quick attack. Most of the twenty-eight jets that survived had already turned back to the carrier.

Jong's jet, along with two other J-11s, remained on combat air patrol to maintain visual observation of the burning enemy ships.

Jong pushed down on the yoke, leveling the jet at 1,000 feet, turning in the direction of one of the troop transports. The ship's bow was rising out of the water. The stern had already disappeared.

Jong brought the jet down to 500 feet and turned into yet another loop for a closer look.

There were dozens of them. Specks in the water with arms flailing, splashing desperately to stay afloat. These were the Taiwanese Marines and sailors who were to lead the assault on Itu Aba. Some had life vests. Many did not.

It did not matter whether they had life vests. The ones who did not drown would die from having their limbs and bodies ripped apart by man-eating whitetip sharks.

Jong put the plane into a climb just as the first troop carrier disappeared under the surface, a momentary bubbling marking the spot.

He switched on his radio frequency for direct contact with the carrier.

"*Shi Lang* Control. Cougar Leader."

"Cougar Leader. *Shi Lang* Control. Go ahead."

"*Shi Lang* Control. One of the troop ships just sank. The other troop ship and destroyer are burning out of control, under no propulsion, with all systems disabled. Be advised I've just observed a major explosion from the destroyer. Possibly from her magazine rack."

Jong glanced over his right shoulder at the crippled destroyer. Two angry fires ravaged the ship, one being from the explosion in the aft section.

"Cougar Leader. *Shi Lang* Control. Excellent work. Break off patrol and return to the carrier."

The White House

4:45 a.m. local time

The black Lincoln with the "US Government" tags rolled under the north portico of the White House, which was bathed in floodlights, making the old mansion stand out against the dark of the early pre-dawn.

This was not Wylie Shepherd's first visit to the White House. But this was the first time he had been driven to the mansion in a government limousine, and now ... yes ... he was about to have his door opened by a United States Marine! Something was up.

"Good morning, sir," the Marine, in sharp dress blues and white gloves, said as he opened the door for him.

"Morning," Wylie said. He did not say, "Good Morning, Corporal," or "Good Morning, Sergeant," or whatever the Marine was, because frankly, he could not tell the difference between a corporal and a general.

"Mister Brubaker is waiting at the main entrance, sir."

"Thank you, Officer ..." Wylie stepped out of the car.

"That's Sergeant, sir. Sergeant Melesky."

"Sorry, Sergeant. I'm not familiar with Marine Corps officer ranks."

"Thank you, sir, but I'm not an officer."

"Morning, Wylie!" The recognizable voice was that of White House Chief of Staff Arnie Brubaker, who was walking out the front door of the White House. "I'll take him from here, Sergeant."

"Yes, sir," the Marine said.

"Wylie, we've gotta teach you the difference between an officer and an enlisted guy in the Marine Corps." Brubaker, the consummate politician, patted Wylie's back.

"Arnie, you know I'm a hopeless lib. The only corps I know is the Peace Corps." He cut to the point. "And it sounds like there's not much peace going on right now in the South China Sea."

"Walk with me," Brubaker said. He led the reporter in through the front door of the White House, onto white marble, past two more stiff-looking Marines.

"Where you taking me?"

"Situation Room to meet with the president."

"Must be serious."

"I'll let the president talk to you about it," the chief of staff said.

Brubaker led the way down several hallways, past a small army of Marines, Secret Service agents, and White House policemen. Brubaker was carrying on and chatting with meaningless small talk, but all the time avoiding any mention of the South China Sea.

"You ever been in the Situation Room?" Brubaker asked.

"They never let me get past the press room, Arnie."

"First time for everything." Arnie pushed open the double doors, which caused the president, the vice president, the secretaries of state and defense, and the chairman of the joint chiefs of staff all to rise, as if Wylie himself were the president entering the room.

"Thanks for coming, Wylie." The president extended his hand. "Please sit here next to me."

"Thanks for inviting me, Mister President." Wylie sat in the swivel chair next to Surber. "Looks like you gentlemen are busy."

"Unfortunately we are," Surber said. "You saw Tang's speech?"

"Yes, sir, I did."

"Well, part of what he said is true."

"May I ask which part?"

Surber exchanged glances with the secretary of defense. "It's true that things are heating up in the South China Sea. It's also true that our navies have exchanged fire. We have shot down several of their planes."

"What part of it isn't true?"

"It's not true that we captured that freighter for no reason. The freighter has evidence of crimes against humanity committed by the Chinese."

"Crimes against humanity?"

"Yes. I'm going to go into more details about all that when I address the nation this morning. But I also want you to know that what you heard about Stephanie ... that's also true."

Wylie studied the man's face, looking for some sign of human emotion, a parental concern.

Nothing. Just a straight jaw and steely eyes.

"Mister President, why are you telling me this?"

"Because we don't think the Chinese know that she's aboard the *Emory Land*. This isn't just about Stephanie. I've got hundreds of other parents and wives and husbands and children with relatives aboard that ship that I am responsible for. We think that if this information gets out, this jeopardizes our chances of saving the ship and the crew."

Wylie thought about that. "Because, I take it, they feel they would have more leverage?"

"Precisely."

"And … I take it you want me to sit on this information?"

"I can't tell you to sit on it. This is America. As president I took an oath to defend the Constitution. Last I checked, the First Amendment is still in the Constitution. But I'm asking you to consider all the lives involved—American lives—that would be in much greater jeopardy if this leaks out."

Wylie exhaled. "I can understand that, Mister President. But this is a big story. I have a responsibility to my viewers and to my network."

"Wylie," Secretary of Defense Lopez said, "how about if you consider holding the story about Stephanie being aboard until we're able to rescue the ship. Then you and your network can be the first to confirm that she is on board. We agree not to comment on the issue and will give you first dibs on the story just as soon as we've rescued this ship."

Wylie didn't like where this was going. The opportunity to break a story like this was the type of thing that could propel him to network anchor. On the other hand, he was going to have to work with this president and his press secretary for the better part of the next three and a half years. A favor now might bring huge dividends in the future.

But how could he trust these people to keep their word?

"Tell ya what, Mister Secretary. How about if you all promise to give me first dibs, plus give me the first exclusive interview with Stephanie and the president if the ship is rescued *and* with the president and First Lady if the ship is not rescued."

"Deal," the secretaries of state and defense said at the same time.

"Mister President?" Wylie looked into Surber's eyes.

"You have my word, Wylie." Surber extended his hand.

"Okay, I'm not excited about it, but with your word that I get first dibs on the story and those interviews, I'll do it."

The president grabbed Wylie's hand, squeezing it in a vice-like grip. "Thanks, Wylie. I won't forget this."

H ow bad is it, Admiral Wong?" Taiwanese President Lu felt sick.
"The situation is dire, Mister President," Admiral Wong Lu-Chen said. "We have lost two troop transport ships and one destroyer. We count ten Communist warplanes shot down, Mister President. The remaining three ships had to change course to avoid further risk."

President Lu stood and began pacing. "They threw their entire air wing at us from that new aircraft carrier of theirs?"

"Yes, Mister President. That's where we miscalculated. We didn't think they would risk their entire air wing."

Lu turned and looked out the window at the late-afternoon rush-hour traffic starting to clog Chongqing South Road. "So our armada is decimated. We have damaged part of their air wing, but if we press on to Itu Aba, we run the risk of losing the rest of our ships." He spun around and looked at the members of his national command structure. "I am reading this situation correctly?"

"Yes, sir," said Lien Chan, chief of the general staff.

Lu sat back down. "Where do we go from here?"

"If I may make a suggestion, sir?" Mark Huang, the minister of foreign affairs, said.

"Certainly."

"Sir, we must ask the Americans for military assistance."

Lu thought about that. "The Americans do not officially even recognize us. And they go to great lengths to play both sides of the fence."

"True, Mister President," Mark Huang said. "But at the same time, they have done more for us than anyone else. They sold us every one of the ships lost in today's attack. We do not yet know much about Douglas Surber, as his presidency is so new. We have nothing to lose by asking, sir."

"Very well," Lu said. "Mister Secretary, prepare a communiqué to President Surber requesting military assistance from the Americans."

"Yes, Mister President."

Presidential Palace
Zhongnanhai Compound
Beijing, People's Republic of China

5:15 p.m. local time

General Shang stood in front of a large map, aiming a pointer at the last recorded positions of allied and enemy ships and aircraft. "And so, Mister President, although we lost ten aircraft from the carrier's fighter wing, our mission succeeded. I am pleased to report" — the general turned and faced the president — "that the remaining ships of the task force have turned and are running like rats. My congratulations to Admiral Zou." Shang nodded at his naval colleague. "And to the People's Liberation Navy for the great naval victory that we have won today in a battle that will forever be known as the Great Battle of the South China Sea!"

A broad grin crept across the face of the Raging Dragon. He stood, closed his eyes, held his arms out, and lifted his palms up, as if he were a divine beatific figure.

"Yes!" His black eyes scanned the faces in the room. "The Great Battle of the South China Sea! Where Taiwan was defeated and humiliated! This after the American cruiser, the *Vicksburg*, ran from us in fear! Let it be said from this day forward that on this day, China was born as a military superpower!" He slumped back down into his chair.

The grin disappeared. His face turned quizzical, then took on a determined look. "But we must not stop now." He looked at Shang. "General, what is the status of our nuclear forces?"

"Our nuclear forces, sir?"

"Yes, General. I want to know the status of our ICBMs."

"Our ICBMs?" Shang glanced over at Admiral Zou. What was this about?

"Yes, General. I want to know about our new DF-31A intercontinental ballistic missiles. I want target recommendations against America."

"Mister President." Shang felt a queasiness. "Sir, I am not certain that it would be wise to begin targeting the Americans with our nuclear forces. My concern is that we would be escalating the conflict beyond the current realm of proportionality."

Tang cocked his head, twisted his mouth, and stared hard at Shang. "General. It is *my* job to decide if and when this conflict is escalated beyond the current realm of proportionality. May I remind *you* that someone—America or Taiwan—already escalated this conflict when they killed my brother." He leaned back in the chair. "Effective military leadership of a great superpower involves preparedness for every possibility. Leadership that is effective involves—no, requires—delivery of a knockout punch."

He leaned forward and peered hard at Shang. "Now then. I want a briefing on our DF-31A intercontinental ballistic missiles. I want specific target recommendations against the United States. If you don't think you can do that, General, I will find someone who can."

Admiral Zou shook his head just subtly enough that Shang sensed that Zou was sharing his concerns about the president's request.

"My apologies, Mister President." He cleared his throat and took a deep breath. "Our new Dong Feng 31A has a range of well over 5,000 miles, sufficient to hit targets along the entire West Coast of the United States and in several Rocky Mountain states. It incorporates design aspects similar to current-generation Russian missiles on which it is based. However, much of the advanced technology for the missiles was acquired from the USA during the Clinton Administration.

"Each Dong Feng 31A can deploy three nuclear warheads. We currently have twenty-four such missiles in our arsenal, Mister President. The missiles are mobile and can be launched from mobile platforms from any location in China. They are operated by the Second Artillery Corps, which is headquartered in Luoyang, in Henan province."

The Raging Dragon just sat there, not reacting in any way. He raised an index finger. "Very well. I am ordering you, General, as a precautionary measure, to target five DF-31A missiles against the American West Coast. Have the missile crews ready to launch if I give the order."

Shang considered objecting on the grounds that the order would create a dangerous hair-trigger situation that could put China on the brink of nuclear holocaust. America may have been weakened economically, but her ICBMs could still wipe out all of China. But based on Tang's current state of mind, now wasn't the time to object.

"Yes, sir, Mister President," Shang said. "I will pass your order on to Second Artillery Corps."

Officers Country
USS **Emory S. Land**
South China Sea

5:20 p.m. local time

Captain Wang Ligin of the Marine Corps of the People's Liberation Army-Navy, the Chinese officer in charge of the occupied American warship *Emory S. Land*, moved through the passageway, rifle pointed forward, with two rifle-bearing corporals behind him.

He was in command of the seventy-five Chinese Marines on board the *Emory Land*. Most of his men were concentrated around the ship's nerve centers — the bridge, the engineering compartments, communications and weapons areas, and on the main deck. These were the nerve centers that allowed the Marines to control the ship.

Some Marines were guarding the *Land*'s officer quarters, which, combined with control of the vital nerve centers, gave them complete control of the ship.

Still, the *Emory Land* was a big ship, with many compartments and passageways. His Marines, while controlling all the important nerve centers, were not sufficient in number to occupy all the different compartments on the vessel. The fact remained that most of the ship remained unoccupied by Wang's Marines.

This made Wang nervous. Two of his Marines were unaccounted for.

"Sergeant!"

There was no answer.

"This is the passageway he was guarding, sir," one of the corporals said. "One of the women officers is in the stateroom on the far right at the end of the passageway."

"On the far right?"

"Yes, sir. This is where we left him."

"Let's go." Wang suspected that the sergeant may have decided to take advantage of the woman officer, who was quite attractive and even had seemed familiar. A smile crossed Wang's face at the thought.

"Is this it?"

"Yes, sir."

Wang knocked on the door. "Sergeant." He knocked again. Nothing. "Sergeant! Open the door."

Nothing. He tried the door. It was locked.

"Corporal, open it."

"Yes, sir."

The corporal kicked the door open. Wang stepped into the empty stateroom. "Are you certain this was the stateroom, Corporal?"

"Yes, sir."

"Captain!" The other corporal bent down and pulled on the corner of a blanket that was sticking out from under the rack. "Look! Is that blood on this blanket?"

Wang looked down at the dark stain on the gray blanket. "Pull it out."

"Captain! A body! It is the sergeant!"

The Situation Room
the White House

5:23 a.m. local time

Secretary of State Mauney hung up the phone. "Mister President, President Lu Yen-Hsun of Taiwan is requesting a video conference."

"When?" Surber asked.

"Now, sir. Right now."

Surber looked at his advisers. "Gentlemen? Cyndi?"

"Let's hear what he has to say," Secretary Lopez said.

"Agreed," Vice President Morgan said.

"Very well," Surber said. "Arnie, get President Lu on the flat-screen."

"Yes, sir."

Arnie Brubaker picked up the phone and mumbled some instructions. A few seconds later, the flat-screens all along the conference table and on the walls lit up with a bright blizzardy image that looked like a heavy snowstorm, and then a live image of the president of Taiwan appeared.

Surber said, "Mister President. This is Douglas Surber. Can you hear me, sir?"

A second passed. "I hear you, Mister President, and now I see you," Lu said. "Thank you for taking my call."

"Tell me, Mister President, how may I be of service to you this morning?"

Another second passed—the delay from the electronic signal traveling halfway around the world. "We need your help, Mister President. Half of our fleet sailing to Itu Aba to retake the island has been destroyed. The attack by the regime in Beijing came from the aircraft carrier *Shi Lang*. We have been forced to abandon our mission ... for the time being. The carrier has resulted in a major swing in the balance of power in the South China Sea and poses a grave threat to the Republic of China.

"Mister President, your government has been the blanket of protection for the Republic of China since the Communist revolution. We are the only hope for democracy to ever return to the mainland. This you know."

Surber looked at Mauney and Lopez. He looked back at the screen. "What would you like me to do, Mister President?"

"Mister President, this carrier is a threat not only to the Republic of China but also to America, to the United States. Remember, Mister President, I know why you seized the *Shemnong*. You did so for good reason. Remember too, sir, that it was our government that asked for a US Navy doctor to be flown to the *Shemnong*. We know of China's mass atrocities. We are aware that this carrier has launched attacks on two of your ships, the *Emory Land* and the *Vicksburg*. There is a reason why they call Tang the Raging Dragon. I understand how dependent your country has become economically upon Communist China.

"Tang must be stopped. He is a charismatic genius whose goal is world domination. He started this current crisis with his unprovoked attack on Itu Aba. You and I, our countries, we are forever bonded together. Please help us, Mister President. The future of both of our countries depends on it."

Surber looked around at his advisers.

"I think we need to talk it over," Vice President Morgan said. Others nodded.

"Mister President," Surber said, "I am sympathetic to your cause. You make some good points. I am preparing to address our nation in about two hours about the situation in the South China Sea. I will discuss your request with my advisers and get back with you yet today. And please know that you and your staff and the people of the Republic of China are in our thoughts and prayers."

"Thank you, Mister President."

Entrance to engine room
USS Emory S. Land
South China Sea

5:30 p.m. local time

They worked their way down through the ship, steel ladder after steel ladder, the droning roar of the ship's engines growing louder as they approached the bottom of the ship.

"Last deck," Stephanie said.

Gunner's shoe touched the steel-grated deck. He looked up. Stephanie was almost all the way down the ladder.

"This is it," Stephanie said. "The engine room is through those doors."

Gunner looked around. No sign of anyone. "I don't think they're in there, but anything's possible. I'm going to step in and make sure the coast is clear." He handed her the pistol. "If one of them shows up, take 'em out."

"Aye, sir."

He stepped into the engine room, into a labyrinth of pipes, boilers, flashing lights, steam gauges, and electronic control panels.

"Commander!"

Gunner looked to his left. A senior chief boiler technician, wearing the nametag "Roberson," was standing behind one of the control panels.

"Anybody else with you, Senior Chief?"

"Three of us, sir. Me and a couple of first classes. Guys, come out here!"

Two petty officers, decked out in blue camouflage uniforms, joined the senior chief.

"Any sign of the Chinese?"

"A couple were down here an hour ago. They walked around with their rifles. Looked like they were searching for somebody. Then they left."

"Did they see all three of you?"

"They just saw me," the senior chief said. "They didn't see my men here."

"Did they say anything?"

"No, sir."

"Stay right there, Senior Chief."

"Yes, sir."

Gunner opened the engine room door and motioned.

The First Daughter of the United States, packing a .45-caliber pistol and with a Chinese assault rifle strapped over her shoulder, stepped into the engine room, drawing wide-eyed reactions from the senior chief and the two petty officers. Gunner sealed the hatch behind her.

"You okay, ma'am?" the senior chief asked.

"I'm fine," Stephanie said.

"You got any weapons down here?" Gunner asked.

The senior chief hesitated. "Well, that might just depend, sir."

"Depend on what?"

"Well, sir ... it might just depend on whether some officer is ordering me to be a cooperative senior chief and turn those weapons over to the Chinese. Because if that were the case, sir, I'd say no, no weapons down here."

"How about if the senior officer were to tell you that we need every weapon available to go along with the ensign's pistol and these two assault rifles we took off some dead Chinese in order to start picking off Chinese Marines and take this ship back?"

A grin crawled across the old sailor's face. "I'd say for a cause as worthy as that, sir, we just might be able to round up three .45-caliber pistols and about sixty rounds of ammo."

"Excellent," Gunner said. "Okay, here's the deal. They'll try a manhunt all over the ship to find their two missing Marines. We'll probably get a visit soon. We need those guns ready. We need to get your two petty officers, me, and Ensign Surber out of sight, ready to ambush them. We need to kill 'em, take their weapons, and get those weapons into the hands of our guys.

"To keep the noise down, avoid attracting a crowd, I'd rather take them out without firing a shot. But if we have to fire, we fire."

The senior chief grinned. "Well, it just so happens, sir, that I've got silencers for two of those pistols."

"Excellent," Gunner said. "Let's get moving. They'll be here soon."

MSNBC Capitol Bureau
Sixteenth Street, Washington, DC

5:35 a.m. local time

He thought of the bold audacity of the great American journalists who had broken the great stories in the last hundred years. Ben Bradlee — the Pentagon Papers. Seymour Hersh — the My Lai Massacre. Woodward and Bernstein — Watergate. Nick Davies — Murdoch and NewsCorp.

In each case, he thought, these brave journalists broke their stories to the embarrassment of the administration sitting in power.

They were lions of the field — destined for the Mount Rushmore of journalism.

And now he — Wylie Shepherd — was poised to set his name above his contemporaries in the annals of journalistic history.

He donned a navy blazer and stepped into his producer's office.

"Bob, I need to talk to you."

"About what, Wylie?"

"I need to go on air."

"When?"

"Right now."

USS Emory S. Land
South China Sea

5:45 p.m. local time

Captain Wang Ligin, accompanied by two enlisted Marines with rifles cocked in firing position, moved through the passageway four decks below the main deck.

As the senior Marine aboard the ship, Wang was the onboard commander of Operation Counterpunch at its point of attack. And while the attack and capture of the large ship had gone smoothly, the murder of one of his Marines and the disappearance of the young woman officer had changed the dynamics of the mission. He feared that a rebellion had begun. The question was whether he was dealing with an organized rebellion or an isolated incident.

He had to find the woman. She was at the center of it. The body of his Marine was found in her stateroom. He would find her and kill her.

They moved through the passageway, slowly and deliberately.

The shrill beeping in the distance sounded like a fire alarm. Perhaps a radiation alarm.

Wang stopped and held up his hand.

"What is it?" he asked.

"An alarm?" the sergeant said.

"It's that way," the corporal said.

"Let's go."

They moved toward the sound. Step by step. "Isn't this the sick bay?"

"Yes, sir," the sergeant said. "This is where we brought Corporal Li's body."

"It is coming from in there," the corporal said.

"Cover me," Wang ordered. He pushed open the door and stepped in, rifle first.

The body of a Chinese Marine was sprawled out on the deck in a pool of blood, a gash in his neck.

"Sergeant! Corporal! Get in here!"

The two rushed in, weapons drawn.

Wang turned his attention to the beeping. It was coming from a canvas bag on the floor in a corner. He picked up the bag and looked in. He dropped the bag and jumped back. A cylindrical device was flashing and beeping.

"A bomb?" the sergeant asked.

Wang carefully opened the bag and studied the device. "No, I don't think so. Looks like a homing device." He tried pushing several buttons on the side of it. Nothing. "Get back." He set the beeping cylinder down on the deck, over in a corner. He grabbed his pistol and worked the action. "Step out into the passageway."

"Yes, sir."

Wang took several steps back, trained his pistol on the device, and pulled the trigger.

**The Situation Room
the White House**

6:00 a.m. local time

Mister President," Arnie Brubaker rushed back into the Situation Room, as he had been doing throughout the night. "I'm sorry for interrupting, sir, but MSNBC is advertising that Wylie Shepherd is about to go on the air live."

"I don't like the sound of this," Surber said.

"Me neither," Secretary Lopez said.

"Did they say why?" Secretary Mauney asked.

"They say major breaking news about the naval war in the South China Sea."

"If he does what I think he's about to do, I'll kill him myself," Surber said. "Put on MSNBC."

"Yes, sir."

The flat-screens around the room, displaying a satellite image of the South China Sea, switched to MSNBC. The desk anchor was speaking. "And now, with major breaking news from a rapidly escalating naval war in the South China Sea, a war which is pitting the United States against China, here's MSNBC's Wylie Shepherd."

The screen switched to Wylie Shepherd standing in front of a map of the South China Sea.

"Thank you, Dick." Wylie Shepherd looked into the camera. "That's right. The Chinese president, Tang Qhichen, appeared on television last evening to describe events of what appears to be a naval war brewing in the South China Sea between the United States, Taiwan, and China.

"President Tang reported that China has captured a United States warship, the USS *Emory S. Land*, a submarine tender, which supplies materials such as food and weapons to submarines."

A photograph of the *Emory S. Land* appeared on the screen.

"MSNBC has learned that President Tang's claims about the capture of the *Emory Land* are correct. Moreover, this reporter has learned, and indeed has verified, that Ensign Stephanie Surber, the daughter of US President Douglas Surber, is an officer on board the *Emory Land*." A photo of Stephanie in her dress white naval uniform flashed on the screen.

"I'll kill him myself," Surber said.

"Let me repeat. This reporter has learned, and indeed has verified, that Ensign Stephanie Surber, the daughter of US President Douglas Surber, is an officer on board the *Emory Land*. We do not believe the Chinese are aware that Ensign Surber is on board, as there has been no indication of that. No mention has been made of her presence. No demands have been made by the Chinese regarding the president's daughter. President Douglas Surber is to address the nation at eight this morning. Stay right here on MSNBC for all the latest in this developing story. The president's speech will be carried live on MSNBC at—"

A telephone on the conference table rang. Admiral Jones picked it up and spoke softly.

"Turn that trash off," Surber ordered.

"Yes, sir," Arnie said.

"Mister President, interesting news," the admiral said.

"Let me guess. SEAL Team Six is on the way to take out Wylie Shepherd?"

"No, sir, but possibly to board the *Emory Land*."

"Talk to me, Admiral."

"Our satellites just picked up a homing beacon. It's the same homing beacon that broadcast when Commander McCormick was lost at sea. Those devices sometimes shut down for hours at a time to save the batteries, then fire back up. We think that's what happened. We got a fifteen-minute burst, and then it went dark again. But that was long enough to get coordinates. USS *Shiloh* is in the area, and we're going to launch a drone to the coordinates to check it out. It's getting dark over there right now, but if we can find the ship, we've got a shot, sir."

Mister President, big news out of Washington, DC, which I think you will find fascinating," General Shang said.

"Surber is acquiescing to my demands and will exchange the *Emory Land* for the *Shemnong*?"

"Not yet, sir. But Surber might be more willing to negotiate after what we have just learned."

"Out with it, General."

"An American reporter on their television claims that President Surber's daughter, Stephanie Surber, is an officer on board the *Emory Land*!"

"What?" Tang stood up behind his desk. "This is a trick! Why would a reporter reveal such crucial information to the enemy in the midst of a war?"

"Well, Mister President" — Shang stroked his chin — "many in their press corps are ... socialist in their leanings."

"Is this information true?"

"There is a woman officer on board who fits the description, but we cannot find her at the moment. The American reporter, Wylie Shepherd, is reporting that it is true! Said he has confirmed this information!"

Tang let out a belly laugh. "This is too good to be true. If I were not an atheist, I might believe in God! What a glorious opportunity! General, have the propaganda ministry prepare immediate press releases to all the American television networks that we have captured the Surber girl. And that unless Douglas Surber releases the *Shemnong*, the Surber girl will be executed!"

"But, Mister President," Shang said.

"You have a problem with that, General?"

"No, sir. With all due respect, sir, my duties are to advise you on military matters. And the key to the successful prosecution of any military operation is managing the military conflict with careful proportional escalation."

"Your point, General?"

"My point, Mister President, is that if we make mention of Surber's daughter and threaten her execution, that would come across as inflammatory and would escalate the conflict with the Americans beyond what is necessary at the moment. Moreover, there are Geneva Convention concerns about threatening the execution of a prisoner of war."

Admiral Zou nodded in agreement. But Tang, whose eyes bored into Shang's, apparently did not notice the admiral nodding.

"My dear General." Tang's voice rose. His lips trembled. "Have you forgotten that the Americans have killed my only brother by their imperialist aggression? By interfering in our area of influence? Have you forgotten that?"

"No, sir."

"And are you saying that the life of the daughter of the American president is more important than the life of the brother of the Chinese president?"

Shang hesitated. "No, sir. Of course not."

"Then carry out my directive!"

"Yes, Mister President."

**Third-floor dining room
the White House**

6:15 a.m. local time

Hope-Caroline Surber, fighting sleeplessness for the last three hours, walked into the third-floor dining room, the private dining room reserved for the First Family. She sat alone at a small mahogany table covered with a white linen tablecloth.

"How may I be of service to you, Madame?" Charles, the elderly black waiter, smiled at her.

"I need something to settle my stomach, Charles. Maybe ginger ale?"

"Of course, ma'am."

"And Charles?"

"Yes, ma'am?"

"Would you turn on Fox, please?"

"Of course, ma'am."

The waiter picked up the remote control, pointed it toward a flat-screen television on the wall, and pressed a button.

Tom Miller, in a light-blue dress shirt and wearing his traditional wire-rim glasses, appeared on the screen.

"This just in. Chinese authorities are confirming the report from earlier this morning that Ensign Stephanie Surber, a naval officer on board the USS *Emory Land* and the First Daughter of the United States, is not only on the ship but, according to the Chinese, she has been captured and is in the custody of the Chinese.

"According to communiqués received by the US Embassy in Beijing and copied to US media outlets, if President Surber does not order the release of the Chinese freighter *Shemnong* within the next two hours, then Ensign Surber and several other officers aboard the *Emory Land* will be immediately put on trial for war crimes.

"Again, according to the communiqué," Miller looked up at the camera, "that war crimes trial could take place as early as today on board the *Emory Land*. A Chinese court would be convened aboard the ship. Anyone convicted of war crimes under Chinese law could be subject to execution, which sources say could be carried out aboard the ship … today.

"Still nothing from the White House, but we understand that President Surber is set to address the nation at eight this morning, in an hour and forty-five minutes."

Hope-Caroline reached over and grabbed the remote control and flipped off the television. She prayed for the strength not to faint in front of the White House kitchen staff.

"Your ginger ale and tea, ma'am."

She looked up and saw Charles standing nearby holding a silver tray with a glass of ginger ale and steaming hot tea.

"I'm sorry, Charles. I've got to find my husband."

"I'll be here for you, ma'am."

Engine room
USS **Emory S. Land**
South China Sea

6:17 p.m. local time

Huddled in a semicircle, Stephanie and the others listened closely to Gunner McCormick as he spelled out his plan for retaking the ship.

"Here's the deal," Gunner said. "We've gotta hurry. They've got a whole lot more guns than we do. But thanks to this schematic diagram of the inside of the ship the senior chief provided, we know where all the ladders and compartments are. And they don't. And that gives us a huge advantage.

"So here's what we do. We split up and head up separate ladders, out of the main corridors. We'll hide in the cracks and crevices of the ship, and when one of their Marines strays from the rest, we'll pick him off. We'll get 'em, one by one. We'll take the guns off the dead bodies and give them to our sailors. We'll take this ship back. Now that their choppers are gone, we can do this."

"Let's move!... Ensign Surber, you stay here."

"Commander!" Stephanie protested.

"No time for that, Stephanie," Gunner shot back.

Gunner eyed each member of the small group. "Ready?"

"Ready!" they replied.

Stephanie could only marvel at the speedy recovery Gunner had made. He seemed so strong and confident for someone who just yesterday was suffering from severe dehydration.

He reminded her of Bobby Roddick, and tears threatened to spill. She bit her lip to regain her composure. Now was the time for strength. She would do this for the XO.

"Stephanie, be on your guard. We don't need you to become a trophy. And no buts. Stay out of sight. There are plenty of places to hide. I'll be back. But if anyone shows up before I return, you know what to do. Understand?" He put a hand on her shoulder.

"I'll put a bullet between the eyes, Commander."

President Douglas Surber listened to the debate raging among his national security advisers.

"This guy's a nut," Vice President Morgan said.

"Yes, but I think he's bluffing about this war crimes thing," Secretary Lopez said.

"But do we know he's bluffing?" This was from Secretary Mauney. "I know that he's crazy and therefore dangerous."

"Admiral, any word on that homing signal we picked up?" the national security adviser, Cyndi Hewitt, asked.

"We've launched a drone from USS *Shiloh* to explore those coordinates. No news yet."

"Excuse me, Mister President?"

Surber turned around. His chief of staff had just walked into the room.

"What is it, Arnie?"

"I apologize, sir, but the First Lady is outside. I told her that you were busy, but she insisted. She wants to see you."

Surber checked his watch: 6:26 a.m. "Gentlemen, Cyndi, excuse me for a minute." He got up and stepped out the double doors of the Situation Room.

Hope-Caroline was outside, accompanied by a Secret Service agent. "Doug, we need to talk."

"Let's step over here." He put his hand on her back and they walked away from three Secret Service agents who were standing closest. "Give us some privacy, gentlemen."

"What is it? I've got an international crisis."

"Yes, I know. I heard Tom Miller say that they've got Stephanie, and that they're going to kill her if you don't release that ship."

Her words felt like someone had dumped a bag of crushed ice all over him.

"Doug, this is our daughter! I don't know why you captured that freighter ... but ..."—tears streamed down her face—"I didn't sign up for this."

He pulled her close to him. Her body shook. And now the sobbing overpowered her ability to say anything.

"Mark." He motioned to one of the Secret Service agents who was standing off to the side.

"Yes, Mister President."

"Please call Sarah down here." He was referring to Sarah Edwards, Hope-Caroline's personal aide.

"Yes, sir. Right away."

He held her tight, and as they stood there, the words of his own secretary of state, spoken just four hours ago, danced in his head: "With respect, sir, I agree with the secretary of defense. We don't want Stephanie to become a pawn giving greater leverage to the Chinese. But if they discover that she is on board ..."

Maybe they were right. Maybe God was giving him advice through his advisers. Maybe it wasn't all worth it. Was he really going to stop these baby-killing atrocities by exposing the horrific evidence on board that ship? Maybe he should instruct Bobby Mauney to contact the Chinese and negotiate the release of the freighter. At least that might save the American lives on board, including his only child.

Sarah Edwards walked into the waiting area and came over to them. "Sarah's here. I need you to go with her now."

Sarah put her arm around Hope-Caroline's shoulders and gently led her away.

With clenched jaw and insides shredded into a million pieces of confetti, Douglas Surber stepped back into the Situation Room.

Engine room
USS **Emory S. Land**
South China Sea

6:35 p.m. local time

Under bright fluorescent lights, crouching behind a steel drum off to the side of the engine room, Stephanie had a clear view of the passageway running down the middle of the spaces and of the port entrance to the engine room.

She was alone. Gunner had taken the senior chief and the two petty officers topside to hunt Chinese Marines, get as many weapons as they could.

She was not afraid to be alone, yet the sight before her, all the steel and wiring and flashing lights and haze gray paint, somehow hit a nerve, made her realize the extreme danger. Tears started streaming down her face.

The hatch of the portside entrance swung open and a Chinese Marine stepped into the engine room. She hunkered down a little tighter and aimed her pistol for a clear shot. Just then a second Marine walked in. And a third.

She slid down farther behind the huge steel drum. Her heart pounded as she calculated the math. One pistol with fifteen rounds versus three assault rifles with at least forty-five rounds, and that was in the first wave. They could reload. She could not.

For this to work, she had to be fast … and accurate. If she missed or took out only one or even two of the three, a .45-caliber pistol versus an assault rifle could be suicide.

Should she wait it out? Wait for them to leave? Stay hidden?

No. Not a good idea. The Chinese had attacked the ship. They killed Bobby. Yes, she was outnumbered, but she still had the element of surprise—which might be gone if she didn't act now.

She heard them talking. Their boots clicked on the deck. They were coming closer. She figured they would fan out and search the engine room. If she was going to fire, now was the time before they got spread out too far.

She eased around the drum and saw them, standing together. She drew a bead on the head of the first one.

She squeezed the trigger three times and ducked back down behind the tank. The deafening blast of gunfire echoed against the labyrinth of steel beams and pipes.

She heard a harrowing primordial scream.

Thump. Thump.

Then … silence. The only sound was the roar of the ship's engines, the wash of the sea against the steel hull. Her heart was pounding.

She thought she had hit two. Still no sound. Maybe all three.

She waited, then, gun leading, she crawled to the end of the steel drum for a look.

The head of one Chinese Marine came into view. Her bullet had hit him right between the eyes. Blood had pooled under his head. His eyes and mouth were frozen open.

Staying low, she crept a bit farther. The second Marine was over the leg of the first, face down.

Where was the third?

A shot rang out!

Hot pain seared her left arm. She fell back. She'd been hit!

Her gun? Where was it?

There! On the deck!

She lunged for it and rolled, then looked up.

The third Marine was standing almost over her, his rifle aimed right at her head. The front of his uniform was soaked with blood.

The explosion of gunfire slammed her head back against the steel deck.

US Navy "Fire Scout" MQ-8B robotic helicopter
over the South China Sea
altitude 18,000 feet

6:45 p.m. local time

The gray "Fire Scout" robotic helicopter, a small pilotless aircraft with elements of stealth technology, chopped through the dusky sky over the South China Sea at 18,000 feet, its infrared camera focused on the waters below.

More than one hundred miles to the east, Navy Lieutenant Bradley Lucas sat in an electronic cubicle in the Combat Information Center aboard the *Ticonderoga*-class cruiser USS *Shiloh*. Holding an electronic joystick, Lucas controlled the Fire Scout and monitored live images being fed from the high-powered in-flight camera.

The GPS computer feeding data to the screen showed that the Fire

Scout was about to approach the position matched by the homing beacon signal that had been briefly picked up by US satellites.

Daylight was fading, but so far, the weather had cooperated. Visibility was clear with no cloud cover to obstruct the greenish seascape below.

Lucas pulled back on the control stick. On the screen, still nothing but a green expanse below.

And then ...

The outline of a ship. A warship!

And then a second ship! Much larger than the first. The *Emory S. Land*!

A third ship, same design as the first, was on the other side of the *Emory Land*. The Chinese were guarding the *Emory Land* with a destroyer escort on each side.

"CIC to Bridge."

"Bridge. Go ahead, CIC."

"Good news, Skipper! Fire Scout has located the target!"

CHAPTER 30

The Situation Room
the White House

6:55 a.m. local time

Admiral Roscoe Jones hung up the telephone. "Mister President, we've found the *Emory Land*."

"Okay!" Surber's heart raced. "That's a positive step." He wanted to feel relieved, but could not. Finding the ship did not mean that Stephanie was safe or that she would survive a firefight to retake the ship. "Recommendations, Admiral?"

"Are you asking for my recommendations on how we should try to recapture the ship?"

"That's precisely what I'm asking you."

Admiral Jones glanced at the secretary of defense, and then back at Surber. "Mister President, the Chinese are guarding the *Emory Land* with two destroyers, one on each side. They aren't moving at the moment, just maintaining their position in the water.

"The nuclear sub USS *Georgia* can be in that location in about thirty minutes. The *Georgia* has a SEAL team aboard, which can approach the *Emory Land* in a mini-sub launched underwater from the mother sub.

"As long as the drone flying above the targets remains undetected, we have an opportunity to take out the destroyers with cruise missiles launched from the USS *Shiloh* and coordinate that attack with a SEAL assault against the *Emory Land*." The admiral removed his wire-rim glasses. "However, Mister President, even if we are able to recapture the ship, I cannot guarantee the safety of the officers and enlisted personnel on board."

Surber hesitated. "Admiral, I know what you're saying. The Chinese might kill my daughter during the course of this operation. Right?"

"Well, sir ..."

"Listen. And this goes for all of you. Am I worried sick about my daughter? You bet I am. And does a part of me as a father scream on the inside to give in to Tang's demands? Of course. But I believe that the right thing to do, ethically and morally, is to not turn over the *Shemnong*. Therefore, I cannot let my actions as commander in chief be dictated by the fact that my daughter's life may be in danger, especially when others who serve also are in danger.

"I'm ordering all of you, until this is over — and I know you mean well — but I don't want you feeding me special information about Stephanie above and beyond the general military situation at hand. Is that clear?"

"Yes, sir, Mister President."

"Yes, sir."

"Now then," Surber continued, "Admiral Jones. Are you recommending that I authorize this mission to try to recapture the *Emory Land*?"

"Yes, sir."

"Very well. Execute the order. The minute that operation is under way, I'm going on national television, even if that's before 8:00 a.m. Americans are waiting to hear from their president, and I've waited too long already."

"Yes, Mister President."

Interior Ladder 4
USS Emory S. Land

7:00 p.m. local time

With the .45-caliber pistol stuffed into his back belt and a silencer screwed into the barrel, Gunner climbed the steel utility ladder.

According to the senior chief, this ladder would lead straight up to a hatch that would open onto the ship's main deck, about thirty feet from the bridge, but not within direct sight of the bridge. Chinese Marine guards would be milling about on deck in the area.

He stepped off the ladder onto an inner deck. The hatch was over to the right. It had a porthole in the middle of it, allowing a view of the outside.

Gunner pulled the gun from his belt and pressed his back against the interior bulkhead. He slid over close to the hatch to get a look out the porthole.

So far, nothing outside but sky.

He decided to go outside and scope out the situation. He could always return to the ladder if he needed an escape. He put his hands on the latch to push open the hatch.

Two Chinese Marines, with rifles slung over their shoulders, walked by, heading forward in the direction of the bridge. As Gunner started to open the hatch, two more walked by.

He quickly opened the hatch, climbed out and aimed his pistol. He squeezed the trigger four times. The gunshots were muffled by the silencer, barely audible over the evening sea breeze.

The four Chinese dropped to the deck, piled on top of each other, with bullets in the back of their heads. He had to move quickly.

He grabbed the four assault rifles and lined them up against the bulkhead.

Yanking one body off the pile, with his boot, he shoved the Marine under the steel safety wire and over the side of the ship. By the time the fourth body splashed into the sea below, the only evidence left was blood on the deck.

He slung the four rifles over his shoulder and stepped back inside the ship just as one of the petty officers from the engine room was rushing up the ladder.

"Commander! You've got to come quick!"

"What wrong?"

"It's Ensign Surber, sir. She's been shot!"

Control Room
USS Georgia

7:15 p.m. local time

When the 1991 Strategic Arms Reduction Treaty with Russia forced the Navy to reduce its big Trident missile submarines to a total of fourteen, a decision had to be made on what to do with four submarines whose presence would have exceeded the maximum number.

To comply with the START treaty, rather than scrap these billion-dollar boats, the Navy removed their ballistic-missile silos in order to reconfigure them for another mission.

In the aftermath of 9/11, the subs were reconfigured for special operations in the war on terror. Carrying SEAL teams of up to sixty members, the reconfigured super-subs were equipped with multiple SDVs—the Navy acronym for SEAL Delivery Vehicles—which were open-water mini-subs allowing SEAL units to strike anywhere, anytime, on any open water in the world.

Three of the submarines selected for reconfiguration—nicknamed the "Tactical Tridents"—were the USS *Ohio*, USS *Michigan*, and USS *Florida*.

A fourth, the USS *Georgia*, under the command of Captain Roger Stacks, United States Navy, was currently operating in the South China Sea.

From the command post in the boat's control room, Stacks contemplated the *Georgia*'s role in the mission that was about to unfold.

Georgia had been ordered to launch a SEAL team assault on the USS *Emory Land* in order to recapture the ship from Chinese Marines and rescue the daughter of the president of the United States.

"Mister Moore. Range to target," Stacks said.

"Range to target, two thousand yards, sir."

"Very well. All ahead one-third."

"All ahead one-third. Aye, sir."

"Up scope."

"Aye, sir. Up scope."

Stacks waited a few seconds for the boat's periscope to reach the surface. Then, as the sub's engineers carried out his commands to slow their approach to one-third power, he stepped behind the periscope for a look up top.

The infrared images on the screen showed not one, but three ships. The ships were barely moving. They had settled outside the heavily trafficked sea lanes in an area where they were less likely to be spotted by other ships or aircraft.

In the center was the large fat-bodied *Emory Land*. Stacks had seen this very same image in the periscope yesterday morning, just before the *Georgia* was resupplied by *Emory Land*. On each side of *Emory Land*, lying lower in the water, a Chinese destroyer stood guard.

The destroyers were targets in this operation, but they were someone else's targets. Right now, the *Georgia*'s mission was to get SEALs on board *Emory Land*.

Captain Stacks stepped back from the periscope. "All engines stop!"

"All engines stop!"

"All engines stop! Aye, Captain!"

"Mister Moore, is the SEAL team prepared to launch?"

"Aye, sir. SEAL team in place in tubes one and four, ready for launch."

"Very well," Stacks said.

Combat Information Center
USS Shiloh

7:20 p.m. local time

Fire Scout. Bridge."

"Go ahead, Bridge." Lieutenant Bradley Lucas, sitting in the *Shiloh*'s Combat Information Center, continued to monitor the three ships on the screen that were 18,000 feet below the Fire Scout drone helicopter that he was piloting remotely.

"Fire Scout. USS *Georgia* reports SEAL team deployed. Initiate targeting."

"Roger that," Lucas said. "Initiate targeting." Lucas punched two buttons on his control panel. The first was the ACTIVATE LASER button. The second was the TARGET LASER button.

Within seconds, miniature laser beams shot down from Fire Scout into the superstructure of each of the two Chinese warships. They provided precise targeting information back to the Fire Scout, which fed data to the fire-control computer aboard USS *Shiloh*. That computer fed targeting data into the internal guidance computers of four Tomahawk cruise missiles that were in launch position on the *Shiloh*.

"WEPS. Bridge."

"WEPS. Go ahead, sir," the missiles officer said.

Lucas listened to the open communications over his headset.

"Prepare to launch Tomahawks One and Two."

"Tomahawks One and Two. Prepare to launch on your order, sir."

"All hands. This is the XO. Prepare for missile launch in fifteen seconds."

"WEPS. Bridge. Stand by to launch in five seconds ... four ... three ... two ... one ... Fire missiles!"

"Fire missiles! Aye, sir."

Lucas glanced to the right of the center monitor, at the monitor set to show the Tomahawk launch via closed-circuit television all over the sub.

A massive burst of fire, followed by billowing white smoke, filled the screen. Two Tomahawk cruise missiles streaked into the darkening night sky.

"Stand by to launch Tomahawks Three and Four in five seconds ... four ... three ... two ... one ... Fire missiles!"

"Fire missiles! Aye, sir."

More smoke and fire on the screen. Two more Tomahawks fired off into the night sky.

The Tomahawks, all four of them, would initially ascend and then descend to level off at fifty feet above the sea, flying to the east, destined for a deadly rendezvous with the two Chinese destroyers.

Lucas looked up at the center screen. This was a risky surgical-strike attempt.

The descending time clock in the lower right corner of the center screen showed initial impact with target—now T minus nine minutes.

For this to work, those Tomahawks had to strike with absolute precision. If the targeting sequence malfunctioned, if any of the missiles veered off course and struck the *Emory Land*, the results would be catastrophic.

The Situation Room
the White House

7:25 a.m. local time

His guts felt like tangled spaghetti, but Surber set his jaw, focused
on the flat-screen, and listened as the chairman of the joint chiefs,
Admiral Roscoe Jones, explained the military operation that was unfolding half a world away.

"Mister President, we'll be watching this operation in real time,
from a high-tech camera on board a stealth Navy drone flying 18,000
feet above the ships."

Although Surber heard every word, his eyes and his mind and his
heart were glued on the image of the big ship in the middle. Through
the eye of the powerful infrared camera, the ships on the screen glowed
whitish against the dark water, replicating the sensation of viewing an
illuminated X-ray. Crew members, taking on a glowing, ant-like appearance from the camera's altitude, could be seen moving about on all
three ships. Somewhere within the middle ship, she was there—so
deceptively close by the surrealistic image on a television screen, yet so
impossibly far away.

As he prayed silently, memories and visions swirled within him—of
Steph as a little girl, of their travels as a young family at a more innocent time when he was a young naval officer in San Diego. Memories of
him spinning her on the merry-go-round at Coronado's Glorietta Park
to her chants of "Faster, Daddy, faster!" Of chocolate smeared all over
her chubby little cheeks on those "secret" daddy-daughter excursions
to the chocolate factory in La Jolla, when they would get away while
"mummy" was at the Mission Valley mall buying designer clothes. And
of their East Coast vacation to Hilton Head when, as a four-year-old,
perched high up on his shoulders, her big brown eyes as big as pancakes
at her first sighting of a live alligator, she defiantly proclaimed, "Alligator! She won't bite me!"

She was a daddy's girl then, and she was a daddy's girl now.

She was just like him. Defiant. Determined. Hardheaded. And she
was smart.

Followed him into the Navy over Hope-Caroline's pleadings ...

"As I have explained," Admiral Jones continued, "this is a risky and dangerous operation. Our success depends on the accuracy of those Tomahawks. If the Tomahawks strike the Chinese destroyers, this will give cover to our SEAL team to board *Emory Land*.

"The SEALs are en route to the ship aboard small open-water mini-subs launched from USS *Georgia*, submerged about a mile astern of the ships. The SEAL teams should be in place now. So, to recap, the success of this mission depends on accuracy, chaos, and surprise." Jones paused. "Any questions, sir?"

Surber thought for a second. "Admiral, on the missile strikes. What do you estimate our percentage of success?"

"You mean how do I rate the chances that those missiles strike the Chinese destroyers and not the *Emory Land*?"

"Precisely."

"We're operating in tight quarters here, sir. As you can see, these ships are all floating within about one hundred yards of each other. The good news is they aren't moving much in the water. They've cut their propellers to make them harder for passive sonar to pick up. A stationary target is easier to hit. But the ships are still jam-tight together, and there's a chance the missiles could get confused on targeting.

"As long as we don't have any hitches, I'd say the chance of all four Tomahawks finding their targets is about 70 percent. But if something goes wrong with that drone, it's a crapshoot, sir. And if *Emory Land* gets hit ..." Jones slipped on a pair of glasses. "Mister President, if you want to cancel the missile strike, we can detonate the Tomahawks midair. But you have to tell me now, sir."

Surber looked up at the screen. In the lower right of the screen, the digital countdown running in reverse order displayed: TIME TO IMPACT ... 2:23 ... 2:22 ... 2:21 ...

"We've got about two minutes before the missiles strike?"

"Correct, sir. Two minutes fifteen seconds to initial missile strike. If you're going to abort, sir, we need to know within the next thirty seconds."

The screen went blank, all except the countdown clock in the lower right.

"What the—" Admiral Jones picked up the hotline to the Pentagon.

Combat Information Center
USS Shiloh

7:26 p.m. local time

L ieutenant, what's going on down there?" the skipper's voice boomed over the radio headset.

"Not sure, sir!" Lieutenant Lucas punched a series of backup codes into the control panel. "We've lost contact with the drone!"

"What's the problem?"

"I'm not sure. Maybe they shot it down! We've lost targeting feed to the missiles!"

"Well, get it fixed, Lieutenant! Last thing we need is for one of those Tomahawks to slam into the *Emory Land*!"

The Situation Room
the White House

7:26 a.m. local time

S ir we've lost all contact with the drone," Admiral Jones told the president in a cool, matter-of-fact voice.

"Explanation, Admiral?" Surber watched the clock tick down.

1:30 ...

   1:29 ...

"We've lost real-time targeting feed to the Tomahawks. The missiles will fly to the last position beamed to them from the drone. If they miss, their internal radar will start looking for targets. It could get dicey."

"Is it too late to abort?"

"Yes, sir. Too late."

"Jesus, please help us." Surber wiped cold sweat drops from his forehead.

Combat Information Center
USS Shiloh

7:27 p.m. local time

Come on, baby!" Brad Lucas said.

"T minus one minute to impact." The automated voice from the fire-control computer.

"Come on ... come on ..." Lucas punched yet another backup code onto the uplink keyboard.

"Lost Connection ..."

"Let me think."

He stopped a second. "God, please help me."

Officers crowded behind Lucas in a semicircle. He felt their breath on the back of his neck.

"Let me try one more thing." He thought, trying to remember.

"T minus forty-five seconds to impact," the automated voice announced.

"There was a reboot code the instructor came up with," he said, more to himself than to anyone else. "Wasn't in the manual. Just something the instructor told me about as a last-ditch effort. What was it? ... God, help me to remember this."

The Situation Room
the White House

7:27 a.m. local time

Against a black screen with the words *COMMUNICATIONS MAL-FUNCTION* flashing in the center, the chronometer continued its countdown.

29 seconds ...

28 seconds ...

The president of the United States, the most powerful man in the world, felt paralyzed in his chair at the end of the table. He prayed silently.

The phone rang from the Pentagon.

"Admiral Jones ... what? ... when?"

The black screen morphed into something resembling an electronic meteor shower. And then ... the images of the three ships reappeared!

15 seconds ...

14 seconds ...

"Hang onto your seats, gentlemen," Admiral Jones announced, hanging up the phone. "We've reestablished contact!"

3 seconds ...

2 seconds ...

From the left and the right, two Tomahawks flew into the screens and exploded in the Chinese ships. A split second later, two more Tomahawks finished the job.

Smoke clouds billowed so large over each destroyer that their outlines became invisible.

"Bull's-eye!" Admiral Jones said.

The line from the Pentagon rang again.

"Jones ... Roger that ... Keep me posted." He hung up. "Mister President, Navy SEALs are now boarding the *Emory Land*."

Surber exhaled in relief. He could do no more. The fate of his daughter, and of every member of the crew, was now in God's hands—and in the hands of SEAL Team Six.

"Very well," the president said. "Let's get up to the Oval Office. I've got a nation that's waiting for some answers."

**Third Floor Dining Room
the White House**

7:32 a.m. local time

I t'll be okay, Mrs. Surber." Sarah Edwards sat with Hope-Caroline at the small table in the private presidential dining room on the third floor of the White House. "The president's a good man," Sarah said. "Besides, we're going to pray that Stephanie and the whole crew of that ship will be safe."

Hope-Caroline gazed into the kind face of her forty-year-old personal aide. "You know you don't have to call me Mrs. Surber." She smiled at her. "Hope-Caroline will be fine."

As Sarah took Hope-Caroline's hand, Charles walked up to the table. "Mrs. Surber, the president is about to address the nation. Would you like to watch?"

"I thought that was supposed to be at eight o'clock."

"Yes, ma'am. I think they decided to go on early."

"Yes. Turn it on, please."

Charles nodded. A second later, Fox anchor Tom Miller appeared on the screen, saying, "And now, from the Oval Office, the president of the United States."

The screen cut to the Oval Office, where her husband, having donned a navy blazer, sat behind his deck in front of the bay window overlooking the South Lawn.

"My fellow Americans.

"Pope John Paul II once said that 'Radical changes in world politics leave America with a heightened responsibility to be, for the world, an example of a genuinely free, democratic, just, and humane society.'

"Just a few short days ago, naval forces of China attacked Itu Aba Island, a small island in the South China Sea, an island that has been controlled by Taiwan since 1950.

"Because it is not in the best interests of the United States or the world for China and Taiwan to be at war, I sent several US Navy ships into the region to deter a war before it could get started.

"As the first elements of our naval forces were arriving, Taiwan stopped a Chinese freighter, the M/V *Shemnong*, because they suspected that the *Shemnong* was transporting weapons to reinforce Chinese forces on Itu Aba Island.

"As it turned out, the Taiwanese were right. But weapons were not the only cargo found on board the *Shemnong*.

"The Taiwanese made a shocking and gruesome discovery. In the bowels of the *Shemnong*, in a refrigerated cargo bay, there literally were thousands of dead babies preserved in fluid in large glass containers inside shipping crates marked 'Medical Supplies.' Some of these infants died before birth. Some died after birth. All were girls.

"Taiwan asked for our help. So we sent a US Navy medical team on board the *Shemnong*. Our examination of these babies revealed something even more shocking. All had been murdered. A document we obtained revealed that these bodies—these babies—were to be sold on the black market.

"This crime against humanity was so despicable that I ordered the *Shemnong* seized to preserve evidence of these atrocities, to ensure that the monsters who murdered these babies are brought to justice, and to ensure that the bodies of these babies get a proper burial.

"As you may know by now, China retaliated by attacking and seizing a US Navy warship, the USS *Emory S. Land*. The *Emory Land* is a submarine tender without the weaponry to defend herself against overwhelming forces. Unfortunately, the *Emory Land* was in the wrong place at the wrong time, as we did not have ships in place to defend her at the time of the attack.

"However, I can report that at this very moment, US Navy SEALs are executing a rescue operation to retake the *Emory Land* from Chinese Marines.

"I warn China that any further attacks on American naval forces will bring about severe consequences. I call upon China and Taiwan to immediately cease fire and to negotiate a diplomatic solution to the crisis in the South China Sea.

"As far as President Tang's demand that we immediately return the *Shemnong*, well I can tell you that this is not going to happen. Not until after we expose to the world the evidence of these shameful atrocities that have been going on in China. And not until after we are assured that the murderers who committed these crimes will be brought to justice.

"Thank you, and may God bless America."

The screen lingered on Surber for a second, and then switched back to Tom Miller at Fox.

"That's enough, Charles. Thank you."

Presidential Palace
Zhongnanhai Compound
Beijing, People's Republic of China

7:49 p.m. local time

Mister President," General Shang said, "we have received a radio broadcast from our Marines aboard the *Emory Land*. The Americans have launched an attack to retake the ship. They have also launched missile attacks against our two destroyers guarding the *Emory Land*."

"What did you say, General?" Tang stood up behind his desk. "How can this be? I thought we were hiding the ship in the open sea outside of the lanes so it could not be easily found!" He looked at Admiral Zou. "Admiral, you yourself suggested that we keep the ship on the open seas to make it harder to find. How do you explain this?"

"We believe that someone on the ship activated a distress beacon that the Americans picked up, sir."

"So what is our situation now? We are repelling these attacks. Are we not?"

"Mister President," Admiral Zou said, "we have lost all contact with both destroyers. The radio broadcast that we received from the *Emory Land* indicated that both destroyers are aflame from multiple missile attacks. It appears we will lose those ships. Also, US Navy SEALs have boarded the *Emory Land*, and a shootout is going on right now.

"Our Marines are suffering heavy losses. It appears that the Americans may retake the ship."

There was an empty cup and saucer on his desk. This was the cup that his young aide, Captain Lo Chen, had brought his tea in. Tang picked it up and slammed it into the glass window behind his desk. Shards of porcelain flew all over.

He spun back around and glared at his military commanders. "How did the Americans launch this missile attack?"

Admiral Zou said, "The cruiser USS *Shiloh,* the sister ship to the *Vicksburg*, steamed into the area. We believe that our destroyers were sunk by a cruise missile attack launched from the *Shiloh*."

"Is the *Shiloh* now within range of the jets on board the *Shi Lang*?"

"Yes, Mister President. But barely within range."

"Then sink the *Shiloh*."

"Yes, Mister President."

Combat Information Center
USS Shiloh
South China Sea

8:00 p.m. local time

The mood of celebration in the ship's CIC, buoyed by the successful Tomahawk strike against the two Chinese destroyers, was doused by a sudden announcement over the 1MC.

"General Quarters! General Quarters! All hands to Battle Stations! Radar showing four inbound bogies! Stand by to launch missile batteries. This is not a drill."

Bridge
USS Shiloh
South China Sea

8:01 p.m. local time

Captain! Missiles in the air, sir. Eight inbound, sir. From those jets! Looks like they're throwing everything they've got at us."

"Very well," Captain Jamie Neely said. "Prepare to launch interceptors on my command."

"Prepare to launch, aye, sir."

"XO!"

"Aye, Captain."

"FLASH message to USS *Carl Vinson*. Request fighter cover ASAP. Get those birds out here! We need all the help we can get."

"Aye, Captain!"

"WEPS. Bridge."

"WEPS. Go ahead, Captain."

"Launch interceptors! Now!"

"Aye, sir. Launching interceptors!"

Bridge
USS Carl Vinson
South China Sea
100 miles astern of USS Shiloh

8:03 p.m. local time

Scramble! Scramble! USS *Shiloh* is under attack! Navigator! Turn the *Vinson* into the wind!"

"Turn into the wind. Aye, Captain!"

The commanding officer, Captain J. Scott Hampton II, barked

orders into the 1MC microphone. "CAG, we need two jets in the air immediately! *Shiloh* is under attack! Requesting immediate air cover!"

"Roger that, Skipper," the CAG commander said. "We've got two Hornets on the cat! Ready for launch."

The Situation Room
the White House

8:05 a.m. local time

"Should we tell him?" Admiral Jones asked.

"He said he didn't want to know," Secretary Lopez said.

"Wouldn't you want to know if it was your daughter?" Cynthia Hewitt said.

"He'll know soon enough," Lopez said. "He doesn't want to be influenced by the appearance of favoritism. Not that it would do any good at this point anyway. Besides, we need to make sure that he keeps a clear head with the *Shiloh* under attack!"

Third Floor Dining Room
the White House

8:05 a.m. local time

Hope-Caroline's hands trembled. She could no longer contain the tears.

"It's going to be okay." Sarah Edwards reached across the table and took her hand. "Dear Jesus. Please. Protect the crew of that ship. And protect Stephanie from harm. And be with our president in this time of crisis, guide him so that he will be full of wisdom to make the correct decisions that are in the best interests of our nation and the world."

Her head bowed, Hope-Caroline felt Sarah's gentle embrace.

"And please be with my friend Hope-Caroline. Give her your supernatural comfort."

Bridge
USS **Carl Vinson**
South China Sea
99 miles astern of USS **Shiloh**

8:06 p.m. local time

"Clear the deck! Prepare for takeoff!"
"Clear the deck! Clear the deck!"

From the flybridge, Captain Hampton peered down at the fire brewing in the end of the twin turbo-fan engines of the two F/A-18 Super Hornet jets on the cat. Off to the front of the jet on the right, the "shooter," the officer in charge of giving the hand signal for launch of the aircraft, was on one knee.

With crash helmet on and his green flight jacket blowing in the night breeze under the carrier deck lights, the "shooter" gave the take-off signal—a straight arm and finger pointed straight out.

The first Super-Hornet roared, fire blazing from the back of its engines, and with a mighty *whoosh* of steam from the powerful launch catapult system, the jet shot off the bow into the night, its twin after-burners marking its ascent into the dark sky over the sea. A few seconds later, the second jet followed the first, and flight crews began pushing two more into place.

The Situation Room
the White House

8:10 a.m. local time

"Ladies and gentlemen, the president." Arnie opened the door to the Situation Room.

"Sit," Surber said. "No time for that. Admiral? Secretary Lopez? What's our status?" He sensed hesitancy between them. They just looked at each other, as if uncertain about something.

"Two matters of urgency, sir," Admiral Jones said.

"Let's hear it, Admiral."

"First, our SEAL team has taken control of the bridge of the *Emory*

Land. We also control the engine room, CIC, and communications. In short, we've retaken control of the ship, and Captain Auclair Wilson, the CO, is in control on the bridge."

"Thank God," Surber said.

"Our SEALs are scouring the ship for any Chinese Marines who may be hiding out. However, you should know that we've taken casualties, and we're sending choppers from the *Carl Vinson* to medevac crew members who need urgent medical attention."

That statement hit Surber hard. How he wanted to ask, "Is my baby okay?" but he didn't. "Do you know how many wounded, Admiral?"

"Several, Mister President. Some seriously. We've lost several crew members, sir."

Dear Jesus, no.

"Is the ship able to steam on her own power?"

"Yes, Mister President. There was little damage to the bridge and engineering during the attack. She's now en route at full power toward the Philippines."

"Okay, good. What else?"

"Sir, the USS *Shiloh* is currently under attack by the Chinese. They've launched at least four jets from their carrier, the *Shi Lang*. Last I heard, eight missiles had been launched from the jets against the ship. We've scrambled four jets from *Carl Vinson* to provide air cover, but it looks messy, sir."

Surber shook his head. This was getting out of hand. "That carrier is getting to be a problem, isn't it?"

"Yes, it is, Mister President," Admiral Jones said.

"We got a sub anywhere within range?"

"The *Boise*'s right on her tail, sir. The carrier doesn't even know we're there."

The phone rang from the Pentagon. Admiral Jones picked it up. What now? Jones was cursing about something. Jones hung up the phone. "Mister President, the *Shiloh*'s been hit. One of the Chinese missiles got through. Don't know how bad it is yet, sir. We've taken out all four of the jets, but I imagine they'll just send four more to try to finish the job."

Surber thought for a second. "Is the *Boise* close enough for a shot at that carrier?"

"Point-blank range, Mister President. Just give the word."

"That carrier's done enough damage. Send the order to the *Boise*. Take her out."

"Yes, sir, Mister President."

Control Room
USS **Boise**
South China Sea
depth 100 feet

8:25 p.m. local time

S ir, FLASH message in from National Command Authority."

"Thank you, Mister Roberts." Commander Graham Hardison read the FLASH message, then folded it and put it in his front shirt pocket. "XO, take the boat to General Quarters. Prepare to fire torps. The president just ordered us to take that carrier out. I want shots out of all four tubes."

The XO picked up the 1MC and flipped a switch, sounding alarm bells throughout the nuclear attack sub. "General Quarters. General Quarters. All hands to Battle Stations!"

Fantail
USS **Shiloh**
South China Sea

8:28 p.m. local time

A ll hands to the fantail! We need all the help we can get!" The XO's voice boomed over the 1MC, and after the explosions that had rocked the *Shiloh*, it was a miracle the 1MC was even functional.

Lieutenant Brad Lucas, who had seen so much of the action on a monitor in his electronic nest as he controlled the Fire Scout drone 18,000 feet above them, headed out of the Combat Information Center, out of the superstructure, and into the night air.

Flames leaping into the tropical sky cast a long reflection in the water off the port side of the ship. The Chinese missile had ignited an inferno from hell in the midst of the sea. He heard the desperation in the voices:

"More water!"

"Get some more hoses back here!"

"Watch your head!"

"Move! Move!"

The crew of the *Shiloh* was battling flames on the ship's stern that, if not contained soon, would engulf the magazine room, setting off an explosion that would send them all straight to the bottom.

Another explosion lit the skies in the top of the superstructure, this one not as large as the first. Lucas began to think that he might not survive the night.

Control Room
USS **Boise**
South China Sea
depth 30 feet

8:30 p.m. local time

U p scope!" Commander Hardison ordered.

"Up scope! Aye, sir!"

Hardison brought his eyes to the viewfinder of the periscope. "Yeah, baby! I'll teach you to launch air strikes on US warships." *Boise* had swung out broadside of the carrier and was lying in wait like a vicious wolf about to pounce. The *Shi Lang*, the new flagship of the Chinese fleet, appeared oblivious of what was about to happen.

"WEPS. Status on torps."

"All tubes flooded. Ready to fire on your command, sir."

"Very well. Fire torps one and two!"

"Fire torps one and two! Aye, sir!"

The sub jumped once ... then again as she fired the first of four Mark-48 torpedoes that had the *Shi Lang*'s name written on them.

"All right, these next two are for you, Bloodhound! Fire torps three and four!"

"Fire torps three and four. Aye, sir."

Two more jolts to the sub. Now four deadly Mark-48 torpedoes raced through the water at the *Shi Lang*. Just one, accurately placed, would do the job. But Hardison wasn't taking any chances.

"Time to impact?"

"Thirty seconds, sir!"

Fantail
USS **Shiloh**
South China Sea

8:30 p.m. local time

Four men were standing, one scrunched behind the next. Lieutenant Brad Lucas was third in line, sandwiched between two petty officers and behind a fireman chief, who was at the front of the line. They hung onto the high-pressure fire hose, spraying pressurized seawater up high into the ship's superstructure, battling the flames from the latest explosion.

Two other fire crews poured more water on the orange-red flames billowing from the fantail.

Even twenty yards back from the flames, the heat from the burning ship was oppressive. But Lucas would stand his ground. He would die by fire, or he would die by water. But if he was going to die, he would die fighting.

Control Room
USS **Boise**
South China Sea
depth 30 feet

8:31 p.m. local time

Time to impact ... eight seconds ...

"Seven seconds ...

"Six ...

"Five ..."

Commander Hardison gripped the guide bars and watched the illuminated aircraft carrier.

"Two seconds ...

"One ..."

A giant explosion lit the night sky from across the water near the carrier's bow! Then, a second explosion amidships!

"Bull's-eye!" Hardison muttered.

Cheering erupted as real-time images of the flaming carrier appeared on control-room screens.

This was followed by a third explosion ... and then a fourth!

All four torps had landed on mark! *Shi Lang* did not stand a chance. She was going down!

"Down scope!" Hardison ordered.

"XO. Notify CINCPAC. USS *Boise* reports, bull's-eye times four!"

"Aye, Captain."

"Helmsman. Dive to two-zero-zero. Set course for two-seven-zero. All ahead full!"

CHAPTER 31

Presidential Palace
Zhongnanhai Compound
Beijing, People's Republic of China

9:00 p.m. local time

The two men walked together, their spit-polish black shoes click-ing down the marble corridor as they approached President Tang's office. Though the political infighting between the Chinese Army and Navy had often been fierce, these two men had formed a special bond. At least General Shang felt that way.

Perhaps the bond had been forged by a common, yet unspoken, understanding that the two of them, together, represented the only real counterbalance against the man known as the Raging Dragon.

Of course they could never say this, because if such talk were over-heard by vicious, backstabbing subordinates anxious to get in Tang's good graces, they could wind up on the short end of a deadly power play.

Now, together and united, they faced the dreadful responsibility of informing Tang of the single greatest Chinese military disaster in a hundred years.

This loss, in Shang's opinion, was solely on Tang's shoulders. He had become too aggressive, too quickly, believing propaganda spewed by the party machine branding him as a "military genius" or, as some said, as the "Chinese Napoleon."

Tang would never acknowledge his own responsibility in this. His massive ego would not allow it. Shang wondered whether either he or

Zou would survive the news they were about to deliver. He should have ordered young Captain Lo Chen to remove Tang's revolvers from his desk.

Of course, Shang even worried about Lo Chen's loyalties. Although it had been he—Shang—who had gotten Lo Chen the job with the president, after Tang oddly requested a younger male officer for his attaché, Shang worried that Lo Chen may have fallen too far under Tang's spell.

"My General," Admiral Zou said as they approached the entrance to the presidential office, "no matter what happens, I wish to say that it has been an honor to work with you."

Shang smiled at his friend. "These are my sentiments toward you also, Admiral."

"Sir," Zou said, "the *Shi Lang* was a naval vessel. There is no point in both of us taking the fall. Let me accept responsibility. China needs you to remain at your post."

The men stopped in front of the door to Tang's office. Shang put his hand on Zou's back and lowered his voice to keep out of earshot of the two officers guarding the entrance to the office. "Admiral, I admire your character. But I am minister of national defense. Ultimate military responsibility is mine. I will not, if I can help it, let you take the fall for this."

Zou nodded.

"Ready, Admiral?"

"As ready as I can be."

They stepped forward, and one of the officers opened the door. The other announced their arrival.

As the senior officer, Shang stepped in first. Tang was sitting behind his desk. Off to the side, young Captain Lo Chen was pouring some nuts into a bowl. He then began preparing another evening drink for the boss, which was a recipe for a fire-on-gasoline tantrum.

"General. Admiral. Sit!" Tang ordered. "I take it you have good news from the South China Sea. Let me speculate." He took a swig of liquor. "Our flagship, the *Shi Lang*, has sunk this American cruiser the *Shiloh*!"

Shang and Zou exchanged glances. "Sir, our planes have scored a direct hit on the *Shiloh*. We believe it has sustained considerable damage. However, I must inform you," Shang said, "of very tragic news."

"Tragic news?" Tang stood up. "You are not going to tell me that the Americans have recaptured the *Emory Land*, are you?"

Shang hesitated. "Mister President, the Americans have in fact retaken the *Emory Land*. But that is the least of our troubles. There is tragic news, sir."

"Tragic news," Tang said. He reached into his top drawer and extracted one of the pearl-handled .38-caliber revolvers he kept in his desk, which he had become enamored with when, as a student at Harvard, he saw the movie *Patton*. "Now then"—Tang blew on the silver barrel of the .38—"what is this tragic news of which you speak?"

"Mister President, I regret to inform you that the *Shi Lang* has been sunk."

Showing no emotion, Tang took the gun and pointed it at Shang. "Did you just tell me, General, that the Americans have sunk the flagship of the Chinese fleet? The great capital ship that we spent more than a dozen years building after we purchased it from Ukraine?"

Shang did not flinch. "Sir, I did not say the Americans sunk her. All we know is that she was torpedoed multiple times, the suspected work of a submarine."

Tang spewed a bloodcurdling scream. "Of course it was the Americans, General. You know that! You are not that stupid!" He pointed the revolver at his own right temple.

"Mister President! Don't!"

"What do you expect me to do?"

Tang aimed the revolver at the wall and fired. He fired again. Another shot hit the wall. Then a third shot busted a lamp on a side table. The bulb exploded.

The two guards rushed into the office, weapons drawn. "Mister President!"

"It's okay," Shang said to the guards. "Stand down and return to your posts outside."

"Yes, sir."

The president aimed the revolver at the liquor glass for a final shot. The glass shattered in another deafening explosion.

After the shooting spree, a strange calm overtook Tang. Gently, he laid the revolver in his desk drawer.

"Sometimes," he said in a soft voice, "this sort of thing is necessary to deter would-be assassins."

"Of course, Mister President," young Lo Chen said, sounding like a dutiful lap dog.

"Surber has made the mistake of attacking our flagship. But Surber should have read the *Art of War*." Tang looked at Shang. "General, what would Sun Tzu do if he were here?"

Shang thought for a second. "Mister President, Chinese military philosophy, embodied in Sun Tzu's classic work *Art of War*, underscores above all the need for decisiveness in military action."

"Precisely. And when I wrote that two thousand six hundred years ago in the reign of Emperor Quianlong, it was true then and is true today. Great military minds, such as Napoleon, MacArthur, and Mao, have drawn from my words."

Shang did not respond.

"Why do you look so incredulous, gentlemen? You do not believe in reincarnation?"

No response.

"Consider yourselves fortunate. Only a few know the truth." He rose from his chair, towered over them, and declared, "I am Sun Tzu! Tang Quichen and Sun Tzu are one and the same! And I have come to redeem for China what I began twenty-six centuries ago!"

It was as if some spirit had taken over his body. "But the time for my revelation has not yet come. Soon, but not yet. Therefore, I order you to say nothing until I expose this truth to the world!"

"Of course, Mister President."

"Now then," Tang's voice turned chilly cool. "Admiral Zou."

"Yes, sir."

"What is the Americans' largest base on their West Coast?"

"That would be San Diego, sir."

"And I seem to recall that San Diego is the homeport to several aircraft carriers?"

"Yes, sir," Zou said. "USS *Ronald Reagan*, USS *John Stennis*, and USS *Carl Vinson*."

"Admiral, how many of those carriers are in port now?"

"Two, I believe, sir. *Stennis* and *Reagan*."

"Very well. Has my order to arm five DF-31A missiles and have them ready for launch been completed?"

"Yes, sir," Shang said.

"I want all five targeted on San Diego. Armed with nukes. If they are going to take out our carrier, we are going to take out theirs. I want those missiles launched in one hour." He looked at his watch. "It is about 6:00 a.m. there now. I think we should treat San Diegans to a rather spectacular sunrise."

"But Mister President ..."

"Do you have a problem, General?"

"No, sir. But I do have a suggestion."

"Speak, General."

"Well, sir, in deference to Sun Tzu's philosophy of decisiveness in military action—"

"That is my philosophy!" Tang screamed. "It is *my* creation!"

"Yes, sir," Shang said. "And in deference to your philosophy, rather than limiting the strike to five missiles, which would obliterate San Diego but leave the Americans with a capacity to strike back, I would suggest an all-out barrage with over twenty-five missiles against various civilian and military bases. If we're going to strike, let us make sure that we cripple them to the point they cannot retaliate."

"An excellent idea, General Shang!" Tang's eyes sparkled. "You have studied my philosophies well! But I do not wish a long delay."

"The delay would not be long, sir. I would need to present a list of targets for your approval, which will take about an hour to assemble, and then we program more missiles for those targets. We can be ready to deliver a fatal blow to the Americans within three hours. This is my recommendation, sir."

Tang leaned back and grinned. Shang could feel the stare of Admiral Zou.

"Very well!" Tang said. "Meet me back here, General, in one hour with target recommendations."

"With pleasure, sir!" Shang said. "And I shall make sure Captain Lo prepares lots of tea and food. We are in for a long night, Mister President, but we look forward to a glorious morning for China!"

Presidential Palace
Zhongnanhai Compound
Beijing, People's Republic of China

10:00 p.m. local time

Once again, for the fourth time in the last twenty-four hours, General Shang was walking down the long hallway leading to the president's office. But this time he did not have disastrous news to deliver. And this time, he did not have Admiral Zou at his side. No point in having the admiral here. Not yet anyway.

"Is the president in his office?"

"Yes, sir," the chief guard said. "Shall I announce your arrival, General?"

"Not quite yet," Shang said to the guard. "I'm waiting on Captain Lo Chen."

Just then, Lo Chen rounded the corner, carrying a silver tray with hot tea, coffee, sugar, fruits, and pastries.

"Captain, I need to have a word with you. Major, will you take the tray for a moment while I speak with Lo Chen?"

"Yes, sir."

"Step over here a moment, Lo Chen."

"Yes, General."

"I have fabulous news! I am recommending you for promotion to Colonel!"

"Really, sir?"

"Yes, and this will be one of the fastest promotions in the history of the Army! I have spoken with the president and he approves. But I want to do this right now. We want history to record that you bore the rank of colonel at the moment of the great victory that we are about to achieve."

"Thank you, sir."

"Take this letter to my chief of staff. Right now. We will expedite your promotion before sunrise. I will tell the president where you are."

"Thank you, General!" The boy-wonder captain shot an enthusiastic salute, then took the letter and hurried down the hall.

Admiral Zou joined the general just as Lo Chen was leaving. "Where is he going?"

"I sent him on an errand. Are you ready, Admiral?"

"Yes, sir."

"Major, I'll take the tray. Please announce our presence."

"Yes, sir."

The major opened the door to Tang's office.

"Good evening, Mister President," Shang said.

"Do you have targeting recommendations?"

"I do, sir. All of our missiles are programmed, but I realized that we targeted only the American mainland. So I sent Lo Chen to deliver orders to target Pearl Harbor also."

"Excellent!" Tang said. "Excellent!"

"As I recall, you take your tea with one packet of sugar, sir?"

"Yes, and I need a caffeine shot to counteract some of that liquor that Captain Lo was feeding me." Tang laughed.

"It is going to be a great night for China, sir." Shang emptied the packet into the president's tea. "And a great sunrise in the morning! All of our missiles are ready, except the missiles to target Hawaii, and I would like to spend a few minutes going over our targeting options, starting with our West Coast targets and moving east."

"Excellent." Tang took a sip of his tea. "I take it that Los Angeles and Seattle will also be targeted this time?"

"Yes, of course, Mister President, as well as San Francisco. San Diego and Seattle represent their largest West Coast naval installations."

"I ... I ..." Tang's eyes began to cross.

"Mister President? Are you feeling okay?"

"I ..." Tang slumped over in his chair, then tumbled to the floor.

Admiral Zou stood and started to head over to Tang, but Shang motioned him back. "Stay back, Admiral."

"But—"

"Admiral, do you suppose he forgot the last words of chapter three that he wrote twenty-six centuries ago? Those words ... do you remember?"

"'If you know neither yourself nor your enemy, you will always endanger yourself.'"

CHAPTER 32

Mister President, you have a call from Beijing," Arnie Brubaker said. "Is it Tang?"

"No, sir. It's General Shang Xian, the minister of national defense."

Douglas Surber looked at the members of his national security team. "That's odd. Do we know this guy?"

"I've met him," Admiral Jones said. "Seems reasonable enough."

"Put him on speaker, Arnie."

"Yes, sir."

"General Shang, this is President Surber. What can I do for you?"

"President Surber. It is a pleasure. I am calling because China would like to accept your invitation to negotiate with the US and Taiwan, and we are prepared to enter into an immediate cease-fire as a measure of good faith."

Surber hesitated. Was this a hoax? "I welcome your words, General, but if I may ask, where is your president?"

"Aah. Unfortunately, President Tang is very ill. The doctors tell us he has suffered from an aneurysm and is indefinitely incapacitated. The Chinese military is temporarily in charge of the operations of the government until the People's Congress can appoint a replacement. But you have my word as an officer that I speak for the government, and we would like to negotiate a quick settlement."

Surber looked at the secretary of state, who nodded.

"When and where would you like to meet, General?"

"I've always wanted to visit Hawaii, Mister President. Perhaps your government would consider hosting an emergency summit there."

"Tell you what. Let us contact President Lu of Taiwan and we will get back with you."

"Very well. I look forward to hearing from you, sir."

CHAPTER 33

Punchbowl National Cemetery
Honolulu, Hawaii

48 hours later

Under rich blue skies and surrounded by luscious greenery, the podium had been erected just in front of the marble statute of Lady Columbia, which had inscribed upon it the immortal words of Abraham Lincoln to Lydia Bixby, who lost all four sons in the American Civil War.

The solemn pride that must be yours,
to have laid so costly a sacrifice upon the altar of Freedom.

President Douglas Surber glanced at the words once more before stepping to the podium, where he was flanked by the Chinese defense minister and the Taiwanese president.

"My fellow Americans and to our friends around the world. We have chosen these hallowed grounds to announce the terms of this historic agreement as a solemn reminder of the costs of war, and as a reminder that peace and life ... precious life ... must be preserved over war and death.

"This is a place where, in the words of President Abraham Lincoln, so many 'have laid so costly a sacrifice upon the altar of Freedom.'

"We have also chosen these hallowed grounds because many of the Americans buried here fought alongside the sons of China and the sons of Taiwan in liberating the Pacific from the brutal and tyrannical hand of Japanese imperialism in World War II.

"America and the two Chinas have joined hands together in the past, and there's no reason that we should not join hands now and in the future.

"Today, we are here to announce the Honolulu Accords between the US, China, and Taiwan, signed earlier today at the governor's palace here in Honolulu.

"The terms agreed to by the parties are these:

"China has arrested and will turn over for international prosecution members of the Qinzhou Medical Group, the group responsible for the murder of over two thousand baby girls, whose bodies we found on the freighter *Shemnong*.

"China will join the world in working to eliminate the practice of killing babies as a form of population control and will make the practice of selling deceased babies on the international markets illegal.

"China will allow US and UN monitors to monitor the practices within that country regarding the treatment of children.

"China will give full diplomatic status and recognition to the Republic of China located on Taiwan and will no longer insist upon a 'One China' policy.

"The United States will give full diplomatic recognition to Taiwan, will immediately open an embassy there, and will enter a mutual defense pact with that country.

"China will administer Itu Aba Island, and China and Taiwan will share equally in all natural gas extracted from the South China Sea within a fifty-mile radius of the island."

Surber looked up from his notes and out at the crowd of press members, camera crews, and dignitaries. "Within the hallowed grounds of this beautiful place are the stories of those buried here, some who are known, like the great war correspondent Ernie Pyle, or Hank Hansen, one of the Marines who first raised the American flag over Iwo Jima. And there are many others whose actions are just as heroic, but whose names we will never know.

"But whether we know their names or not, we hear them today, all of them, calling from the graves and reminding us that peace is preferable to war, and that life, and especially the lives of innocent children, must be protected at all costs.

"May God bless the Republic of China, God bless the People's Republic of China, and God bless America."

EPILOGUE

Decked out sharply in summer white uniforms, high-ranking naval officers, the brain trust of the United States Pacific Command, stood at parade rest under sunny skies in a warm afternoon breeze.

Behind the senior officers stood ten rows of junior officers and enlisted men, awaiting commencement of the festivities.

Twelve uniformed policemen riding motorcycles rumbled in pairs into the circular driveway in front of CINCPAC headquarters, followed by three Honolulu PD vehicles, followed by two black Suburbans with tinted windows.

The black Cadillac limousine following the second Suburban flew two flags on its hood. The flag on the right side of the hood was the flag of the United States of America. The navy blue flag on the left had on it an embroidered seal of the president of the United States.

Men in black suits and wearing dark shades jogged alongside the limousine, and when the limo rolled to a stop in front of the entrance, a Marine sergeant stepped forward and opened the back door.

"Attention on deck!" Every sailor and Marine snapped to erect attention.

"Ladies and gentlemen, the president of the United States."

The US Navy band played "Ruffles and Flourishes" as the president stepped out of the limo, then transitioned into "Hail to the Chief." A crowd of several hundred civilians greeted him with enthusiastic applause. The president exchanged salutes with the base commander and several other high-ranking officers standing near the podium that had been set up.

Before the band had finished and as the Marine honor guard cracked off its twenty-one-gun salute, the president stepped to the podium. His eyes seemed to glance at each and every sailor and Marine, and when the Navy band finished playing, he broke into a big smile.

"Admiral Gardner. Captain Eleya. Thank you for having me at Pearl Harbor today. I've come to express my appreciation to all of you. But before I get into my remarks, I see there's some personal business I need to attend to." He broke into another big smile. "I'll be right back."

The president stepped away from the podium and walked through the first row of officers, saying, "Excuse me, gentlemen."

Then he barked an order to an officer in the second row. "Drop that salute and give your daddy a big hug!"

She fell into his arms, unable to contain the tears.

"How are you, Steph?"

"I'm just great, Daddy. Now ... I'm great."

"How's the arm?"

"Still sore. They got the bullet out. And I took out the guy who shot me. You taught me well, Daddy."

He stepped back and looked into her eyes. "That's my girl."

"Daddy, I want you to meet Lieutenant Commanders Gunner McCormick and Fred Jeter. Gunner led the takeover of the ship. He had the situation under control even before the SEALs arrived. And Dr. Jeter was on the *Shemnong*. They flew him off the *Shemnong*, and he performed emergency surgery to remove the bullet."

The president looked at Gunner and Fred, standing to the left and right of Stephanie. He shook their hands. "Gentlemen, I'm grateful to both of you."

Her tears started again, and to hide them, Stephanie threw her arms around him once more. "I'm so proud of you, Daddy. You stood for life. You did the right thing."

He kissed her on the cheek and then the forehead.

"I love you, Steph. Welcome home."

BACKGROUND OF THE NOVEL
THE RISE OF COMMUNISM IN CHINA

When civil war first erupted in China in the early twentieth century, more than ten years had passed since the start of the Bolshevik Revolution in Russia. In both conflicts, in Russia and in China, massive amounts of blood would be spilled by thousands over the issue of Communism.

But unlike the Bolshevik Revolution, which was quick and decisive, the civil war in China was long and drawn out. The first period of the war started in 1927 and raged for ten years to a bloody stalemate in 1937.

When war broke out with Japan in 1937, the Chinese suspended their infighting and unified to fight the Japanese in yet another war that would last for nine years.

But after World War II ended, the Chinese civil war reignited in 1946. American-backed nationalists, led by General Chiang Kai-shek, battled power-hungry Communist rebels, led by Mao Zedong and backed by the Soviet Union.

As the fighting wore on, Chiang Kai-shek lost power and Communist rebels asserted control.

On October 1, 1949, Mao Zedong declared the establishment of the Communist People's Republic of China, with its capital at Beijing.

By December of 1949, Chiang Kai-shek, along with two million nationalist Chinese, fled to Taipei on the island of Taiwan, where they claimed legitimacy as the official government of China in exile.

Thus, the "two Chinas," consisting of the "Republic of China" (ROC) on Taiwan and the Communist "People's Republic of China" (PRC) in Beijing, were pitted in bloodthirsty hatred against each other, separated by a strip of water seventy-five miles wide known as the Taiwan Strait.

The Taiwan Strait separates the two Chinas

The United States at first recognized Taiwan as the official government of China in exile. It would not acknowledge the Communist government in Beijing. But in 1979, the US finally recognized the People's Republic as the official government of China.

While the US technically broke diplomatic relations with the

Republic of China on Taiwan, it maintained close military and economic ties with the Taiwanese.

All this left the United States tiptoeing back and forth across a delicate diplomatic and military tightrope between the "two Chinas," each of which it is economically dependent upon and each of which would destroy the other if they could get away with it.

By 2010, the Navy of the Communist People's Republic of China had more ships than the United States Navy. And the US owed China trillions, having sold Treasury bonds to finance American debt.

The relationship between the "two Chinas" remains an explosive powder keg.

The Navy Justice Series

Available in stores and online!

Black Sea Affair

Don Brown

As the U.S. Navy searches for weapons-grade plutonium that has been smuggled out of Russia by terrorists, a submarine mishap escalates the international crisis. With the world watching, JAG Officer Zack Brewer is called to Moscow to defend submarine skipper Pete Miranda and his entire crew. It is a heart-stopping race against the clock. With Russian missiles activated and programmed for American cities, Brewer stalls for time as the U.S. Navy frantically searches the high seas for a floating hydrogen bomb that could threaten New York Harbor.

The Malacca Conspiracy

Don Brown,
Author of the Navy Justice Series

Set in Singapore, Indonesia, Malaysia, and the United States, The Malacca Conspiracy is a bone-chilling tale of terrorism on the high seas, of political assassination, and nuclear brinkmanship.

Available in stores and online!

Share Your Thoughts

With the Author: Your comments will be forwarded to the author when you send them to *zauthor@zondervan.com*.

With Zondervan: Submit your review of this book by writing to *zreview@zondervan.com*.

Free Online Resources at
www.zondervan.com

Zondervan AuthorTracker: Be notified whenever your favorite authors publish new books, go on tour, or post an update about what's happening in their lives at www.zondervan.com/authortracker.

Daily Bible Verses and Devotions: Enrich your life with daily Bible verses or devotions that help you start every morning focused on God. Visit www.zondervan.com/newsletters.

Free Email Publications: Sign up for newsletters on Christian living, academic resources, church ministry, fiction, children's resources, and more. Visit www.zondervan.com/newsletters.

Zondervan Bible Search: Find and compare Bible passages in a variety of translations at www.zondervanbiblesearch.com.

Other Benefits: Register to receive online benefits like coupons and special offers, or to participate in research.

ZONDERVAN®

ZONDERVAN.com/
AUTHORTRACKER
follow your favorite authors